Nathan B. Young

and the Struggle over Black Higher Education

Missouri Biography Series
William E. Foley, Editor

Nathan B. Young

and the Struggle over Black Higher Education

Antonio F. Holland

UNIVERSITY OF MISSOURI PRESS
COLUMBIA AND LONDON

Library of Congress Cataloging-in-Publication Data

Holland, Antonio Frederick, 1943–
Nathan B. Young and the struggle over black higher education /
Antonio F. Holland.
p.   cm. — (Missouri biography series)
Summary: "Examines Nathan Young's 20-year academic career, during which
he attempted to uphold W. E. B. Du Bois's vision of liberal arts education for
blacks while balancing it with the agricultural/vocational education advo-
cated by Booker T. Washington, adhering to high standards for black higher
education despite powerful and entrenched opposition"—Provided by
publisher.
Includes bibliographical references and index.
ISBN-13: 978-0-8262-1679-3 (hard cover : alk. paper)
ISBN-10: 0-8262-1679-X (hard cover : alk. paper)
1. Young, Nathan B., 1862–1933. 2. African American educators—
United States—Biography. 3. African Americans—Education (Higher)—
History.   I. Title.
LA2317.Y73H65 2006
378.1'22092—dc22
[B]
2006020035

∞ This paper meets the requirements of the
American National Standard for Permanence of Paper
for Printed Library Materials, Z39.48, 1984.

Designer: *foleydesign*
Typesetter: Crane Composition, Inc
Printer and binder: Thomson-Shore, Inc.
Typefaces: Baltane and ITC Stone Serif

The University of Missouri Press offers its grateful acknowledgment to an
anonymous donor whose generous grant in support of the publication of
outstanding dissertations has assisted us with this volume.

In memory of my parents,
Garnett G. and Carmen T. Holland

CONTENTS

ACKNOWLEDGMENTS

I wish to gratefully acknowledge the guidance and criticism of Dr. Arvarh E. Strickland, who supervised this study in the dissertation stage. Dr. John L. Bullion also read the manuscript and offered many helpful suggestions. The other members of my committee, Dr. William M. Wiecek, Dr. Winfield J. Burggraaff, and Dr. Michael D. Woodard, were also helpful and supportive. Numerous librarians and their staffs helped immensely, and I thank everyone at the State Historical Society of Missouri, the Western Historical Manuscript Collection, Missouri Historical Society, University of Missouri, Washington University, the Archives of Oberlin College, University of Virginia, the Archives of the University of Florida, Savery Library, Talladega College, Manuscript Division of the Library of Congress, the Carver Research Foundation of Tuskegee Institute, the Amistand Research Center, Dillard University, the Florida Department of State, Division of Archives, History, and Record Management, and the Southern Historical Collection of the University of North Carolina Library. An examination of the Black Archives, Florida A&M University was essential to this study. Leedel W. Neyland, John W. Riley, and James Eaton were very helpful. Especially important was an examination of the Archives of Lincoln University and the Special Collection on Black History in Inman Page Library. I also would like to thank John Waide of Saint Louis University Archives, Pope Pius XII Memorial Library for guiding me through the Nathan B. Young Jr. Collection. Besides the librarians, many of the faculty, staff, and students at Lincoln University proved to be supportive in one way or another. Especially helpful were the late Dr. Lorenzo J. Greene, emeritus professor of history, who read the entire manuscript and made many useful suggestions. Likewise, Dr. Noel Heermance, professor of English, and especially Dr. Rosemary Hearn, professor of English and former vice president of Academic Affairs, both read the manuscript and offered valuable criticism. At the University of Missouri–Columbia, Dr. Walter C. Daniel, Dr. Carolyn A. Dorsey, and others were helpful. Two fellow members of the Missouri National Guard, Timothy R. Roberts and Barbara Mulkey, were also supportive and helpful. Ms. Darlene Dixon typed the manuscript in the dissertation form from the beginning to the end, including drafts. I would like to acknowledge permission of the University of California Press to reprint from *Agriculture History,* vol. 65, no. 2, 1991 by the Agriculture History Society my article on Nathan B. Young at Florida A&M College. In addition I must especially thank the late Judge Nathan B. Young, Jr., and the late Nathaniel Sweets of St. Louis for their aid and encouragement. Dr. Helen Nash of the same city was also helpful. Special thanks must be given to the many people who allowed me to interview them. They are too numerous to mention here but their contributions are recognized in the footnotes and bibliography of this study. In preparing this manuscript for publication I would like to thank Elizabeth Wilson and Carmen Beck of Iman E. Page Library, and also Candy Buford, Helen Huhman-Hart, and Debra Foster Greene at Lincoln University of Missouri. At the University of Missouri Press I would like to thank Clair Willcox, Jane Lago, John Brenner, and the rest of the staff as well as publisher Beverly Jarrett. For reviewing the manuscript I would like to thank William E. Foley and an unknown reader. Last, I must thank my family, my late parents, Garnett and Carmen Holland, my in-laws, the late Nolan and Anna Turner, and especially my wife, Carolyn, stepson Bradley Wilkins, and son Erik for their support.

Nathan B. Young

and the Struggle over Black Higher Education

CHAPTER 1

Early Life and Education

Nathan Benjamin Young, born a slave in Alabama, was a member of that select group of freedmen who dedicated their lives to the uplift of their race through education. Young, like many other young freedmen, had the advantage of his mother's encouragement and inspiration, but he also had what was lacking in many of the other cases, the opportunity to pursue a formal education. His educational experience led him through the usual period of doubt in determining his life's work. In the end, however, Young was convinced that he could make a significant contribution to racial advancement by becoming a teacher.

Young, the son of Susan Smith and a father whose identity is not known, was born in Newbern, Alabama, on September 15, 1862. His mother was the most important influence on Nathan's life. Susan Smith, the daughter of an African mother and a father of mixed blood, was born in slavery in Chatham, Virginia, in 1843. When she was twelve years old, her master died, and in the settlement of his estate, she was given the choice of being sold to a local master who had the reputation for abusing his slaves, or being sold to a slave trader. Her mother persuaded her to take her chances with the slave trader. In the fall of 1856, Susan was sold for $750 and taken from the plantation without having the opportunity to say a final good-bye to her mother. She would not see her parents again until after the Civil War.[1]

1. Nathan B. Young, "The Quest and Use of an Education," typewritten manuscript, 83, hereafter cited as "The Quest." Young manuscript, Joint

1

The slave trader left immediately for Alabama with his human merchandise. He walked Susan and his other Virginia purchases to Greensboro, North Carolina, where they were held in a slave pen until a larger number of slaves were gathered for the walk to Alabama. In Newbern, Alabama, near Mobile, the slave trader sold her to a cotton planter for more than a hundred percent profit.[2]

Susan spent her remaining years as a slave in the vicinity of Newbern. After the Civil War began, her owner sold her to his overseer. Either just before or soon after this sale, Susan gave birth to Nathan, whom she named after her father. Neither Susan's nor Nathan's account of this period of her life provides any substantial clues as to the identity of Nathan's father, although he was likely the offspring of the first master or one of his family members. Susan's new master, the overseer, was a draft dodger until the war was nearly over and was ostracized by his white neighbors. Although these neighbors made life difficult for the slaveholder and his wife, they fed Susan and her son.[3]

Even though Susan's master did not support the Confederacy, he refused to give up his slaves at the end of the war and planned to take them to Texas, where he believed slavery would continue to exist. Susan learned of her master's plan, however, and ran away, taking three-year-old Nathan with her. By walking all night and receiving the aid of a friend, she succeeded in reaching the next county near Tuscaloosa, where she began a new life.

She left young Nathan with an old woman and went into Tuscaloosa seeking aid and work. A black artisan's family provided her refuge and assistance, which enabled her to return to the old woman's house to get her child. The artisan was a well-to-do member of the black community. He learned the building trade from his master during slavery and was permitted to hire himself out. In

---

Collection–University of Missouri, Western Historical Manuscript Collection, State Historical Society of Missouri. L. S. Curtis, "Nathan B. Young, A Sketch," 107. "Handwritten statement of Mrs. Susan Young," in Young, "The Quest," 83. In Susan's handwritten account she claims she was eleven when sold to the slave trader. Young's more detailed account sets her age as older.

2. Young, "The Quest," 91–92.

3. Ibid.; "Handwritten statement of Mrs. Susan Young." Susan said that her son never saw his father after she ran away.

time, he improved his skills to the point that he became a master builder.[4]

Within a few years, Susan met and married Frank Young, a tenant farmer. During the Civil War, Frank's youthful master had taken him into the Confederate service as a body servant. Actually, he worked with numerous other slaves in labor battalions building breastworks for such Confederate strongholds as Mobile. After their marriage, Susan and Frank established a home near Tuscaloosa, and Frank became a good father to young Nathan. He was a hard worker and provided well for his family, even though he was something of a spendthrift. This bad quality was checked, however, by Susan's good business sense and thrifty nature. Her son never knew her to be without money, which she generously shared with him. She was a "gadfly" for both her husband and son.[5]

Ambitious for her son, Susan decided to show him the wider world and, in 1875, she took Nathan for a train trip and family reunion to Virginia, where he met his grandparents for the first time. During the twenty years since she had been sold away from her parents, she had irregularly kept in contact with them.[6] The train trip from Tuscaloosa to Chatham, Virginia, was a great adventure for young Nathan. Throughout his life he continued to remember every stop, layover, and change of trains. The first stop was Birmingham, then just a village recovering from a recent smallpox epidemic, which, at this time, plagued the South. Although the first signs of industrial growth were evident, Birmingham had not yet developed into a great steel center of the New South. Much of the center of the town was dominated by open fields. From Birmingham they went on to Chattanooga, a much more developed city than Birmingham. From Chattanooga, the Tennessee, Virginia and

4. Young, "The Quest," 91–92. Nathan B. Young, "A Slave Girl's Escape from Slavery," Young manuscript.

5. Curtis, "Nathan B. Young, A Sketch," 107. Among blacks, tenant farming became widespread after the war. Bond, *Negro Education in Alabama,* 120. Young, "The Quest," 93.

6. Young, "The Quest," 75–76. Young carried on this correspondence as soon as he could write. Young points out that his parents' boss, a planter, showed him how to properly address an envelope and a white tenant boy on the same farm gave him instruction in math and long division. Horace Mann Bond suggests that although there was antipathy between the poor white class and the black population, it was overplayed by the conservatives. Bond, *Negro Education in Alabama,* 25–26, 64, 69–72.

Georgia Railroad carried them to Bristol and on to Lynchburg, and finally to Chatham, Virginia.[7]

The ride between Chattanooga and Chatham was filled with adventure and exciting new sights for Nathan. During the first night, a group of black musicians passed the time by singing about the passage of the Civil Rights Bill of 1875. Reaching Lynchburg, they learned that they had missed the train that would take them the final leg of their journey. Here Nathan watched mule teams transporting wagon loads of tobacco through the hilly streets of the city. The next day Nathan and his mother arrived at the station an hour ahead of time for the midafternoon train to Richmond. Young did not get to see Richmond, however, for their journey ended in the hill country of Virginia at the Chatham station. Young was so disappointed not to see Richmond that his mother had to pull him off the train.[8]

In Chatham, Susan Young was reunited with her mother and father, and visited with her many brothers and sisters. She even visited her former master's family. Meanwhile, Nathan spent his days fishing in the ponds and runs with his cousins and uncles and roving the countryside. This would be the family's last reunion; soon its members joined the migratory movement north. In 1876, a year after the visit, Susan's father died, and five years later her mother died.

When Nathan returned to Tuscaloosa, the fact that he had taken this journey made him something of a hero to the rest of the youngsters. He had been away from home for more than seven days and traveled nearly one thousand miles by train. He impressed the other youth with his tales of the sights and sounds beyond their hometown. After this experience, Nathan always

7. On the economic and industrial growth of Alabama and Birmingham during this period see Bond, *Negro Education in Alabama*, 39–45, 126; and Young, "The Quest," 75–77.

8. Young, "The Quest," 78–79; John Hope Franklin, *Reconstruction*, 201–2. Franklin provides a good general discussion of the Civil Rights Bill of 1875. Also see Eric Foner, *Reconstruction, American's Unfinished Revolution, 1863–1865*, 553–56. Young claimed that the only time he was late for a train was when he was traveling with Booker T. Washington: "He [Young] and Washington had to run to catch the slowest train in Alabama. Dr. Washington specialized in being late for trains, just as he [Young] specialized in not being late for them."

found traveling to strange and different places exciting and adventurous.[9]

Growing up in a larger town like Tuscaloosa assisted Young in seeking an education. The city was the home of the University of Alabama, and the university added greatly to the cultural life of the community. Many of the early faculty of the school were Yale graduates, and those teachers gave the town a Yankee "flair." As a result, the town attracted many educated whites, some of whom were interested in seeing that the freedmen received an education.[10]

There was in Tuscaloosa, however, a general hostility toward the black community. The students at the university often paraded through the black community and taunted the residents. Moreover, during the Reconstruction period, the Ku Klux Klan was a powerful force in this area, and the Klansmen tried to enforce their social and political will by violence. As a youth, Nathan saw more than one of his neighbors killed by the night riders. He witnessed the murder of a carpentry shop owner in whose yard he had played, and whose wife was a friend of Nathan's mother. This man was shot down in the middle of the road during the daytime, and Nathan stood by the neighbor's dead body and wondered what it all meant. Another victim personally known to Young was a woman who was called out of her home and made to stand on a box in her yard. The Klansmen then shot her in the face. The father of a friend of Nathan's was also killed by the night riders.[11]

In desperation, the black population fought back. Nathan's own home was barricaded against the arrival of the Klan, and there were gun ports cut into the walls of their cabin. His father was always armed and prepared to defend their home. An incident that stood out in Young's memory was when a settlement of blacks met the Klan and slaughtered both Klansmen and their horses.

---

9. Young, "The Quest," 92, 83, and 80. After this Young would always enjoy trains and he rode them frequently. Later, he owned a car but never learned to drive. Interview with Judge Nathan B. Young, Jr., July 1981, in St. Louis.

10. Young, "The Quest," 11–12.

11. Ibid., 13. There was a deep conviction among whites that the black race was inferior, morally, mentally, and physically, because of slavery. Bond, *Negro Education in Alabama*, 11–12. On Klan violence in Alabama see Eric Foner, *Reconstruction: American's Unfinished Revolution, 1863–1877*, 426–30.

Such resistance made what was once sport become very dangerous and greatly aided in stopping the Klan's terror. In this section of Alabama many Klansmen did not return from their night rides.[12]

Before the violence started Young had enjoyed some of the political parades and outings of the Reconstruction period. In his childhood, he would even declare himself to be a "Democrat" for the pleasure of local whites and a few pennies. The witnessing of the brutal treatment of black politicians and the violence of the "Democrats," however, soon made Young conscious of their anti-black bias.[13]

The violence of the Alabama countryside made Nathan's mother anxious that her only son get an education in order to better his lot in life. Her concern for her son's education increased greatly when she realized that he could not count accurately even using his fingers. He had made her aware of this weakness by failing to get the proper number of beets from their garden. In order to make it possible for Nathan to attend school, she convinced her husband to give up tenant farming and to move nearer to town. Frank Young took a job at a mental hospital, and moved his family within three miles of a school.

Young's parents enrolled him in a one-teacher school, which was conducted by a college-educated, Southern white Baptist minister. To Nathan his Southern schoolteacher became "a philosopher, guide, and friend," and he would always remember him as that "iron gray school master in black." The school was ungraded and accepted both children and adults as students for the payment of one dollar per month tuition. The school started in a small tenement owned by a black man, but it was moved frequently. The only time the school was located in a building designed for school purposes was when it was situated in a building formerly used as a school for white children. Equipment for the school consisted of a long desk and benches without backs. There was no teacher's desk nor blackboards. The students recited while standing next to the teacher's chair.[14]

---

12. Young, "The Quest," 13. The Klan was very bitterly opposed to any black advancement on economic, educational, political, or social levels. Bond, *Negro Education in Alabama,* 12. On the resistance of black communities to Klan violence see Steven Hahn, *A Nation under Our Feet,* 280–85.

13. Young, "The Quest," 84–85.

14. Ibid., 1–3. There was virtually no formal education for Alabama's blacks before the Civil War. There was no regular schooling until the Radi-

Young characterized his first teacher as democratic and informal in dealing with his students, and as a skillful and effective teacher.[15] The course of instruction was liberally spiced with religion and classic illustrations from Greek and Roman mythology. The stories of the Olympian gods and goddesses instilled in Nathan a desire to receive a classical education and to be able to read Greek and Latin. To give added emphasis to the students' spiritual development, every Friday afternoon the last hour of school would be devoted to the reading and interpretation of the New Testament. Nathan found these interpretations to be clear and understandable. The teacher used as his textbooks Webster's *Blueback Speller, National Readers,* Monteith's *Geography,* and Davie's *Arithmetic.* There was no set daily schedule or regular curriculum to be followed. Although there was very little in the way of corporal punishment, the few sleepers would be tapped. The teacher taught each student separately, and each would be called upon in turn to recite.[16] After Young's first two months in school, his mother became discouraged with his progress. He was excited about school, but he was not making much headway in reading. She let Nathan know that either he would have to do better in his studies or give up school. The life of a student was much more attractive to Nathan than that of farm worker, and he quickly began making remarkable progress in his reading.

The white Southern minister closed his missionary school for blacks, but his place was soon taken by a Northern woman teacher. She had come south to join the faculty of Stillman Institute, a black school founded by the Presbyterian church, but she

---

cal Republicans established a public school system in 1868. Black parents bore much of the cost of educating their children, paying tuition cost from 50 cents to $1.50 a month or about one-tenth the wages of an agricultural worker. There was a considerable campaign to replace Northern teachers with white Southern teachers. This was aimed at providing employment for educated white Southerners and more importantly to see that the blacks did not receive a radical education. Peter Kolchin, *First Freedom,* 79. Bond, *Negro Education in Alabama,* 24–25, 111–14; and Albert B. Moore, *History of Alabama,* 514–19.

15. Young, "The Quest," 3. There were other whites interested in the educational uplift of blacks. Not all of the whites interested in black education were reconstructed Southerners. There were also unreconstructed Southerners equally interested in black education. See Bond, *Negro Education in Alabama,* 24–25; and Henry Lee Swint, *The Northern Teacher in the South, 1862–1879,* v.

16. Young, "The Quest," 4–5.

soon left Stillman to open her own school. The students who had attended the school operated by the Southern minister now resumed their studies with this new teacher. The new teacher operated her school more systematically than her predecessor and modeled it after the graded schools of New England. She had trouble, however, classifying students like Nathan, who had become accustomed to the informality of the upgraded system. Nathan, for instance, only wanted to work on subjects that interested him, such as arithmetic, reading, and geography, because he had no interest in history, general science, and grammar. To solve this problem, Nathan was finally placed in a class by himself for as long as he was at school. Then, because other duties permitted Nathan to attend school for only about three months a year, he continued to study on his own at night throughout the rest of the year.[17]

Despite Nathan's irregular attendance, the teacher recognized his abilities and suggested to his mother that Nathan be permitted to continue his education at Stillman Institute. Both Susan and Nathan were anxious to follow this suggestion. Susan had high aspirations for her son and wanted him to get more education, and Nathan did not want to follow in his stepfather's footsteps and become a sharecropper. While Frank Young was not convinced that his son needed to be educated beyond the basics, Susan prevailed and plans were made to send Nathan to Stillman. A local white doctor, who had taught Young in a Sunday school he conducted for blacks in the white Presbyterian church, assisted in getting Young admitted to Stillman.

Stillman Institute was founded in 1876 by Dr. Charles A. Stillman. It was originally called Tuscaloosa Institute, and its primary purpose was to train ministers for the black Presbyterian churches.

17. Ibid., 6, 7–9; and Swint, *The Northern Teacher in the South*, v. It is interesting that Young would later become a teacher of history and English. Immediately after the war most Southern whites opposed any type of education for blacks. Some white Southerners only became interested in black education when they saw that the Northerners were going to provide the education. Mainly Northern teachers provided the first education for blacks in Alabama. Kolchin, *First Freedom*, 80–83; and Bond, *Negro Education in Alabama*, 82–83, 115–19. Interview with Judge Nathan B. Young, Jr., July 1981. Although Nathan's mother dreamed of him becoming a medical doctor, he later rejected this idea because he had never seen a black doctor. Young would later become a trustee of Stillman College.

Earlier, in 1865, the General Assembly of the Presbyterian Church in the United States had approved the licensing of qualified blacks as ministers. During Reconstruction, blacks, displeased with worshipping in the balconies of white churches, began to form their own churches. In 1875, the Presbyterians got the General Assembly to recognize the need for trained black ministers and this resulted in the establishment of the school. In 1893, the name of the school was changed to Stillman Institute in honor of its founder. Because of the low educational level of the black youth, the course of study at Stillman was basic academics. The school operated as a secondary missionary institution where the students could work their way through school. At Stillman, Young paid for his education by working as a "buggy boy" for Dr. Stillman. Young was only a part-time student here because he did not want to become a minister. He was, however, inspired by his scholarly teachers to continue his education.[18]

To meet the urgent need for black teachers for the public schools, normal schools grew up throughout the South after the Civil War. At this time, the largest and most successful secondary and normal school in Alabama was Talladega College. It was only natural in 1880 for Young to select Talladega as his next step up the educational ladder.[19]

Talladega College was founded in the small eastern Alabama town of Talladega in November of 1867 with three teachers and 140 students. The school was located in the middle of the Black

18. L. W. Bottoms, "The Policies and Rationale Underlying the Support of Negro Colleges and Schools Maintained by the Presbyterian Church in the United States," 264–73; and Young, "The Quest," 10. This was the only time Young was ever hired out. Because of her slave experiences Susan was strongly opposed to such service.

19. "The Quest"; Horace Mann Bond, "Negro Education: A Debate in the Alabama Constitutional Convention of 1901," 49–50. In 1889–1890, black children in Alabama received 44 percent of the school's money appropriated in the state, although they were only 43.8 percent of the population. Therefore, black children received 50.2 percent and white children 49.8 percent. In 1929–1930, black children received only 36 percent of the school's fund and on the average white children received 64 percent of the distributed funds. For the gradual restrictions of black political rights throughout the South see C. Vann Woodard, *Origins of the New South, 1877–1913*, 321–95; and Young, "The Quest," 37–39, on the deliberate use of Negro public school funds to advance the white public schools. Kolchin, *First Freedom*, 88, 90, 95.

Belt of Alabama. The nine surrounding counties had no schools for black children after the Civil War. The new school replaced an earlier one established by two former slaves from Talladega, William Savery and Thomas Tarrant. General Wagner Swayne of the Freedmen's Bureau aided the American Missionary Association in purchasing a thirty-four-acre tract and a large brick building that had been built in 1852 to serve as a high school academy for upper-class white boys.[20]

Talladega was intended to produce black teachers for the surrounding counties. The first principal, the Reverend Henry Brown, an 1861 graduate of Oberlin College, was asked by the people in the black communities in the surrounding counties to send them teachers. Brown, in turn, asked that the communities send him their most promising young people with enough corn and bacon to feed them, and he would educate them. At first the school was little more than an elementary school, with no living quarters. It was so crude that only missionary teachers performing a labor of love would find it acceptable.[21] Because the school was firmly rooted in the basic tenets of the American Missionary Association, Talladega was consciously dedicated to God and the brotherhood of man, and thus the school's faculty treated their students as fellow human beings.

At Talladega, the level of work deliberately proceeded slowly. In 1868, the year after the school was founded, a church was opened and courses established for the training of black ministers. By 1873, a department of Bible study was established. It was not until 1879 that college work was even planned. In that year, the Reverend Henry Lee De Forest, a Yale man, became president, and under his leadership college work was gradually added to the curriculum. No outline of a college course appeared in the school catalog until 1890. In 1892, only two students out of a total of 510 were admitted to a college program, and they received degrees in 1895. De For-

---

20. Young, "The Quest," 14–19; and Dwight Oliver Wendell Holmes, *The Evolution of the Negro College,* 97. Addie Louise Joyner Butler, *The Distinctive Black Colleges: Talladega, Tuskegee and Morehouse,* 16–18.

21. Butler, *The Distinctive Black Colleges,* 18. Augustus Field Beard, *A Crusade of Brotherhood: History of the American Missionary Association* 173. Swint, *The Northern Teacher in the South,* 12; Holmes, *The Evolution of the Negro College,* 98.

est's seventeen years as president of Talladega College proved to be the formative years of the school. He established a single normal department and streamlined the theological, college preparatory, and industrial departments. Talladega was a Christian Missionary School that aimed at development of "hand, head and heart."[22]

Nathan Young received his first systematic education at Talladega College. Young enrolled in the normal school program, and here, for the first time, he remained in school for a period longer than three months. The school year ran for nine months, and Young's studies were not interrupted by farm and household duties. Talladega had a staff of Northern white teachers under the leadership of De Forest.

President De Forest was well qualified in both background and attitude to lead this effort in black education. He was of Puritan ancestry and a member of an influential Connecticut family. During the Civil War, De Forest resigned an instructorship at Yale to join the Union Army with many of his students. After the war and a brief ministry in the Midwest, De Forest joined the American Missionary Association (A.M.A.) and went south to teach the freedmen. He was without racial prejudice, and his life was devoted to the service of his fellow man. He was especially interested in the educational uplift of the rural blacks and became an early advocate of the kind of rural common school projects later carried on by the Jeanes, Slater, and Rosenwald funds. Believing that blacks should be educated as high as their potential would permit, De Forest took a militant stand against educational inequality. He spoke out against blacks being educated for a certain station in life, and he challenged all of his students to aspire to the highest and best education. "The disabilities of the past," said De Forest, "make the more urgent the demand for superior training."[23] De Forest felt the black

22. Holmes, *The Evolution of the Negro College,* 98–99. Many Yale graduates were among the Northern teachers who went south to educate the freedmen and to establish some of the better colleges. Willard Range, *The Rise and Progress of Negro Colleges in Georgia, 1865–1949,* 22. Talladega College, *Annual Catalog, 1882–83* (Talladega, Alabama, 1883), 22; *Catalogue of Talladega College, 1894–1895* (Talladega, Alabama, 1895), 32–33 (Talladega Archive); and Butler, *The Distinctive Black College,* 24–25.

23. Young, "The Quest," 15–17, 18–19, 118–19. One of De Forest's students at Yale and a fellow soldier was Edmund Ware, the founder of Atlanta University. Young considered these soldiers turned schoolteachers as the

race would be saved by its exceptional men and women and that these persons needed to be liberally and broadly educated as leaders. De Forest was a supporter of all educational efforts for the freedmen, and he was an early backer of Booker T. Washington of Tuskegee.

Talladega College was an exciting center of black education during the early 1880s. Some of the leading organizers of black educational efforts in the South visited Talladega. Many of these leaders, drawn to Talladega because of President De Forest, often spoke to the students. Among the first of these speakers was Dr. A. D. Mayo, a New Englander who was trying to sell the South on the common public school. He was to the South what Horace Mann was to New England. Dr. Mayo was soon followed by Professor Spence of Fisk University, who left a professorship in a great Middle West university to teach the freedmen at Fisk and who occasionally traveled to other Southern colleges in order to share his philosophy and knowledge.[24]

Some of these visitors provided Talladega's students with more than intellectual and spiritual uplift. Atticus G. Haywood, for example, visited Talladega in the 1880s as a member of the Slater Fund, which had just started providing small loans to worthy students who were trying to get through school. Young was given such a loan from the fund, to be paid back after he had finished his education. He paid the loan off in 1892 to Haywood's successor, J. L. M. Curry, a man who also was one of the visitors to Talladega.[25]

While at Talladega, Young, like most black college students, taught school in the rural areas during the summer. Young's pay was poor, but it provided him with enough money to return to college in the fall. These teaching experiences made Young realize not only that

---

real emancipators of blacks. Butler, *The Distinctive Black College,* 24–25; and Beard, *A Crusade of the Brotherhood,* 207. Young kept a batch of letters that De Forest had written him through the years encouraging him to seek the best possible education in the best schools and to aim high. De Forest died in 1896. Even then, De Forest and Young were planning a rural education program. Nathan B. Young was devoted to the A.M.A. ideals. Interview with Judge Nathan B. Young, Jr., July, 1981. See Beard, *A Crusade of Brotherhood,* 146–47 for the ideals of the A.M.A. De Forest quoted in James M. McPherson, *The Abolitionist Legacy,* 220.

24. Young, "The Quest," 114–15.

25. Ibid., 115–17. Young paid off his loan in 1892 when he started teaching at Tuskegee Institute.

he needed more education, but also that he was ambitious for a higher status than that of a teacher in an ungraded rural school.[26]

On July 4, 1881, Young opened his first school in a former slave cabin in Coaling, Alabama. The schoolhouse was located on the Clements' plantation, the owner of which was supposedly a relative of Mark Twain. The school was located in a cotton field, and at the close of school each day Young picked cotton for his board. Young stayed with a family headed by a preacher and successful farmer. In his cabin school, Young started his teaching career, by "keeping a school." Although he was paid only sixty dollars for the three months, he felt that his students were cheated because of his lack of training and knowledge. This experience inspired him to want more formal training.[27]

Young's next summer teaching occurred at Appling, Alabama, located in the hill country of his home county. There had been an attempt to operate a school for blacks more than ten years earlier, and Young's summer school was the second attempt at providing an education for the black youth in this area. There were very few blacks in this community, and the black population's pro rata share of the school fund was sixty dollars. To be paid the full amount, Young had to have a certain number of students in attendance daily. He had a difficult time maintaining adequate attendance, and to keep attendance up, he admitted students from adjacent townships. Frequently, he went out into the countryside encouraging families to send their children to his school. The schoolhouse, a log cabin located in an isolated spot, was originally built to be a school for whites. The nearest family lived three miles away. Many of Young's students had to walk five or more miles to attend school.

In this community, both blacks and whites lived under primitive conditions. Young's landlady, who was more than fifty years old, had never been to the nearest large town, forty miles away. Her husband made a "pilgrimage" to the town once a year. Young lived on cooked and uncooked peaches from his landlady's orchard.

---

26. Ibid., 118–19, 18. Many black college students found the summer teaching experience more rewarding than Young. See Louis Harlan, *Separate and Unequal,* 214–15, and W. E. B. Du Bois, *The Souls of Black Folk,* 55–64.

27. Nathan B. Young, "A Fifty Year Jaunt along the Educational Road," Young manuscript (typewritten). No pagination. Young, "The Quest," 42–44.

Once a week, he walked several miles to the post office, general store, and blacksmith shop that represented the community's center.

Here many local whites were hostile to the idea of education for blacks, and Young became the direct object of racial prejudice. The mountain whites asked Young all types of questions to test him. Some of the whites were friendly, but most were hostile. The whites' questions would reveal their contempt for an educated black. Young recalled that one of the questions he was asked was: "A hog is one hundred feet from a tree, and he jumps halfway toward it at each jump. How many jumps will the hog take to get to the tree?"[28] The greatest expression of prejudice toward Young came from a local white farmer who particularly delighted in quizzing Young on a wide variety of subjects, even though his farm was not located in the township where Young taught. The farmer had several black families working on his farm, and Young had persuaded these families to send their children to his school. The farmer did not permit the children to attend school regularly, and when he found out that the town had paid Young the children's pro rata money, he tried to prove that Young had falsified reports. The farmer was successful in having a grand jury indict Young for obtaining money under false pretenses. This became a frightful experience for Young, even though the legal authorities did not take the matter too seriously. Because Young and his family were well known and the amount of the money was small, the indictment was dismissed without a trial. From this experience Young realized how deep were the prejudices of some Southern whites against the blacks receiving an education.[29]

The next summer Young faced hostility from the superintendent of schools in his home county. Young had spent the first month of his summer vacation looking in vain for a teaching position in his home county and in nearby counties. The superintendent of schools of Tuscaloosa County, Young's home county, did not want him to teach in the county, because Young did not trade in the superintendent's store. Young was saving his money to return to Talladega. Because black public schooling was not popular in the county, whites did not care about the qualifications of school offi-

28. Young, "The Quest," 44–45.
29. Ibid.

cials. The chief qualification of the superintendent was that he had served in the Confederate Army and had reached the rank of captain. The superintendent's attitude forced Young to seek a position outside the state.

With the aid of a friendlier white, Young spent the summer teaching in western Mississippi. Fortunately, Young had been tutored by the Reverend D. C. Rankin, the principal of Stillman Institute. Rankin gave Young a letter of introduction to the Reverend M. Archer, pastor of the Presbyterian church and county superintendent of schools in Greenville, Mississippi. Archer sent Young to a school forty miles away on a plantation located on an offshoot of the Mississippi River. This school was held in another former slave cabin and was to last for five months. Young closed the school, however, after two months because of a case of malaria.

Besides malaria, Young considered this a very undesirable experience because of the physical and moral environment, where most of the blacks were laborers on the plantation, with a few blacks making a living as tenant farmers and with many of the workers actually fugitives from justice, shielded by planters in exchange for their labor. There were only three legally married couples, and two of the white plantation owners had common-law black wives that they called housekeepers. These loose moral arrangements were upsetting to Young, and this experience helped convince him that he did not want to spend his life as a county grade-school teacher.[30]

Leaving this frightening experience, Young returned to Talladega for his last year and graduation. After graduating, Young taught for the summer in Alexandria, Alabama, near Anniston. The school was a newly built one-room log cabin, called the Chester Kirkley School, after the black man who had built it. Young was the first teacher in this school, but he did not stay beyond the summer. Before graduating from Talladega he had accepted a position for the fall in Jackson, Mississippi.[31]

After closing the Kirkley School, Young went to Jackson, Mississippi, where he was to become principal of a school taught in a benevolent society hall. Later this school would be called the

30. Ibid., 47–48.
31. Young, "A Fifty Year Jaunt."

Smith-Robinson School. He reported to the superintendent of schools for Hines County, a Mr. Wolfe, who told Young that he was not old enough for the position. The situation at the school was unusually bad, in that the former principal was involved in a morally compromising situation. Young convinced the superintendent that he could handle the challenge. Since Young was under appointment he was given a chance. Young had charge of half a dozen teachers and workers, all of whom were older than he was. This was Young's first teaching and administrative experience in a graded school, but he was unhappy with his performance. The black school board, however, was pleased with his work and renewed Young's contract for a second year, but Young refused to accept the contract because he had decided to return to school. He determined that "one cannot teach what one does not know."[32]

Young's year in the Jackson school was also his year of decision-making about his life's work. This was a year of indecision about the vocations of medicine, law, theology, and teaching. Young gave some thought to the idea of becoming a lawyer. During Reconstruction, the black man in Mississippi had been influential in politics. The state sent two blacks to the U.S. Senate and a black congressman to the House of Representatives. There were also black lawyers in Jackson. After the end of Reconstruction, however, the political rights of blacks declined throughout the South. Young had also witnessed acts of violence against black politicians in his native Alabama. At any rate, for the time being he gave up the idea of studying law.[33]

Young also considered studying medicine. As he was growing up in Tuscaloosa, a Judge E. W. Peck had urged him to enter medicine at those times when he had played marbles and other games around the judge's house. Each year when he returned from Talladega, then, Young would visit the judge, and the judge would encourage Young to study medicine so that black people would receive proper care. Because many Southern white doctors refused to give blacks medical care, Young was moved to accept the judge's

32. Ibid., 2; Young, "The Quest," 49. President De Forest also guided Young toward teaching as his profession.

33. Young, "The Quest," 49. Young later made a small effort toward reading law while principal of the Thomas Elementary School in Birmingham.

advice, but, in the end, Young could not think of himself as a black doctor since he had seen so few role models of black practitioners in the course of his own life.[34]

Another white Southerner, the Reverend D. C. Rankin, urged Young to enter the ministry and offered him a scholarship. But Young did not think of himself as saintly enough to be a minister. In the end, he decided to make teaching his life's work and to return to college for additional training.[35]

Having decided on a teaching career, Young had to select a school in which to continue his studies, and he had a difficult time choosing between Yale and Oberlin. Because De Forest was a Yale man and Young's educational patron, and because De Forest preferred that Young also attend Yale, Young seriously considered going to Connecticut. However, despite the advice of De Forest, he finally decided to go to Oberlin, primarily because some of his other teachers at Talladega were Oberlin graduates and they promoted that school's history of open race relations. Young, in fact, said that he selected Oberlin because of the school's record in this area.[36]

Since before the Civil War, Oberlin was noted for its efforts in educating black people. Later, the trustees of Oberlin reiterated "that the education of the people of color . . . should be encouraged and sustained in this institution." In 1900, W. E. B. Du Bois reported that of 390 black graduates of white colleges, 128 had been educated at Oberlin. More than a hundred others had attended Oberlin without graduating. The white college to graduate the second-highest number of blacks was the University of Kansas, with only 16.

Oberlin advertised and promoted its open-door policy. From 1878 until the 1930s, the college catalog proclaimed: "The educational facilities at Oberlin have always been open to all applicants, without regard to sex or color." Despite the open-door policy, however, the numbers of black students at Oberlin were always small. In the ten years following the Civil War, black students were never as high as 8 percent of the enrollment. By 1885, when

34. Ibid., 22–24.
35. Ibid., 24. Young said that his pastor thought it was foolish for him to return to college because his education was already "head and shoulders above the rank and file of his race."
36. Ibid., 26.

Young entered Oberlin, the percentage of black students, because of the school's high standards, had declined to no more than 6 percent.[37]

Another reason for Young's selection of Oberlin was his mother's preference for that institution. Oberlin, Ohio, was much closer to Tuscaloosa, Alabama, than was New Haven, Connecticut, and, for a mother as close as Susan was to her son, distance was important. Then, too, Oberlin's reputation as an evangelistic college appealed to the highly religious mother. Young also worried that studying at Yale might make him unfit for service in the South. He had already decided that upon graduation he would return to the South and teach. Young had seen other blacks educated in the East who could no longer return to the South.[38]

In choosing between Yale and Oberlin, Young had to consider expenses. The cost of an education at Oberlin was inexpensive when compared to Yale. At Oberlin students were encouraged to work and be self-supporting. The college prided itself on providing poor, hard-working young people an opportunity for an education. In 1885, the college advertised that as little as $100, added to the pay of one or two hours' work a day, would meet all the necessary expenses for tuition, incidentals, board, room, fuel, light, and washing for an academic year. While Oberlin may have been making the expense picture too rosy, it was much cheaper than Yale. Even a decade earlier Yale cost more than $4,000 a year while Oberlin cost from a low of $900 to a high of $2,100 a year.[39]

At Oberlin, for the first time in his life Young was competing against members of the white race. Young found that he was competing academically against some of the best-prepared white youth. Oberlin was a school that left its door open wide, and there were students from all over the world there. Since the faculty taught to the general student's abilities, Young not only found himself matched but also, at times, overmatched. He had to catch up academically. Young worked hard, often studying late into the night. From this experience Young began developing the convic-

37. W. E. Bigglestone, "Irrespective of Color," 35–36. W. E. Bigglestone, "Oberlin College and the Negro Student, 1865–1940," 198.
38. Young, "The Quest," 26.
39. John Barnard, *From Evangelicalism to Progressivism at Oberlin College, 1886–1917,* 17–18.

tion that black youth had to be educated in the same manner as white youth.[40]

In the 1880s, religion was a pervasive influence at Oberlin. The students were required to attend one of the Protestant churches in the town of Oberlin. Students did not attend classes on Monday so that Sunday would be free of lesson preparation. Each class started with an opening prayer or hymn. Travel and recreation were prohibited on Sunday, and violators were dismissed from the college. Oberlin students were expected to spend most of their out-of-class time in religious activities. In 1881, a YMCA was established and during the 1880s, the YMCA and its religious activities averaged four hundred student members. At this time, 25 percent of Oberlin's male graduates were ministers.[41]

At Oberlin, Young said that he found "an atmosphere favorable to all seekers of knowledge and the way to the 'higher life,' regardless of race or economic condition." He found an opportunity to take part in all the activities of the school. Young thought Oberlin was the ideal place where rich and poor were treated the same. The school was dominated by the Christian democracy of the earlier abolitionist movement. Here there was "simple living and noble thinking."[42]

In the 1880s Oberlin was, however, undergoing a transition from the old evangelistic college to the modern college. The older brick buildings were being replaced by stone buildings, but more importantly, changes were being made in the school's curriculum. Oberlin's curriculum was being modernized by the beginning of the elective system. Younger men were being hired for the school's faculty with advanced degrees from Harvard, Yale, Johns Hopkins, and the German universities. Also during this period Oberlin students were demanding that they be taught the current sciences, social sciences, and modern foreign languages. At this time, juniors and seniors were allowed to elect courses, while freshmen and sophomores were required to follow the traditional classical requirements. No freshman could become a sophomore without passing Professor William G. Frost's Greek test, which combined one hundred

40. Young, "The Quest," 26.
41. Barnard, *From Evangelicalism to Progressivism*, 25–31.
42. Young, "The Quest," 27.

questions on Greek syntax. Further, freshman mathematics blocked many students from the sophomore class.[43]

Young majored in classical studies at Oberlin. His course of study was very similar to classical courses dating back to the founding of Oberlin in the 1830s. His instruction consisted of courses in Greek, Latin, mathematics, religion, and science. Young went to summer school during 1886, and only spent three years at Oberlin, 1885–1888. Because of a lack of dormitory space, Young lived off campus, first at 12 South Professor Street and then, during his upperclassman years, at 27 East Mill.[44]

The courses in history, economics, and science that Young took in his junior and senior years represented modern trends in those disciplines. Such teachers as James Monroe, professor of political science and modern history; Lyman B. Hall, professor of Latin and history; Frank F. Jewett, professor of chemistry; Charles H. Churchill, professor of mathematics and natural philosophy; and Albert A. Wright, professor of zoology, geology, and natural history, were leading Oberlin toward a modern curriculum and into the front ranks of American colleges. Some of the students experiencing these new adventures in education would go on to establish themselves as outstanding teachers at Oberlin and other colleges and universities. Among their numbers were Robert A. Millikan in physics, William B. Chamberlin in biology, and John R. Commons in sociology and social science. Of this period Commons noted that Oberlin underwent an awakening, with better teaching methods, higher academic standards, and the "enthusiastic spirit of scholarship." During the 1880s, then, Oberlin was pushing to lead the country in "scholarship and learning," tempered by the old Oberlin spirit of moral righteousness.[45]

Young's contact with several members of the Oberlin faculty and community was to have a decided influence on his later life. Above all others stood James Harris Fairchild, president of Oberlin from 1866 until 1889, who represented the evangelical tradition and the commitment of Oberlin's founders to Christian democracy. Young

43. Barnard, *From Evangelicalism to Progressivism*, 36–39, 40, 42, 43; Young, "The Quest," 27.

44. Barnard, *From Evangelicalism to Progressivism*, 19–20. College transcript of Nathan B. Young, Book 14, 376, Oberlin College Archives.

45. Young, "The Quest," 28; Barnard, *From Evangelicalism to Progressivism*, 68.

considered Fairchild "a good man and a great teacher," a man who practiced the Christian charity he taught in his moral philosophy class. Young claimed that Fairchild's interpretations of the Scriptures were "seasoned with rare common sense and practical piety." He was a quiet and modest man who was scholarly and Christian-like in his behavior to all and who represented the traditional Oberlin spirit where rich and poor alike were treated equally. Fairchild was also an able administrator and teacher, whom Young regarded as a counselor and friend. His personality was to Young ideally suited to bridge the gap between the old and new Oberlin.[46]

Among the teachers who influenced Young was Charles H. Churchill, one of the older faculty members. Starting at Oberlin in 1858 as professor of mathematics and natural philosophy, he taught mathematics, physics, and astronomy until his retirement in 1897. Because Churchill taught so many subjects, Young considered him a "versatile scholar" and a model of character. He was modest and simple in manner, and Young thought him "profound," with "his laboratory a workshop in which many a student found guidance and inspiration to become a scientist."

Robert A. Millikan, a physics student, disagreed with Young's estimation of Churchill. To Millikan, Churchill's science was worthless, though he regarded the man as an excellent personal model for young men. Despite Millikan's opinion, however, Young believed that the "triumvirate" of Churchill in physics, Jewett in chemistry, and Wright in biology produced several outstanding scientists.[47]

There were others at Oberlin who influenced Young. Giles W. Shurtleff was to Young a scholar and Christian soldier. Like many of his fellow faculty members, Shurtleff was also a leader in the local temperance movement. He had fought with black soldiers in the Civil War and was an outstanding teacher in Latin. Possessing a sound business mind, in 1893 Shurtleff became the secretary and treasurer of Oberlin, and a bronze statue of him was later placed before his family home when that building was turned into a college residence hall.[48]

Other teachers who Young remembered were very different from

46. Young, "The Quest," 28–29.
47. Barnard, *From Evangelicalism to Progressivism,* 14; Young, "The Quest," 29. Young believed that Elisha Gray came up with his version of the telephone in Churchill's laboratory.
48. Young, "The Quest," 29.

the "elder statesmen" like Fairchild, Churchill, and Shurtleff. These were recent college graduates, and Young considered these younger teachers as "more *informing* than *inspiring.*" To Young, they were more interested in grades than in the proper spirit, and they were the "wrecking crew" for the underclassmen, often forcing freshmen and sophomores like Young to burn the "midnight oil." There was William G. Frost in Greek, Lyman B. Hall in Latin, and Henry C. King in mathematics, all of whom were Oberlin graduates. Until the turn of the century, in fact, Oberlin often hired its former students as faculty after advanced training elsewhere, a practice that was aimed at preserving the evangelistic spirit of the old Oberlin. These were deeply religious men, who led their students morally as well as intellectually, with Frost and King even organizing religious classes and organizations among their students. Later, Frost left Oberlin and became an outstanding college president at Berea. Hall became head of the history department at Oberlin, a position he retained until his death, and King became president of Oberlin and led the school to the front rank of liberal arts colleges in the United States.[49]

There were others who impressed and influenced Young. James Monroe had been on the faculty before 1866 and took a long leave of absence to engage in politics and diplomacy. He resumed teaching at Oberlin in 1883, after a career as a state representative, U.S. congressman, and diplomat. He was also a leader in the local temperance movement. Young considered him an inspiring teacher of history and economics. Some of his students went on to establish themselves as leaders in these fields. He was a "gentle warrior and honest politician," who made a pilgrimage to Harper's Ferry to return to Ohio the body of one of the black Ohioans who died with John Brown. Young thought he had an equalitarian attitude toward black Americans.[50]

Besides Monroe, there was John Millott Ellis. He taught at Oberlin from 1858 to 1894. An Oberlin College and seminary graduate, he was an ordained Congregational minister. During his career at Oberlin he taught successively Greek, rhetoric, mental philosophy,

49. Barnard, *From Evangelicalism to Progressivism,* 27, 37, 82, 38, 67, 81, 66–67, 75; Young, "The Quest," 29–30.
50. Barnard, *From Evangelicalism to Progressivism,* 32, 33; Young, "The Quest," 30.

and moral philosophy. Ellis was also a leader in temperance movements. He was a dynamic speaker and champion of the old Oberlin values.

Alongside the men of Oberlin stood a woman in shaping character and teaching culture, Mrs. Adelia A. F. Johnston or "Madam J." She was Oberlin's first woman professor and dean of women. Young called her "a virile [sic] woman and a safe leader of women." She had an "eagle eye" that protected the women of Oberlin from any moral compromise.[51]

There were other makers of character besides the faculty. There were young tutors about to become teachers like Charles B. Martin, Frederick Anderegg, Robert A. Millikan, and John Fisher Peck. Young saw Peck as a "prince of pals," who properly guided the students.[52]

There were also the local ministers who influenced Young's development. James Brand, a Congregationalist minister, was one of the college pastors. He had served in the Civil War, where, as a color bearer at Gettysburg, he took part in the fight that defeated General Pickett. Brand was a "preacher of righteousness," although not much of a speaker. He stood in sharp contrast to the other college minister, the Reverend Hutchins, whose eloquence charmed his listeners. Hutchins was the grandfather of the innovative educational leader of the University of Chicago.

Besides formal instruction, Oberlin had a variety of student literary societies. Such organizations were very important during the transition period of the 1880s. As Oberlin moved from an old classical college to a modern university, extracurricular literary clubs filled some of the gaps in the curriculum. Often, these organizations discussed and debated valuable and modern topics. The students would spend many hours preparing for their presentations or debates. Nearly all juniors and seniors belonged to the societies. In these societies the students received valuable training in the art of public speaking and thinking on one's feet. The dues paid by students allowed some of the societies to develop extensive libraries. These organizations were important socially as well as intellectually. The social importance of these organizations was probably due

51. Barnard, *From Evangelicalism to Progressivism,* 12–14, 32; Young, "The Quest," 31.
52. Ibid., 28, 31.

to the anti-fraternity attitude of the officials of Oberlin. Fraternities were seen as antidemocratic in spirit and, therefore, anti-Oberlin. Even those too poor to pay dues were admitted to the literary societies.[53]

Blacks were generally welcomed in the extracurricular literary societies, and Young belonged to the Phi Delta Literary Society, having been unanimously elected in June 1887. Because of Young's poverty, he was excused from two dollars of his induction fee, and he soon became active in the society. On November 23, 1887, for example, he presented an oration before the society entitled "Earth's Benefactors," and, during the quarterly meeting held on June 22, 1888, he read the essay of the evening, entitled "The Philosophy of the Interrogation Point."[54]

According to Young, he did not face any overt prejudice at Oberlin. During his years there the spirit of abolition and reconstruction was still strong, and segregation had not reached its high point nationally. Moreover, Oberlin was an isolated community where change came slowly, and the people seemed determined to hang on to the traditional democratic spirit. President Fairchild was an old Oberlin man who was completely devoted to the spirit of equality for all.

Other black students who attended Oberlin at about the same time that Young was there agreed with his assessment. Mary Church Terrell, for example, attended Oberlin High School and College from 1879 to 1885. Like Young she spent much of her nine years at Oberlin in contact with the black community and had a black roommate for years. Terrell, however, claimed intimate friendship with many of the white female students. For a time she lived in the main women's dormitory, Ladies Hall. She did not feel any discrimination against her while living on campus. She was accepted at all the college social affairs and class receptions. The one complaint she gave of prejudice was her not being elected class orator of her

53. Ibid., 30–31; Barnard, *From Evangelicalism to Progressivism,* 20–22. Oberlin's antisocial fraternity attitude stayed with Young for many years. Young denied an attempt to establish social fraternities at Lincoln University in the 1920s. Later, when the faculty voted for them, Young upheld a higher Oberlin tradition and agreed to the will of the faculty.

54. "Records of Phi Delta Literary Society," Oberlin College Archives. *General Catalogue of Oberlin College of 1833–1908* (Oberlin: Oberlin College, 1908), 501–2, 559.

high school junior class despite the fact that she had been class orator of the freshmen class and felt herself much more qualified than her opponent. She lost after several ballots and determined that her color had caused her defeat.[55]

President Fairchild, writing in the mid-1880s, claimed that black and white students were treated the same. White students were not made to associate with black students or allowed to abuse them. In 1883, Fairchild could not remember any racial problem on the campus except for an infrequent fight between individual black and white students. He did admit that occasionally some of the black students "imagined" racial prejudice on the part of some of the white students.[56]

Like the nation, however, in the 1880s Oberlin was going through a transition in race relations. Despite the efforts of President Fairchild and most of his faculty, prejudice was becoming more evident at Oberlin. In 1882, an Oberlin professor objected to a black student's attempt to room with a white student. A committee of six black students protested the discrimination, but the black and white student were not permitted to room together. This practice was continued for many years. In this same school year, for the first time, white students in the main women's dormitory, Ladies Hall, refused to eat at the same table with black students. As a result, black women students were seated at a separate table. Both black and white alumni strongly protested this sign of overt racial prejudice. This discrimination was eliminated only after much arguing with the white students by the dean of women and President Fairchild.[57]

These were not the only incidents of prejudice at Oberlin. Earlier, an oratorical contest was marred by many white students agreeing not to vote for a black speaker. The incident did not go unnoticed, for in March 1883 a group of black students protested in the school's newspaper, the *Oberlin Review,* against the increasing racial intolerance:

> Although nearly all colleges are now open to colored students there are supposed to be some advantages in studying at Oberlin.

55. Mary C. Terrell, *A Colored Woman in a White World,* 39–55; Bigglestone, "Oberlin College and the Negro Student," 198–199.
56. Bigglestone, "Oberlin College and the Negro Student," 199–200.
57. Ibid., 200.

> We hope that these advantages will increase as only the students can increase them, and that the day will soon dawn when it will not require so much "forbearance" as "brotherly love" and "charity" to tolerate the Negroes presence.[58]

While incidents of discrimination and prejudice continued at Oberlin, they were the exception rather than the rule. The policy and principles of the Oberlin administration and faculty were opposed to discrimination and segregation. In general, a black student was treated on a basis of equality. Despite the prejudices of a few students, as a whole, Oberlin stood for democracy and an absence of special privilege. Historically Oberlin was opposed to the aristocracy of color, sex, wealth, and elitism. It is this better part of Oberlin that Young absorbed and remembered.[59]

It is this model of the more democratic Oberlin that Young tried to establish in the black colleges he would later head. Through the alumni magazine and correspondences with faculty members, Young was always aware of the direction and progress of Oberlin. Young was greatly influenced by his time spent at Oberlin. He took on the Christian democratic attitude of Oberlin.[60]

When Young was about to leave Oberlin, he was asked, at an informal gathering of future missionary workers, in which part of Africa he intended to work. He answered that part located in the state of Alabama. True to his word, in 1888, Young returned to Alabama.[61]

In 1888, Young graduated with a bachelor of arts degree in Classical Studies, and started working on a master of arts degree from Oberlin. At this time, Oberlin followed the practice of many other colleges and universities in conferring the master of arts degree upon those nonresident graduates who subsequently pursued three years of professional study.[62] To obtain his master of arts, Young

58. Quoted in Ibid., 200–201.

59. Donald Love, *Henry Churchill King of Oberlin,* 156–57; Barnard, *From Evangelicalism to Progressivism,* 73; Interview with Nathan B. Young, Jr., July 1981, in St. Louis.

60. Interview with Nathan B. Young, Jr., July, 1981, in St, Louis.

61. Young, "The Quest," 32.

62. *General Catalogue of Oberlin College of 1833–1908,* 1097; *Oberlin Triennial and Quinquennial Catalogue for 1889,* 91; *1900,* 119; *1905,* 151; and *Alumni Register,* 1960, Section 3, Part D, Oberlin College Archives.

had to read in the area of history and write a thesis. A committee of the faculty assigned the readings. In October 1889, Young informed Professor James Monroe, who was guiding Young's reading in modern history, of his progress. Young reported that he had already read the books earlier assigned by the committee. They included Arnold's *Lectures on Modern History*, Youge's *Three Centuries of Modern Europe*, Hausser's *Period of the Reformation*, and Mignet's *History of the French Revolution*. In addition, Young had reread Lodge's *Modern Europe*, read over a large part of Professor Monroe's lectures, and constantly referred to Anderson's *General History*. Young also had to study and read in the area of medieval history. Besides Professor Monroe, Young worked with Professor Wright.[63] In 1891, Young received the master of arts degree in history.

In that same year, he wrote an open letter to his classmates, reporting on his activities. He informed them that he was about to get married, that his year had started well, and that he looked forward to great things in the future. He had done little else since graduating except teach and read history, noting that it even took him three years to finish a two-year course of postgraduate study. He ended his letter endorsing and promising to attend a class reunion at the 1893 World Fair, and throughout the rest of his life, in fact, he would always stay in close contact with his alma mater.[64]

63. Nathan B. Young to Professor James Monroe, October 18, 1889, *Monroe Papers*, Box 15, Oberlin College Archives.

64. "Necrology for Years 1932–33," Oberlin College Archives; Nathan B. Young to Class of 1888, class letters 1891, dated October 28, 1891, 32, Oberlin College Archives. "Questionnaire" from Oberlin College Office of the Secretary dated March 13, 1915, filled out by Young, March 22, 1915, Oberlin College Archives. N. B. Young to H. C. King, August 25, 1915; H. C. King to N. B. Young, September 15, 1915, *Henry C. King Papers*, Box 81, Oberlin College Archives. Young wrote King and asked for his reaction to Young's presidential address before the National Association of the Teachers of Colored Schools, in which he called for a black graduate institution to be established in the South. King was favorably impressed with Young's idea and predicted that it would soon become a reality. N. B. Young to H. C. King, January 28, 1916; Oberlin College, Office of President to N. B. Young, January 31, 1916; and H. C. King to N. B. Young, March 6, 1916, *Henry C. King Papers*, Box 81, Oberlin College Archives; and Rayford W. Logan and Michael R. Winston, editors, *Dictionary of American Negro Biography*, 459–60. Young asked King to recommend an honorary doctorate from Oberlin for Robert R. Moton, who had taken the late B. T. Washington's place as the head of Tuskegee. Oberlin awarded Moton the honorary degree.

After returning to Alabama, Young spent one rather uneventful year as the principal of a rural elementary school in Shelby, Alabama, followed by three "exciting" years as the principal of the General G. L. Thomas School in Birmingham, Alabama. The years Young served as principal of this school were a significant part of his preparation for his life's work as a college teacher and administrator, because they brought him into direct and lasting contact with one of the more advanced and enlightened school systems in the South for both races. Furthermore, these years also brought him into significant contact with Booker T. Washington, and it was from this contact that Young then moved on to Tuskegee Institute in 1892.[65]

---

65. Nathan B. Young, "The Birmingham Public Schools—Colored Department"; Charles W. Dabney, *Universal Education in the South*, vol. 2, 402–3.

CHAPTER 2

At Tuskegee (1892–1897)

The Making of an Educator

From 1892 until 1897, Nathan B. Young worked alongside Booker T. Washington in building Tuskegee Institute. Young played a significant role in charting the direction that Tuskegee's academic program took, but, eventually, he and Washington came into conflict over the philosophy and direction of Tuskegee's academic department. This conflict resulted in Young's leaving Tuskegee.

Young would always regard his years of service at Tuskegee with Washington as his most "eventful and helpful" years. He considered these to be his years of preparation for his later service elsewhere: his "post-graduate years." Here he began his teaching career in earnest, and these five years held a unique place in his heart. No place gave Young exactly the same feelings as he got on his perennial visits to Tuskegee. Even at its fiftieth anniversary in 1931, the memories of the earlier Tuskegee were still strong as Young surveyed the "most remarkable growth" of Tuskegee from "its days of small things." In short, Young had come to Tuskegee at a formative period for him, and his experiences there would leave an enduring mark on him throughout his professional career.[1]

1. Young, "A Fifty Year Jaunt." For an overview of black education see James D. Anderson, *The Education of Blacks in the South, 1860–1935.* The economics of black education is covered in Robert A. Margo, *Race and Schooling in the South, 1880–1950: An Economic History.*

When Young returned to Alabama from Oberlin College to start his teaching career in 1888, he hoped to meet Booker T. Washington and see Tuskegee Institute. Washington's Tuskegee was being talked about by Henry De Forest as an unusual kind of school, and Young was interested in examining it. Young hoped to meet Washington at the Alabama State Teachers' Association meeting in Selma in 1889, but because of the recent death of his second wife, Washington did not attend the conference. In 1890, the next meeting of the Alabama State Teachers' Association was held at Tuskegee. Young attended the conference and saw the campus, but Washington was not present at this conference either because he was off on his spring fund-raising campaign.[2]

Young finally got to meet Washington in 1891, when the teachers' association met at Huntsville. Young led a group of Birmingham teachers to the meetings. In the course of the train ride from Birmingham to Huntsville, Young and his group had to change trains at Decatur, and there they were surprised by the sight of Washington getting off a Pullman in the early morning hours before daybreak. Here Young and Washington met for the first time, and this meeting started an acquaintance that would last between them until Washington's death in 1915. At the Huntsville meeting Young's debating skills impressed Washington, and he invited Young to Tuskegee as a guest lecturer. Young accepted the invitation, but he still did not have an opportunity to talk with Washington, who was off on another one of his fund-raising campaigns.[3]

In January 1892, as principal of the Thomas School in Birmingham, Young was again in contact with Washington. Washington wished to meet with the teachers of the Thomas School sometime during February. Young had informed his teachers of Washington's request, and the teachers were happy to meet with him.[4]

In the early 1890s, Washington was emerging as the leading black educator in the South, and he was trying to attract teachers such as Young to his program. Washington began using the Tuskegee Conference to sell his program. The first Tuskegee Negro Conference was to be held on February 23, 1892, and it was billed as a unique

2. Young, "The Quest," 40.
3. Ibid., 41.
4. Nathan B. Young to Booker T. Washington, January 28, 1892, Booker T. Washington Papers, Division of Manuscripts of the Library of Congress. Hereafter cited as Booker T. Washington Papers.

conference. Washington claimed that his was to be a quiet conference, not of politicians nor the so-called "leading colored people,"
but of "representatives of the masses—the bone and sinew of the
race": the common, hardworking farmers, with a few of the best
ministers and teachers.[5]

Washington had two major goals for the conference. The first
was to determine the real industrial, moral, and educational conditions of the black masses, and the second was to find the most effective way for educators to use their skills to help the masses uplift
themselves. The state of black education, especially in the county
schools, was poor. In these districts, schools were open for only
about three months and students were generally taught in churches
or rough log cabins with no equipment or proper school furniture.
In Washington's view, this first Tuskegee Negro Conference was "a
day memorable in the lives and fortunes of the great bulk of the
Negro population in the 'Black Belt' of the South." He had invited
about seventy-five people to the conference, and four hundred men
and women showed up.[6]

Among other things, Washington and his Tuskegee Conference
drew attention to the poor state of black education in Alabama. At
the conclusion of the conference, a "Declarations of the First
Tuskegee Conference" covering ten major areas of black life was issued. The fifth declaration was on educational conditions. After
noting the shortness of county school sessions and lack of proper
school houses, it pointed out that the teachers were also poorly prepared for their work, with the result that few children attended
school with any regularity. Black citizens were urged to make up
the difference between what the state provided for black education
and what was really needed, including better salaries for their
teachers. Parents were warned to pay particular attention to the
mental and moral fitness of the teachers in their schools and to do
away with all sectarian prejudices in the running of the schools.[7]

5. "A Circular Announcing the Tuskegee Negro Conference," Tuskegee,
Alabama, ca. January 1892, Louis R. Harlan, editor, *Booker T. Washington Pa-
pers,* 13 vols. (Urbana: University of Illinois Press, 1972–84), vol. 3, 209–10.
Hereafter cited as *B. T. W. Papers.*

6. "Samuel Chapman Armstrong to the Tuskegee Faculty," February 23,
1892, *B. T. W. Papers,* vol. 3, 216.

7. "The Declaration of the First Tuskegee Negro Conference," Tuskegee,
Alabama, February 23, 1892, *B. T. W. Papers,* vol. 3, 217–19.

Young and Washington met again on June 8 when Washington addressed the annual meeting of the Alabama State Teachers' Association in Birmingham. His topic was the "Aims and Results of Teaching," and he urged the Alabama teachers to see the school curriculum as a means rather than an end in itself and to see the moral and spiritual uplift of their students as the real ends of their educational efforts.[8]

These meetings and their general agreement about the state of education for blacks led Washington to invite Young to Tuskegee as a teacher in mid August 1892 for $65 per month for nine months or $585 a year. Washington chose Young because he was interested in using his limited resources to hire the best teachers available for Tuskegee. Soon afterwards, Young telegraphed Washington and informed him that he could be in Tuskegee the next day, prepared to teach English and history.[9]

When Young arrived at Tuskegee in 1892, the institute had been established for more than a decade and had grown a great deal from its small beginnings. The Tuskegee of 1881 began with 30 students and one teacher. By the time that Young arrived it had 600 students and 38 teachers. In the beginning there had been no money and no land. By 1892 the school had 1,400 acres of land, 20 buildings (17 of which were built with student labor), and real and personal property worth $180,000. In terms of livestock, in 1881 there was only one weak horse, while in 1892 there were 260 head of livestock.[10] In short, Washington's Tuskegee, which had begun with very little in 1881, had grown appreciably by the year of Young's arrival.

By emphasizing the philosophy of self-help and a program of industrial education, Washington had greatly developed Tuskegee. The school had been established for the instruction of black teachers and youths in various common academic and collegiate branches, with teachers and youths to be taught the best methods of teaching

8. "An Address Before the Alabama State Teachers' Association," Birmingham, Alabama, June 8, 1892, *B. T. W. Papers*, vol. 3, 234–36.

9. Young to Washington, August 6 and 18, 1892, Booker T. Washington Papers.

10. Booker T. Washington, "A Speech at the Memorial Service for Samuel Chapman Armstrong," Hampton, Virginia, May 25, 1893, *B. T. W. Papers*, vol. 3, 317–21.

and the best methods of theoretical and practical industry, which they could then apply to their work in agriculture and the mechanical arts.[11] In short, the school was set up to help teach black students of various ages enough so that they could either teach other black students or make a decent living in one of the agricultural or mechanical trades. Thus part of Tuskegee's appeal to blacks lay in the fact that Washington stressed self- and group-help for the masses of blacks in the South who had suffered through slavery only to find the Reconstruction programs had not really done enough to rectify their earlier, enslaved condition.

Many Southern white leaders found it appealing that agricultural and mechanical arts were to be stressed as much as the liberal arts. Thus, local whites were somewhat assured that Tuskegee would be raising the skill levels of blacks in areas which local whites approved: farming and the manual trades, areas in which blacks had traditionally worked in the South.

The greater physical development of Tuskegee was just beginning as Young arrived. In 1892, Phelps Hall Bible School, a nondenominational school that was the gift of a generous woman in New York, opened. Thanks to her donation, the building housing the school was a large three-story structure containing a chapel, library, reading room, office, four recitation rooms, and forty sleeping areas.[12] The purpose of the Bible School, of course, was to train religious leaders who would return to their communities and help address the spiritual and moral needs of the people in those communities.

Tuskegee was beginning to make a real impact by 1892. There were thirty thousand poor and often ignorant blacks living within a one-hundred-mile radius of Tuskegee, and before the institute's

11. "An Act to Incorporate Tuskegee Normal and Industrial Institute," Montgomery, Alabama, December 13, 1892, *B. T. W. Papers,* vol. 3, 274–77. On February 21, 1893, "An Amendment to the Act Incorporating Tuskegee Institute" was passed by the General Assembly. *B. T. W. Papers,* vol. 3, 299–302. Butler, *The Distinctive Black College,* 60–61, claims that these acts of the Alabama General Assembly not only formally changed the name of Tuskegee but also its nature from a state-supported normal school to a private industrial school receiving state aid but not subjected to state interference. Therefore, Washington could pick his own board of trustees.

12. Booker T. Washington, "An Announcement of the Opening of Phelps Hall Bible School," Tuskegee, Alabama, November, 1892, *B. T. W. Papers,* vol. 3, 271.

existence there seemed to be little hope for them, with schools running only three months a year and most blacks landless and in debt to the crop-lien system. But Tuskegee and its graduates had made a major difference. Since the start of Tuskegee, the institute had reached three thousand students, five hundred of whom had finished the course and had gotten enough training to have significantly improved their skills. These former students were now working as farmers, mechanics, merchants, ministers, and teachers, and they had taught nearly thirty thousand youths in Alabama, Mississippi, Georgia, Florida, Louisiana, and Texas. Such was the impact that Tuskegee had had on the South by the time Young arrived at the school. In short, when Young joined the staff, the overall purpose of Tuskegee was to better the economic, educational, and moral condition of the black community.[13] That was the reason why Young came to Tuskegee.

In the beginning, Young was simply hired to teach English and history, but soon his duties and responsibilities were broadened. Because Tuskegee was a small school, everyone was expected to pitch in and help in whatever areas required attention. Thus in April 1893 Washington asked Young to write some articles about the work at Tuskegee and attempt to get them published in two Alabama newspapers, the *Tribune* and the *Mail and Express*. For his part, Young informed Washington that he thought his idea "a good one" and proceeded to work on the project.[14] Later that month, Young apprised Washington of the results of his efforts in this endeavor. One of the newspaper editors agreed to publish articles about the school.

Young then offered himself for additional service at Tuskegee. After mentioning that Washington had indicated in his last letter that he was planning to institute closer supervision of the academic program, Young offered himself for the position. Young pointed out his experience as an administrator. He had served five years as principal of grammar schools. He said that he had given

13. Washington, "A Speech at the Memorial Service for Samuel Chapman Armstrong," *B. T. W. Papers,* vol. 3, 317–21. "An Account of the Tuskegee Negro Conference," Tuskegee, Alabama, February 21, 1893, *B. T. W. Papers,* vol. 3, 294–99.

14. Young to Washington, August 18, 1892, April 10, 1893, Booker T. Washington Papers.

the matter special study, and concluded, "I think I see your *weak place* here in your academic work." Should Washington give Young favorable consideration, Young suggested that he could hold a teaching position as he then did, with about three classes a day, in addition to his new responsibilities as supervisor of the academic program.[15]

Almost immediately Washington gave Young the responsibilities of head teacher of the academic area. On its most basic, day-to-day level, Young's work as head teacher was mostly concerned with the mundane, routine concerns of a small school. To begin with, Young was still primarily a teacher, one with a full teaching load. In the fall of 1893, for example, he was teaching five regular classes, one speech class, and one study period. It was in addition to all this that he pursued his administrative work. By 1894 the night school had been added to his workload, and his workday now ran from 8:30 a.m. to 9 p.m.[16] Throughout his stay at Tuskegee, teaching continued to be a part of Young's contribution to the school.

Perhaps the most time-consuming and unending of Young's routine responsibilities was his scheduling of classes and courses. When the fall session of 1893 began, for example, the school's program was in very bad shape. In response to this situation, Young offered a plan for a schedule which Washington thought valuable. Washington asked the committee on the course of study to look into the problem immediately, and he suggested specific areas in which he expected improvement. To improve the school's program, Washington asked the committee to pay particular attention to the time of day when studies could best be handled. Washington even asked the committee to take into account that some of the teachers taught in different buildings at a distance from each other. Allowances were to be made for the division of classes into sections, and a course of study was to be laid out to cover all the programs offered in the catalog.

Washington also wanted the fitness of teachers to match the level of work they were teaching, and he wanted each teacher to

15. Young to Washington, April 24, 1893, Booker T. Washington Papers.
16. Young to Washington, August 9, 1893, August 17, 1895, Booker T. Washington Papers.

teach a particular subject. He sent the committee a list of the names of teachers with the amount of work he thought each could be expected to do and the subjects he thought the teachers were capable of teaching. Moreover, Washington said that it was the policy of the school to give each teacher as near as possible a specialized branch to teach and he wanted this policy enforced as much as possible. Washington said that he believed that a "teacher can do the best work when he has but one or two branches." In conclusion, Washington asked the committee to look into all these matters immediately.[17]

Part of Young's duties as head teacher called for him to keep Washington constantly informed. At the start of classes in September of 1894, for example, Washington asked Young to supply him with the schedules of several teachers. In one note, dated September 12, Washington asked to know how many classes three particular teachers heard each day. In response Young wrote the appropriate schedules and promised Washington a full schedule on the following Monday. The same day, Washington asked for the schedule of class work assigned to yet another teacher. In response, Young wrote the appropriate schedule down and then informed Washington that he would have a general program placed in the principal's "office tomorrow (Friday)."[18]

Young's duties as head teacher made it his responsibility to replace teachers and to rearrange the schedule of classes. Because of poor pay, Washington's fault-finding, and failure to reward overtime and extra effort, there was a constant turnover of Tuskegee teachers. On September 9, 1895, Young informed Washington that his department would be ready for opening the next day, only to find out that morning that some of his teachers had not arrived to cover their classes. They were not simply late, and replacements had to be found. Indeed the assignment of teachers to new classes and recommending replacements for resignations was a continuous affair, and at times, this would happen midway through a semester, as happened with the scheduling of Mrs. Booker T. Washington to a Special English class on November 5, 1895. Several weeks later, the

17. Washington to the Faculty Committee on the Course of Study, September 15, 1893, *B. T. W. Papers,* vol. 3, 366–67.
18. Washington to Young, two notes dated September 12, 1894, Booker T. Washington Papers.

schedule had to be rearranged for a new teacher, Miss Melvin, to teach six history classes.[19]

In addition to this sort of routine chaos, Young frequently had extra duties such as scheduling and escorting guest lecturers. Even when the lecturers had been invited by someone else and were lecturing in areas that were totally out of Young's academic area, he sometimes had to take the responsibility. Such was the case with the visiting teacher who was invited from a sister institution and had arrived to lecture on home economics to the upper-class women. Less hectic were the moments when Washington would ask Young to schedule a series of lectures that were planned for the future, as was the case with the weeklong Dulton Lectures.[20]

Personnel matters were a major part of the head teacher's job. Young desired to have only the best teachers in the classroom, and he believed that the best, most experienced teachers should teach the lower grades and classes. Young felt that the lower-level students needed the help the most and that the foundations of future schooling were laid there. He always encouraged the transfer of teachers if it made a better program.[21] Thus, a great deal of Young's time was spent matching teachers and classes, abilities and needs.

One of Young's first major contributions to Tuskegee was his examination of the whole Academic Department. He assessed mathematics as "the *lowest Dept.* in the school," partially because 50 percent of the students in such classes frequently failed. Since the students were successfully passing all of their other classes, Young thought some of the blame indirectly had to fall on the teacher. Accordingly, he asked Washington to approve the transfer of certain teachers to improve the situation in mathematics and to "get a *wide* awake man for the sciences."[22]

19. Young to Washington, September 5, 1895, November 5 and 30, 1895, December 19 and 24, 1895, Booker T. Washington Papers. Louis R. Harlan, *Booker T. Washington,* 281.

20. Young to Washington, February 15 and 19, 1894, Booker T. Washington Papers.

21. Young to Washington, "A Report," May 1, 1896; Young to Washington, June 29, 1896; Young to Washington, Boston, Massachusetts, to Tuscaloosa, Alabama, 1896; Young to Washington, August 15, 1896; Young to Washington, August 25, 1896; Young to Washington, a second letter also dated August 25, 1896; and Young to Washington, December 27, 1895, Booker T. Washington Papers.

22. Young to Washington, March 8, 1894, Booker T. Washington Papers.

On the other hand, there were always individual teachers who did not care for their reassignments, some of whom would go over Young's head and write to Washington. One such case involved a Miss Thompson, who worked in the school's library and was assigned a night class as well. She complained to Washington that she was being overworked, and Young had to explain to Washington that it would be a simple matter to have a suitable student relieve her of some of her library duties, that he needed her special skills in a class that he wanted to be observed by the junior-year students "detailed for the work preparatory to the pedagogy of the senior year," and that the core of the problem was that Miss Thompson simply did not want to teach at night.[23]

Young also had to devise general policy guidelines, as with the question of whether teachers should be allowed to teach in two very different areas. Despite Washington's practice of dividing a teacher's time between the school's two departments, Young demanded that Washington remove teachers from the Academic Department who could not prepare their lesson plans because their time and energies were going to the other department. This became such a serious problem that Young prepared a special statement to Washington, recommending that industrial arts teachers and clerks not be assigned duties in the Academic Department unless they were given a *"definite"* time in which to prepare for the classes and attend academic meetings.[24] These seemingly sensible reforms were not possible or practical given the poor financial circumstances of Tuskegee, and Washington did not make the changes.

Throughout his tenure at Tuskegee, Young wanted to give his teachers sufficient chance to prove themselves. When in October 1895 Washington wrote asking for a list of teachers who were doing unsatisfactory work, Young refused to comply. He would not be forced to make a premature recommendation even by Washington. All the teachers were making an effort to improve their teaching, he noted, and he would inform Washington if any of the teachers began to falter in these efforts. It was not that Young thought that all of the teachers were good. In fact, there were some that he

23. Young to Washington, September 14, 1895, Booker T. Washington Papers.
24. Young to Washington, March 6, 1895, Booker T. Washington Papers.

thought would never make good teachers, and at the proper time he would recommend that they not be reemployed. Young felt, however, that they should be given a "fair chance to show their ability or inability."[25]

Young also sought to keep his teachers from being overburdened by other campus duties. For example, if his teachers were being overworked by the numerous extra duties at Tuskegee, such as "trunk inspection," Young would speak up. Often he would speak up for his teachers even if they had not complained themselves. Young often had to remind Washington that almost all the regular teachers of the Academic Department were carrying a full schedule of class work—six classes.[26]

Young also tried to protect his teachers from having to teach too many classes. In September of 1896, he insisted that Washington issue an order that night school teachers assigned to other departments during the day be let off in sufficient time to allow them to prepare for their night classes. Young found this to be a special problem for two men, and he strongly believed that no one could work all day and successfully teach a night class. He insisted that the school would gain nothing by overworking its teachers.[27]

Yet Young's greatest support of his teachers came less in areas of overwork and underappreciation than it did in the amount of intellectual freedom that he granted them, even when this approach brought him directly into conflict with one of Washington's edicts. In 1896, Washington made it clear that he wanted Young to supervise and control his teachers more closely. As Washington saw it,

> there is need of great improvement in the matter of looking into the class room work closely. Such defects can only be remedied by you looking in detail into the work of each teacher, going into their classes, often looking into their papers, etc. I depend on you to keep close contact with the work of each individual teacher, and the proper results can only be obtained by a close individual inspection of each teacher's

25. Young to Washington, October 19, 1895, Booker T. Washington Papers.

26. Young to Washington, April 16, 1896; Young to Washington, April 29, 1896, Booker T. Washington Papers.

27. Young to Washington, September 22, 1896, Booker T. Washington Papers.

work from week to week. It might be well for you to remain with one teacher several days or a week in order to get that teacher in the right track and correct defects.[28]

Young's response to this order was equally clear, forceful, and articulate: "The question of supervision, raised in your note, is yet an open question," he began. Then he proceeded to explain his perception of education and its management to Washington:

> How far shall a supervisor direct the work of the teacher? Shall he go into the minutia of showing a teacher how to grade examination papers, how to conduct this or that recitation and such question of detail, which doubtless, if entered, will destroy all freedom, all personality of the teacher.
>
> I much prefer the method which I pursue here, and pursued before coming here, of holding the teacher responsible for results, going on the presumption that the teacher has sufficient teaching ability to direct the details of her work, and to take and apply the suggestions offered in private conversations and in teachers meetings or institutions, in my mind, the only successful way of procedure on part of the supervisor. If, among the corp[s] of teachers, there is one who is so obtuse, or so conceited as not to take suggestions, the duty of the supervisor is to recommend (only after fair consideration in view of results) the removal of said teacher.
>
> I try to supervise the work of my associates in such a way to leave them the largest possible freedom in selecting their methods, in offering suggestions as well as in receiving them. I want them to feel free to come to me for suggestions, as freely as I go to them with suggestions. In a word, I strive for the cooperation of the teachers, to impress upon them that I am their co-worker, not their director, or their brains.
>
> I go to their class-room sufficiently often to know that they are doing, and how they are doing—to gather general information as to the progress of the work, and of the difficulties in the way. Finding difficulties, we set about to devise a remedy.
>
> If I go into further details, I cross or check the teacher's individuality. Class-room supervision is a delicate piece of work, and

28. Washington to Young, March 11, 1896, Booker T. Washington Papers.

needs to be done with the greatest precaution, else the work
will be marred by useless personalities.

I have made this lengthy statement, not because I take any exception to your note, but to give you my notion of the functions of my office, regarding the class-room work of the
teachers especially, and thus to explain my policy in dealing
with them. Experience has taught me that this is the best policy
for me, and I can not adopt any other.[29]

Unfortunately, Young's idealistic concepts of academic freedom
were not very practical given the circumstances of Tuskegee. Some
teachers were irresponsible, unenergetic, and even incompetent.
Closer supervision of the teachers was called for in many cases.

Young's educational philosophy was unlike Washington's education philosophy in general; it certainly was not Washington's philosophy at Tuskegee. Washington saw Tuskegee as "an institution
where the will and policy of the Principle are expected to be carried
out even in the remotest corner of the school in the actions of
teachers and students through the head of department." Teachers
and administrators were expected to have "that delicacy of mind
that should enable one to detect even without formal order, the
policy and wish of the one in charge of the school, and seek without pressure to carry out the policy." Eventually, this conflict of values forced Young to leave Tuskegee.[30]

In addition to Young's normal academic responsibilities, there
was, or course, the ever-present concern with supplies. Throughout
his tenure at Tuskegee, Young had difficulty obtaining adequate
supplies. In the mid 1890s, for example, he submitted a request to
the Financial Committee and asked for an electric bell to indicate
the start and close of class periods. He then, however, changed that
request to a considerably cheaper ten-inch gong, hoping, since his
department had made few demands, that this request would "not
be indefinitely postponed." Young then made a second request, for
"respectable black boards." He felt the committee would agree with
him that the present blackboards were a disgrace to the school, and

29. Young to Washington, March 11, 1896, *B. T. W. Papers,* vol. 4, 133–
35.

30. Young to Washington, March 26, 1896, *B. T. W. Papers,* vol. 4, 145–
49.

he feared that the lack of adequate blackboards would keep Tuskegee from achieving the same levels as her sister institutions.[31]

Young was also responsible for the cleanliness of the school rooms, and this issue drew him into conflict with Washington more than once. Before Young came to Tuskegee, the head teacher of the Academic Department had seen to the scrubbing and cleaning of Porter Hall and the classrooms. Young hired a janitor to perform this function, but the overall responsibility remained his. Washington and Young had a policy battle over the question of how often the Porter Hall rooms should be scrubbed. Washington, because he greatly valued cleanliness, ordered in March 1895 that Porter Hall be scrubbed every other day. Young immediately protested strongly against the scrubbing of the rooms in the afternoons during the week. The rooms were used for the night classes, Young noted, and he felt it was unhealthy and wrong to ask students and teachers to sit in a room with a wet floor for two hours. The rooms could be scrubbed on Saturday, Young insisted.[32]

Washington expected an absolute adherence to his wishes in all areas that Young could not give. As Washington's and Young's relationship began to fall apart, "cleanliness" of the school rooms was one of the issues. In accusing Young of choosing to "disregard or disrespect the requests or wishes of the Principal," Washington cited the following example among others:

> Some months ago I asked that special attention be given all through the school to the matter of cleanliness. You did not cooperate in this in a hearty and effective manner. Not only this, but those directly in charge of some part of the cleaning reported to me more than once that you were opposing my policy, and would not cooperate. Almost no attention was given to my request as to the cleanliness, order and attractiveness of the class rooms, etc., until I went into several rooms myself and had the janitor put my policy into effect.[33]

31. Young to the Financial Committee, August 13, 1894, Booker T. Washington Papers.

32. Washington to Young, November 2, 1895, Booker T. Washington Papers, March 5, 1895, *B. T. W. Papers,* vol. 3, 542; Young to Washington, ca. 1896, Booker T. Washington Papers.

33. Washington to Young, March 26, 1896, *B. T. W. Papers,* vol. 4, 145–49.

Like other Tuskegee workers, Young was also occasionally assigned duties that were seen as necessary for the growth and development of the institute. Washington was often away from Tuskegee on fund-raising trips and depended on his close associates to carry out tasks for him. Young, for example, was frequently asked to set up statewide and national conferences, and thus he was the one who principally organized "A Chautauqua for Negroes" at Tuskegee in the summers of the mid 1890s. An article on one event was published in highly respected Northern black newspapers. And it was Young who helped set up some of the Tuskegee Negro Conferences of the 1890s, in particular, one that was attended by almost six hundred persons. Young was also delegated by Washington to arrange Tuskegee's academic exhibit at the Atlanta Exposition.[34]

Young occasionally handled assignments related to Washington's activities in various professional organizations. For example, at times, Young handled some of the affairs of the Alabama Negro Teachers' Association for Washington, and on one occasion, he was specifically charged with getting out the minutes of the organization. Young, however, felt that Washington did not give him enough support to accomplish the job, and he sharply warned Washington that if he was not given enough help the task could not be accomplished at all.[35]

And, of course, Young would frequently initiate activities himself. Some of these activities were to benefit Tuskegee directly and some to benefit the causes of black education and black life, as Young perceived them. A good example was Young's suggestion to Washington in the fall of 1895 that he thought the general catalog needed to be "written up" differently and that he would try to have a new catalog prepared for Washington's review upon the president's return from a trip.[36]

One example of Young's outside professional interests was his

---

34. "An Announcement in the Indianapolis Freeman," *B. T. W. Papers,* vol. 3, 450–51, and "The Negro Chautaugua," *Indianapolis Freeman,* July 7, 1894. "An Account of the Tuskegee Negro Conference," Tuskegee, Alabama, February 20–21, 1895, *Southern Workman* 24 (March 1895): 36–38. See also in *B. T. W. Papers,* vol. 3, 521–30. Young to Washington, September 5, 1895, Booker T. Washington Papers.

35. Young to Washington, March 8, 1894, Booker T. Washington Papers.

36. Young to Washington, November 30, 1895, Booker T. Washington Papers.

own work with the Alabama Teachers' Association. This was an organization cofounded by Booker T. Washington, who was also the organization's third president. Young had been active in the organization for many years, and he would be the organization's fourth elected president and preside over the association's annual meeting in Birmingham in April 1897.[37]

But the most significant example of outside activity was Young's involvement in the affairs of the State Normal School at Montgomery. In this case it may never be known if Young was merely trying to advance himself. But on May 12, 1896, Washington wrote to Young saying that he had learned from various sources that Young was an applicant for the headship of the State Normal School. Washington said that he had understood that Young definitely wanted to maintain his position at Tuskegee, that his position was important, and that Washington therefore needed to know if he could count on Young being at Tuskegee for the next school year. Washington assured Young that he wanted him to stay.[38]

The next day Young answered Washington's inquiry about his alleged candidacy for the presidency of the State Normal School. First, he explained that he had not authorized his name to be used in that context, and that, in any case, he was never a candidate for that post. At the same time, however, Young made it equally clear that he desired that the present head of that school be unseated. The president of the Montgomery school was a white man named William B. Paterson, and he employed only white teachers. Young did not necessarily object to Paterson's color or that of his teachers, but he objected to the weak program at the school. In fact, Young said that the movement to remove Paterson not only had his interest but also had received some direction from him. Young felt that as a citizen of Alabama, he had the right to want change in the administration of the Montgomery school.[39] This dispute over the Paterson administration at the normal school lasted more than a year, and Young was identified by J. L. M. Curry, head of the Slater Fund, as a prime mover. As late as September 3, 1897, Paterson informed Washington that Young was still trying to unseat him as president. Paterson claimed that Young had that very week written the chair-

37. Young to editor of the *Tuskegee Student,* February 24, 1898, Booker T. Washington Papers.
38. Washington to Young, May 12, 1896, Booker T. Washington Papers.
39. Young to Washington, May 13, 1896, Booker T. Washington Papers.

man of the State Normal School's board of directors, criticizing the school's program compared to Tuskegee's. Young had reportedly said that "the contrast between the two schools is painful sharp." Young was, perhaps, falsely accused of saying that Paterson's retention violated the well-established policy of social equality. Paterson ended his letter by hoping that there would be peace between him and Washington. Curry had written Washington three months earlier that he had heard of the efforts to remove Paterson and that Young had been associated with this movement in all the information that had reached him. Curry did not object to Paterson's removal, "but not on the grounds of his color."[40]

Young's responsibilities got him into areas of student policy at Tuskegee, since he, as the head teacher, was concerned with the academic direction of the school while Washington was away on his frequent money-raising campaigns, and increasingly even when Washington was present on campus. Young and Washington most agreed in those areas concerned with student life and with the moral and spiritual atmosphere of the Tuskegee campus. Washington was always concerned about the spiritual well-being of Tuskegee's students. For example, on one occasion, he spoke to Young about "the advisability of having separate evening prayers." Young in turn suggested that the school follow the Hampton plan, whereby the night classes would meet immediately after supper for vesper services in Phelps Hall Chapel and then go directly to class.[41]

Young was also interested in the religious well-being of the teachers. On another occasion, he suggested to Washington that attendance at morning worship exercises should be made compulsory for teachers, as it was for students. Washington hesitated about making the services compulsory and wanted Young to report to him in writing at the end of each week the names of any teacher who failed to attend the services.[42] In his reply to Washington, Young noted that only three members of the faculty, including

40. J. L. M. Curry to Washington, June 15, 1897; W. B. Paterson to Washington, September 3, 1897, *B. T. W. Papers,* vol. 4, 299, 325. Paterson had been involved in a controversy with Washington in 1887 when Paterson's school was moved from Marion to Montgomery, forty miles away from Tuskegee. Harlan, *Booker T. Washington,* 166–68.

41. Young to Washington, September 11, 1894, Booker T. Washington Papers.

42. Washington to Young, February 25, 1895, *B. T. W. Papers,* vol. 3, 531; Harlan, *Booker T. Washington,* 277.

himself, attended services regularly. This situation bothered Young. "In this matter," he wrote,

> We are an exception to the rule of schools devoted to the education of the Negro youth. I *do not think* that it ought to be optional . . . Our non-sectarianism ought not be so straight as to make us non-religious, un-Christian. At present, the tendency seems strongly set in that direction to say the least . . . We are entirely too lax along these lines, for that reason our spiritual life is always at "low ebb."[43]

It is interesting that Young would be so intent on making attendance at worship compulsory for teachers, but rather lenient about supervising their academic performance. This is understandable, however, given Young's earlier education at missionary and evangelical schools such as Talladega and Oberlin. At Oberlin, Young was more impressed by the more *"inspiring"* older, evangelical teachers than the "more *informing"* younger teachers. On the other hand, Washington was more interested in there being close supervision in the teaching area. In the end, however, Washington did make chapel compulsory for all teachers.

Where Washington and Young were most in accord was on the matter of moral behavior. This concern for "moral earnestness" can be seen in a memorandum that Washington sent to several Tuskegee teachers, including Young, regarding any students who were particularly lacking in "moral earnestness in class work, deportment or labor." The teachers were to write the names of the students on Washington's note, stating the student's weakness, and were to return the note to Washington. Young listed eight female students whom he considered "not earnest, and, I fear, morally careless in some instances." Behind the name of two of the girls he wrote, "(especially so)."[44]

Young was very much concerned about all the students on the campus. Margaret James Murray Washington wrote, in one of her frequent reports to her husband informing him of all the happenings at Tuskegee, that Young was one of the few faculty members

43. Young to Washington, February 25, 1895, *B. T. W. Papers,* vol. 3, 532; Harlan, *Booker T. Washington,* 278.
44. Washington to Young, April 22, 1893, Booker T. Washington Papers.

that the students trusted. She reported that there was a good deal of unrest and unhappiness among the female students and that one girl had informed her that the girls felt there was no one whom they could go to for anything except Nathan Young and Mrs. Washington. The unrest among the students resulted from the tight restrictions on their activities, and their being generally treated as children by most of the faculty. On the other hand, Young treated the students more like adults, enforcing the spirit rather than the letter of the rules.[45]

Young also tried to maintain an open relationship with the faculty. He noted this aspect of his professional character in defending himself against one of the frequent accusations Washington began to make toward the end of their relationship at Tuskegee. Because some dissatisfied teachers were going behind Young's back to Washington with their complaints, on October 7, 1896, Young informed Washington that he had provided a space in the Teacher's Weekly Memorandum for registering complaints about the running of the Academic Department. Young wanted to have any problems, mistakes, or complaints brought to his attention first. The teachers were asked to report problems to Young in writing on a weekly basis, and sooner if they were urgent. While he was forced to institute the closer supervision of his teachers, suggested earlier by Washington, Young still tried to be democratic by allowing public expressions of complaints against his administration.

Young made it clear to Washington that he considered himself responsible for the operation of the academic phase of the school and should have the first opportunity to adjust any problems within his department.[46] If Young failed to act to the satisfaction of any teacher, that teacher could then go to Washington or the executive council of the faculty. Young emphasized that his style of leadership was democratic, that he was always willing to listen to his teacher, and that he could not be accused of acting arbitrarily. The only thing that Young felt he might be justly accused of was sometimes diminishing the action of the faculty against the students; but he defended even these actions by noting that he was in

45. Margaret J. M. Washington to Washington, December 13, 1894, *B. T. W. Papers,* vol. 3, 491–93.
46. Young to Washington, October 7, 1896, Booker T. Washington Papers.

closer contact with the students and felt that they should always be treated as men and women. In fact, Young claimed that there was not a teacher or officer at Tuskegee who worked more zealously than he for the welfare of the students.[47]

In addition to Young's conflict with some faculty, Young and Washington generally had differing policy approaches. Perhaps the most notable difference was their antithetical views of the importance of a liberal arts education in an institution that in general had been most concerned about manual and industrial arts. This issue came most clearly to a head in Young's third year at Tuskegee.

The issue first surfaced on November 1, 1895, in a letter from Washington to Young written only forty-four days after Washington's Atlanta Exposition Address, which generated great acclaim for Washington as a proponent of manual and industrial training for blacks.

"MR. Young," the note began:

> From now on I wish an especial effort made to have a more direct connection made between the class-room and industrial work, that is, I wish the one dovetailed into the other. I wish you to be very careful to see that this is done throughout the year. I do not attempt now to lay down rules by which this can be done, I only repeat the instance mentioned in one of the teachers meetings. The students in their composition work can go to the brick yard and write compositions about the manner of making brick or harnessing horses. Many of the examples in arithmetic can be gotten out of actual problems in the blacksmith shop, tin shop, or farm. The physics I think could be made to bear more of the industrial work. I wish as early as possible you would have a consultation with Mr. J. H. Washington on this subject and come to an understanding as far as possible as to the best methods of carrying out this plan.[48]

At first Young made an effort to follow Washington's orders. On November 2, he reported that he planned to "have a conference with Cal Washington regarding 'dove tailing' the work of the academic department with that of the industrial, and shall request the

47. Ibid.
48. Washington to Young, November 1, 1895, Booker T. Washington Papers; see also in *B. T. W. Papers,* vol. 4, 68–69.

teachers to do so where ever practical." By December 4, however, Washington found little evidence of Young's compliance with his order. He asked Young to send to him a report by December 16 showing what progress had been made in this area.[49] Young responded, although little if anything was really being done:

> that as yet no *organized* effort has been made toward this end; but I am sure that *individual* efforts are being made to make the academic work more and more practical—the end to be attained by an organized effort.[50]

On March 26, 1896, Washington raised this policy issue again, and rightly accused Young of being uncooperative and even ridiculing the term "dovetailing." "Some months ago," Washington wrote,

> I announced to the teachers that you and Mr. J. H. Washington would be asked to put into operation the correlating of the literary and industrial work to a larger extent; almost no progress has been made in this as you saw by a letter I sent you a few days ago from the Superintendent of Industries that he expresses himself as feeling that you would not co-operate. Besides this, as many as four teachers told me in person that you went so far in an academic meeting as to ridicule the use of the term 'dove tail' which I had used. Of course this gave these teachers to understand that your heart was not in the matter.[51]

Despite the great respect that Young and Washington held for each other, they increasingly came into conflict on matters of educational philosophy. Young was originally from the Black Belt of Alabama and had helped Washington build up Tuskegee. Even so, Young's educational philosophy was closer to that of men such as W. E. B. Du Bois and John Hope than it was to the viewpoint of Booker T. Washington. Young knew the debate on both sides—

49. Young to Washington, November 2, 1895; Washington to Young, December 4, 1895, Booker T. Washington Papers; see also in *B. T. W. Papers,* vol. 4, 89. There was little being done toward dovetailing. Harlan, *Booker T. Washington,* 280.

50. Young to Washington, December 9, 1895, Booker T. Washington Papers; see also in *B. T. W. Papers,* vol. 4, 90.

51. Washington to Young, March 26, 1896, *B. T. W. Papers,* vol. 4, 145–49.

Washington's industrial arts versus the liberal arts of Du Bois—and Young leaned more toward the liberal arts. In short, it was on this policy issue that Young and Washington parted intellectual company. And it would not be long before the two men would part physical company as well, with Young moving on to Georgia.[52]

Young increasingly felt out of place at Tuskegee. Part of his discomfort had to do with policy differences like that embodied in the "dovetailing" issue; part of it dealt with different approaches to handling people. Young was more democratic and tolerant in his approach to his teachers than was Washington, who desired to have "the will and policy of the Principle . . . carried out even in the remotest corner of the school."[53]

The value of a liberal education, which Young had been taught and which he himself had developed, was confirmed in part by the fact that no year at Tuskegee went by without Young's receiving an offer from another school. This made Washington's anti–liberal arts attitude increasingly oppressive for Young.[54]

Even in the beginning, some events at Tuskegee had been exasperating for Young. As early as January 1894, for example, Washington wrote his older brother, John, who was head of the Mechanic and Trades Department, about a number of routine housekeeping items in preparation for a visit from Dr. J. L. M. Curry. A white Southerner, Curry was the administrator of the Slater and Peabody Fund, upon which Washington depended heavily for money. In the note, Washington said he thought "that the rooms in Mr. Young's house can be cut down from their present size, but the halls can stay the same." This unilateral restructuring of Young's home, plus inordinate delays in its final construction, did not particularly please Young, especially since the room reduction seemed to have been done primarily to please influential white patrons.[55]

Nineteen months later, Young wrote to Washington requesting a salary increase. He pointed out that his workday now ran from 8:30

52. Interview with Judge Nathan B. Young, Jr., St. Louis, July 1981.
53. Washington to Young, March 26, 1896, *B. T. W. Papers,* vol. 4, 145–49.
54. Young to Washington, May 13, 1896, Booker T. Washington Papers.
55. Washington to John Henry Washington, January 5, 1894, *B. T. W. Papers,* vol. 3, 382. Young to Mr. Washington, February 19, 1894, Booker T. Washington Papers.

a.m. to 9 p.m. and that were he to render the same service at any other school, he would not accept less than one hundred dollars per month. He told Washington that he had received several offers from other schools promising him that much per month. Even so, Young said that he was not asking for one hundred dollars per month because he knew that Tuskegee could not pay the full worth of this services and because he personally believed that teachers ought to be willing to serve the school for less than they could demand from other schools. In fact, he said that he generally did not care for that group of teachers who were always crying after money.[56]

In responding to Young's request for more money, Washington said that there were considerations to be taken into account. Chiefly, Washington was concerned with the salaries at Tuskegee not being above those offered to other institutions. He found that Young's salary was about equal to that of other heads of academic departments, and, if Washington was to increase Young's salary, it would go beyond that of the head teacher at Hampton. Clearly, Washington was fearful of criticism by white donors, who frequently were critical of the salaries paid to black teachers. But recognizing the justice of Young's request, Washington added five dollars a month to his salary.[57]

Because of disputes over educational philosophy and lines of authority, Young came into conflict with other members of the Tuskegee family. There was conflict with John Washington, head of the Mechanic and Trades Department. At one point, their clash became so heated that John even complained to his brother Booker that the chickens of some of the faculty and staff were doing damage to "whatever is planted" and that "Mr. Young's are out quite often."[58]

All of this was endurable until Washington's Atlanta Exposition Address in September 1895, but that speech—and the national publicity it brought Washington—seemed to change him and, predictably, Tuskegee. On September 18, 1895, Washington offered his

56. Young to Washington, August 27, 1895, Booker T. Washington Papers.
57. Washington to Young, November 2, 1895, Booker T. Washington Papers.
58. J. H. Washington to Washington, March 9, 1894, *B. T. W. Papers*, vol. 3, 394.

"cast down your bucket where you are" compromise at the Atlanta Cotton State and International Exposition. As a result of this address, Washington was pushed from state and regional recognition to national and international fame.[59]

The last two years of Young's work at Tuskegee, then, were increasingly frustrating and painful. Not only was he at odds with Washington over the issue of "dovetailing" and the related ascension of mechanical arts over the liberal arts, but also he soon found himself being accused by Washington of a host of incompetencies: of not being able to maintain order in his department, of not monitoring his teachers closely enough, of not having Porter Hall and the chapel lamps clean enough, and of not using molding boards and maps in lower-grade geography classes. Furthermore, once this situation became apparent to other members of the faculty, Young's problems snowballed as teachers went behind his back to complain to Washington about any and all issues that involved Young.[60]

Finally, Young could not endure the situation any longer without speaking up. As a result, he wrote the following comments to Washington on October 7, 1896:

> I see in much of the criticism of my administration of this department which come to you the secret purpose of prejudicing you against my spirit towards you and this peculiar work of yours . . . I have not forgotten the *ordeal* thro which I was made to pass last year because of *bare* misrepresentation of my work not only, but of the spirit I brought to this work. I am simply trying to guard myself against a similar experience this year. In this effort, I ask your cooperation, at least, to extent of asking those who come to you with complaints regarding my policy in conducting the affairs of this department whether they have reported or spoken to me about the alleged irregularity—espe-

59. One cannot help but notice in reading the Washington Papers that before September 1895 nearly all the correspondence centered around the activities and development of Tuskegee. After the Atlanta Address, very little of Washington's correspondence dealt with Tuskegee, but rather with him.

60. Washington to Young, February 27, 1896; Young to Washington, February 7, 1896; Washington to Young, October 21, 30, 1896; Young to Washington, November 2, 1895; Washington to Young, November 2, 1895, Booker T. Washington Papers; Washington to Young, March 11, 1896, *B. T. W. Papers*, vol. 4, 133.

cially if the person is a teacher in my department. You will pardon this long, and (you may think) senseless communication; but I see the necessity of it. I do not propose, if I can prevent it, to go through another year of misrepresentation in this school.[61]

Five months later, in response to a very urgent request from Washington, Young submitted a "Partial Statement of the Work of the Academic Department." Young mainly confined this partial report to recommendations for the improvement of the department, but he said that later on he would submit a résumé of the work of the department during his administration. The idea of submitting a résumé of his entire administration sounded very much like Young knew that he would not be at Tuskegee much longer, although nowhere in the report does Young say he is leaving.[62]

Only three months after this all-inclusive "partial" statement, Young addressed a letter of resignation to Washington. In it, he assessed his work and growth, and parted company with Tuskegee. "After due deliberation," he said,

I have decided to accept the position in the Ga. Ind'l College. I therefore herewith transmit to you my resignation of the position of Head Teacher of this institute. I shall put my department in shape to be transferred to whom you may designate. . . . In severing my connection with your work here, I would say that my five years' stay has been reasonably pleasant and profitable to me individually. I have labored as best I could to perform conscientiously all duties assigned me. It is for you my associates to say how far I have succeeded in aiding or hindering the work. I have sometimes thought that the spirit which I have labored here has been misunderstood, because we have sometimes differed as to *methods*. I assure you, that I go away as I came with nothing but good will for you and your work. I regret the necessity which makes it wise for me to heed this fifth *unsolicited* call to a more remunerative service along the line of my profession.[63]

61. Young to Washington, October 7, 1896, Booker T. Washington Papers.
62. Young to Washington, March 3, 1897, Booker T. Washington Papers.
63. Young to Washington, June 11, 1897, Booker T. Washington Papers.

Young was now on his way to Georgia State Industrial College as director of pedagogy, and his period of growth and development at Tuskegee would soon be over. In assessing the significance of his work at Tuskegee in Young's growth as an educator, what stands out is his earlier statement to Washington regarding his educational philosophy and his handling of teachers. In its concluding assertion we find a strength and assurance that Young attained during his tenure at Tuskegee. "Experience has taught me that this is the best policy for me," Young said, "and I cannot adopt any other."[64]

If, indeed, stress and struggle does strengthen, then Young's stay at Tuskegee was clearly a strengthening period for him as an educator and administrator. Young assessed this period many years later as an "eventful and helpful" time. These were his "post-graduate years," on his way to becoming president of Florida Agricultural and Mechanical College and then Lincoln University in Missouri.[65]

64. Young to Washington, March 11, 1896, *B. T. W. Papers*, vol. 4, 133–35.
65. Young, "A Fifty Year Jaunt."

CHAPTER 3

Young and Ideas about Educational Needs for Blacks (1892–1901)

W hen Nathan B. Young arrived at Tuskegee Institute in 1892, his ideas about the education of blacks were already taking shape. Like Booker T. Washington, he was interested in the economic, moral, and intellectual uplift of the black masses, and he believed that education was the key to that uplift. Consequently, he believed that the urgent need of the day was to improve the state of education that existed for the vast majority of black youth in the South, especially in the rural areas. He saw the need for two things: proper training and preparation of competent, dedicated teachers and expansion of common schools into the rural and remote areas of the South.

By the time Young arrived at Tuskegee, he already believed in equality in education and that black teachers should be trained on an equal basis with white teachers. As principal in Birmingham, he had emphasized this and had approved of a policy there requiring black teachers to pass the very same qualifying examination as white teachers.[1] Those most likely to pass would have educational credentials, the foremost of which was a college degree.

After Young began his work at Tuskegee his desire was to develop the Academic Department and provide black graduates with one of the best college degrees in the South. Having been trained in the

---

1. Young, "The Birmingham Public Schools—Colored Department."

liberal arts tradition at Talladega and Oberlin, his bias was for a liberal education for teachers. Because of this bias, disagreement arose early with Washington over the curriculum for teachers, notably over what was known as "dovetailing." To a certain extent, "dovetailing" was simply learning by doing, learning by combining the liberal arts with the industrial arts. In some courses such as mathematics, where students measured the floors for laying carpets, "dovetailing" was useful. In other courses such as history, "dovetailing" was not practical. If "dovetailing" was not totally successful, then it probably did not matter since the concept was used primarily to set a direction and emphasis for Tuskegee. But it did cause some conflict between Washington and Young since Young had become a liberal arts traditionalist.[2]

The conflict did not become critical, however, until after Washington's famous Atlanta Address in September 1895, when Washington apparently began to care more about how outsiders would view his school. Before September 1895, Washington seemed interested mainly in the development and growth of Tuskegee as a school dedicated to educating aspiring black students, and Young's efforts to develop the Academic Department and produce the best-educated graduates and teachers were seen by Washington as a positive complement to his own efforts to assure the existence and growth of the school. After the Atlanta Address, however, Washington was hailed as the leader and national spokesman for Afro-Americans by Southern and Northern white leaders, and he now saw the growth and development of Tuskegee as tied to its being a national model of industrial education.

It became impossible for the liberal arts–oriented Young to stay at Tuskegee after the Atlanta Address. Both Washington and Young soon realized this. Even after Young had submitted his resignation, he protested the continued buildup of the Industrial Department at the expense of the Academic Department. In the summer of 1897, for example, Tuskegee was putting together an exhibit for display in Nashville, and the Industrial Department was receiving most of the money while the Academic Department was receiving very lit-

2. Booker T. Washington to Nathan B. Young, December 4, 1895; Young to Washington, March 6, 1895, Booker T. Washington Papers; Harlan, *Booker T. Washington,* 280.

tle. On June 17, 1897, Young wrote to Warren Logan, treasurer of Tuskegee:

> Mr. Safford had told me that he can not finish that exhibit work. I regret this very much, for I had planned for this to be an important as well as an unique feature of our academic exhibit. I wish that the school might screw itself up to the point of being willing to spread at least *one-thousandth* as much money on getting up a display of its academic work as it spread up [on] its industrial work. At most, your academic exhibit at Nashville has not cost you $15.00. How does that figure compare with that of the industrial? I am very sorry indeed that *all* of that stenographic work has to be thrown away because of an indisposition to pay extra for this extra work. However, if you all can stand it, I can.[3]

But despite differences over the subordination of liberal arts to industrial arts, Young's educational ideas were much influenced by his association with Washington. Later, after Washington's death in 1915, Young would write that whatever success he had as an educational administrator was largely due to what he had learned while observing Washington at work "laying the foundation of the Greater Tuskegee," and he ultimately came to believe that both the liberal arts and industrial arts or the "'cultural and utilitarian' had to be combined to complete the educational process." Finally, he saw the debate over liberal arts and industrial arts as "nimbly contending about opposite sides of the same shield."[4]

If the young blacks who came to Tuskegee were to receive a good liberal arts education, then Tuskegee must hire the best teachers it could find. In Young's judgment the primary qualification for a good teachers was experience. This matter of experience became central to Young's recommendations for hiring and for his class assignments at Tuskegee. He explained that applicants with actual teaching experience, and the more the better, should always be picked over the inexperienced, all else being equal. It was far better, Young insisted, to get experienced teachers, especially for a school

3. Young to Warren Logan, June 17, 1897, Booker T. Washington Papers.
4. Nathan B. Young, "Booker T. Washington," 17 (typewritten), 8, Young manuscript. Nathan B. Young, "A Dream Fulfilled," *Southern Workman* (January, 1916): 53–54, page proofs in Young manuscript.

such as Tuskegee, where the most difficult phases of education and teaching were present. In short, since teaching was an art or professional craft, Young would have preferred that teachers had done their apprenticeship elsewhere before coming to Tuskegee. However, the supply of well-trained, experienced black teachers was small. At that time, most of the black collegiate institutions of the South were merely high schools or junior colleges at best and were not able to produce highly trained teachers. Young knew this, yet he insisted that Tuskegee ran a great risk in employing inexperienced teachers with new degrees, though they might be cheaper.[5]

Faced with the scarcity of well-trained, experienced black teachers, Young was compelled, then, to find a way by which to raise the standards at Tuskegee. He began by transferring teachers from one subject to another until he felt comfortable with the competence of a teacher in a given subject. In some cases, the transfer was between such widely different subjects as mathematics and English. When necessary, Young would hire the wives of Tuskegee workers on a half-time basis as classroom teachers, or as was the case with the sister of M. T. Driver, Tuskegee's business agent, but not until, as usual, he knew a good deal about their qualifications. This insistence upon experience was a hallmark of Young's term at Tuskegee. As late as 1897, in a report to Washington on the status of the Academic Department he reemphasized the need for experienced and trained teachers. He informed Washington in this report that he wanted an experienced teacher of writing and of drawing, which was a weak area. He also notified Washington of the need for a teacher of elocution and advanced reading, but he emphasized the fact that he wanted an experienced teacher and not merely a stage actor.[6]

While experience and credentials were important to Young, he also felt that it was the quality of the individual teacher that made all the difference to students. Because Young put such a premium on a teacher's competence, he and Washington occasionally argued over the teaching assignments of the Tuskegee faculty. In one in-

5. Washington to Young, March 26, 1896; Young to Washington, March 3, 1897, Booker T. Washington Papers.
6. Young to Washington, June 29, 1896; Young to Washington, (Summer 1896); Young to Washington, March 31, 1897, Booker T. Washington Papers; Harlan, *Booker T. Washington*, 276.

stance, Washington wanted to assign a Mr. Jenkins to classes in geometry and arithmetic, but Young refused to make such an assignment. He refused to treat Jenkins any differently than other teachers in his department. He felt Jenkins was not qualified to teach the courses and argued that he would continue to make the class assignments based on the abilities rather than the desires of teachers. Young made it clear to Washington that he did not wish to argue about the situation, but that it was a matter of principle for him and that in such matters he was inflexible. In short, if he was going to be held responsible for the quality of teaching in the Academic Department, then he wanted the power to determine who would be allowed to teach, and he spelled out to Washington this concern in strong, clear terms. On a later occasion, when Washington asked how many classes a Mr. Stevens had, Young answered that "Mr. Stevens has one Bible-class in my department. He is not competent intellectually for any other. I hope you are not thinking of detailing him."[7]

Young also expressed the idea during this period that professional growth was essential to competence and that teachers should stay up to date professionally. He came to believe that one of the best ways for teachers to stay up to date was by subscribing to professional journals. In his evaluation of Miss Pettiford, Young specifically called attention to this aspect of professional growth and the importance that he placed on it. He expected teachers to make a strong effort to improve their teaching through self-improvement by study, teaching institutes, and summer school.[8]

In working on day-to-day problems at Tuskegee and in disagreement with Washington, Young came to believe that the competence of a teacher could be undercut by restricting the teacher's freedom. At times, Young and Washington debated the need for a more "systematic over sight" of the teaching at Tuskegee. Young disliked uniformity. He had come to dislike it and the lack of freedom that followed while he was a public school teacher and principal. Washington, on the other hand, insisted that there was a need for more uniformity of aims and methods. He knew there was some

7. Washington to Young, October 21, 1896; Young to Washington, May 27, 1896; Young to Washington, March 31, 1897, Booker T. Washington Papers; Harlan, *Booker T. Washington,* 275–76.
8. Young to Washington, April 29, 1893, Booker T. Washington Papers.

good teaching at Tuskegee, but he also knew there was "some very poor teaching" there. In fact, Washington cited examples of incompetent teaching in the Academic Department. In one instance, he referred to a report by a Mrs. Logan of her observation of the teaching of a botany class by a Mr. Hoffman. The detailed description of Hoffman's performance left no doubt as to his incompetence. Evidence such as this led Washington to believe that the best method of ensuring good teaching was a rigid and almost absolute control over the individual teacher and every aspect of his teaching. Young, however, believed that such absolute control would destroy good teaching by crippling the individuality and unique talents that a teacher might demonstrate.[9]

When Young left Tuskegee in 1897, he went to Georgia State Industrial College to head the Pedagogical Department. While at Georgia State, he came under the influence of another prominent black educator, Richard R. Wright, Sr., whose ideas of education helped to reinforce the ideas that Young had developed at Tuskegee. Like Young, Wright believed that the training of properly equipped teachers was the urgent need of the black race in America. During his four-year apprenticeship under R. R. Wright, Young traveled all across Georgia promoting teacher training. Young admired Wright, a "man of high educational ideals" who "wore himself out" trying to establish a "decent educational program" at Georgia State Industrial College. Despite the emphasis on industrialism in the South in the 1880s, Wright, an Atlanta graduate, felt as Young did, that the black race needed both liberal arts and industrial education. He divided the school day so that half of the day was devoted to "literary work" and the other half to industrial education and agriculture. He established three departments—industrial, normal, and college. Wright, however, had a board of commissioners who thought liberal education was not what the black race needed. Consequently, for political reasons Wright had to pay attention to the demands of his board, although he believed Georgia's blacks were "sorely in need of broadly educated leaders all along the line."[10]

9. Washington to Young, March 26, 1896, Booker T. Washington Papers.
10. Dorothy Orr, *A History of Education in Georgia,* 373–74; Charles E. Jones, *Education in Georgia,* Bureau of Education, Bulletin No. 4 (Washington, D.C.: Government Printing Office, 1889), 143, 63–64, 231; Thomas J. Jones, *Negro Education,* Bureau of Education, Bulletin 1916, no. 31, 2, 190.

At Georgia State Industrial College, the secondary work was divided between the Normal and College Departments. The Normal Department was a three-year college preparatory course that included Latin, English, mathematics, science, history, education, and physiology. The college program included some high school and college courses.

When Young arrived, the Normal Department and other departments were upgrading their standards. No student under fourteen was received in the school. Students had to be well accomplished in basic English and mathematics for admission. Georgia State Industrial College taught mineralogy and geodesy in addition to the basic sciences, but like other black colleges, Georgia State did not have the funds to properly equip a good scientific laboratory. This was one of the complaints Young had at Tuskegee. Young emphasized the importance of students learning modern science. He thought science was important if the student was going to be a teacher or businessman. Modern science was changing the world, and properly educated students would have to keep up with these changes.[11]

By 1900 the Pedagogy Department, which Young headed, had begun to add the modern sciences and social sciences to its curriculum as well as professional education courses such as the psychology

---

In 1890 the Georgia State Industrial College for Colored was established by the Georgia legislature to end blacks' claims to part of the federal agricultural land grant money of the Morrill Act of 1890. August Meier, *Negro Thought in America, 1880–1915,* 211; Elizabeth Ross Haynes, *The Black Boy of Atlanta: Richard R. Wright,* 70–72; Robert E. Perdue, *The Negro in Savannah, 1865–1900,* 97–98, 192, 133; Young, "The Quest," 56–57, 60–69, 73–74; Willard Range, *The Rise and Progress of Negro Colleges in Georgia, 1865–1949,* 59–64, 117, 135; Logan, *Dictionary of American Negro Biography,* 674–75; Jacqueline Jones, *Soldiers of Light and Love: Northern Teachers and Georgia Blacks, 1865–1873,* 127; W. H. Crogman, "Introduction," in Richard R. Wright, *A Brief Historical Sketch of Negro Education in Georgia,* 1–14, 38. Wright, born a slave in Dalton, Georgia, rose to be one of the most influential black educators in Georgia.

Young considered his "teaching adventures in Georgia second only to those in Alabama." For the four years he was in Georgia, Young considered himself a Georgian. He always counted among his best friends those he met in Georgia through his teaching or business enterprise. Range, *Rise and Progress,* 74–76; Haynes, *Richard R. Wright,* 90; Wright, *A Brief Historical Sketch,* 53–55, 77; Orr, *A History of Education in Georgia,* 374.

11. Range, *Rise and Progress,* 80–81.

of childhood and school economy. Of course, there were still the old standbys in the curriculum emphasizing good morals and manners. Young also established a model elementary school for practice teaching. At Georgia State the college work was an adjunct to the teacher training program. In the 1898–1899 school year the number of college students enrolled was insignificant. That year Georgia State had 12 college, 72 secondary, and 140 primary students.[12] Thus, Georgia was not fertile ground for Young's ideas.

At Georgia State, the all-white board of commissioners opposed all efforts to provide education in the liberal arts for black youth. They insisted that their view of what should be taught should always be followed. Young thought they went to "ridiculous extremes." At a commencement program attended by Young, the reactionary nature of the board became obvious. When the young men walked on the stage to receive their diplomas from the chairman of the board, General Peter W. Meldrim, they were told to get out of their uniforms and into working clothes as "quickly as possible." Young, upon witnessing this, became deeply concerned about the nature of the education that blacks could pursue. Young felt that the implications of the chairman's comments were that education for black youth "must have a very different significance from that offered white youth," and that the board of commissioners only wanted the black students to be taught to work with their hands. Apparently, blacks in Georgia were to have no say in their own education. They were to be educated as whites dictated. This education was not to be "free and unhampered" like that provided for white youth. Young felt there was no regard for the "ability and ambition" of a black youngster, and resented that they were to be "taught what others think is best for them." Whites would tell black youths "what to think and how to think." Neither the black students, parents, or teachers were to have any say. Young saw this as a "hangover from slavery," where blacks were "regarded as a ward," educationally, politically, and economically.[13]

12. Jones, *Negro Education,* 200; Range, *Rise and Progress,* 78–80; W. E. B. Du Bois, ed., *The College-Bred Negro* 12, 14, 16, 17.
13. Young, "The Quest," 57. The members of the board had objected many times to Wright not fitting the students for agricultural and manual labor. The board even wanted to fire Wright for teaching Latin at the school. Board members asked Booker T. Washington his opinion of Wright's

In 1897, shortly after starting at Georgia State, Young gave a significant speech on education in the South before the Alabama State Teachers' Association. In 1896 he had been elected the fourth president of the association. As its president, Young made the major address at the annual conference, and his topic dealt with "Common School Extension," or making primary education in basic reading, writing, and arithmetic available to rural black youth of Alabama.

In this address, Young noted that common school extension was the most vital question facing black Southerners, and for this reason he and the other officers of the association had made a special effort to bring together all those in the state interested in education generally and black education in particular. Young started his speech by making it clear that he was deliberating not on the curricula of school teaching, but on the methods of school extension, perhaps reference to the debate over industrial versus liberal arts education. Young probably wanted no controversy over curricula at this meeting, for he had a program to sell. He divided his address into two parts: one dealing with what was already being done in common school education across the state, and the other dealing with what needed to be done in order to extend that education to many more blacks in Alabama.[14]

As of that moment, Young felt that Alabama and the South were "on the ragged edge of an educational crisis." The public schools in general and black schools in particular were not adequately meeting their mission of providing the ordinary masses with common school education. A large percentage of the black youth of Alabama was reaching adulthood in complete ignorance; many blacks in the state never attended school. The basic literacy problems of the

---

program. When Washington replied negatively, the board almost fired Wright to replace him with a president picked by Washington. See Haynes, *Richard R. Wright,* 90–92. Young, "The Quest," 57–58. Young thought that this type of white paternalism and hostility to free and unhampered education for blacks dominated the board of control of most black state institutions. He felt that the problems he had at Florida A&M and Lincoln University resulted from managing boards dominated by this spirit.

14. The Alabama State Teachers' Association was founded by Booker T. Washington and others in 1882 and Washington became the organization's third president. Harlan, *Booker T. Washington,* 154; Nathan B. Young, *Common School Extension: An Address Before the Alabama State Teachers' Association,* 1–3.

black race were not being addressed in the educational setting that Young believed could best solve those problems.

Young had great faith in education because he believed that education could solve most of the problems of the black race and, at the same time, generate a social and moral revolution among the members, even as they learned the "Three Rs." Indeed, Young denied the truth of Alexander Pope's comment, "a little knowledge is a dangerous thing." He believed that even a little knowledge was an "inspiring thing."[15]

Statistical data supported most of Young's reflections on the status of black education in Alabama. Young had collected this data with the idea of working with his old educational patron Henry De Forest on a program of common school extension, possibly with the intention of seeking funding from a private foundation. But when De Forest died in 1896, apparently so did Young's ambition to carry forth the project. Later, however, Washington would present these very same figures to promote some of the ideas of Young and himself on common school extension to the Jeanes Fund officers.[16]

Young used statistical data because for him "figures you know are always reliable, but figurers are not. 'Figures will never Lie,' but liars will figure, especially when the Negro is the factor and his condition the problem."[17]

Young's figures pointed out the great need for common school extension among the black population. He noted that in the late 1890s there were three times as many black illiterates as white illiterates in Alabama. While 18 percent of whites were illiterate, the figure among blacks was 69 percent. At this time, Alabama had a total population of 1,069,545 above the age of ten, of which there were 107,335 white illiterates and 331,260 black illiterates.[18]

There were other figures which suggested that the vast majority

15. Ibid., 3–4.
16. Ibid.
17. Ibid. In the late 1890s and early twentieth century a large number of anti-black books and monographs were being written. Young made direct reference to Frederick L. Hoffman's *Race Traits and Tendencies of the American Negro.*
18. Ibid., 4. Throughout his career Young used statistical data or surveys to support his ideas and programs.

of Alabama's blacks were untouched by common school education. This group was growing to adulthood in ignorance and in economic, social, and moral conditions similar to those of their slave parents. Young concluded that more than two hundred thousand black youth in Alabama were not in school at all. The need for common school extension in Alabama was therefore obvious.

In fact, Alabama's common school efforts ranked near the bottom in comparison with other Deep South states. Young showed that, on an average, with Deep South had a 60 percent illiteracy rate among its black school-age population, yet Alabama was almost 10 percent worse than the average. In fact, only Louisiana, with a 72 percent rate, ranked lower than Alabama's 69 percent.[19]

Young blamed Alabama's poor educational conditions on the "supposed poverty" of the state and the indisposition to black education by white state and county officials. Alabama was further "handicapped by an anti-educational constitution," whereby the laws were enforced in such a manner that the black youths who needed education the most had the least chance of getting it. For example, in the Black Belt of Alabama, the overwhelming black majority got the shortest school term and the poorest teachers. Here white school boards manipulated school funds to give the white children more than their fair share of the resources.[20]

Young believed that the black citizens of Alabama were contributing their fair share of taxes toward the support of public education, and he discounted the popular Southern argument that white citizens paid more taxes than black citizens and therefore white children should get more than black children from the school fund. After pointing out the direct and indirect taxes paid by Alabama's blacks, Young urged that blacks should vote only for politicians who believed in popular education and actively supported it.[21]

Young went on to emphasize the fact that while the blacks should receive their fair share of the public education funds, they had to begin to do more for themselves. Blacks had to build better schools, and they also needed to extend the school term. In those cases where the state did not provide enough money to build adequate

19. Ibid., 4–5.
20. Ibid., 5–6.
21. Ibid., 6.

schoolhouses, blacks had to be willing to build them, just as they had to be willing to extend the school year. He insisted that black parents had to take greater responsibility for the moral and mental fitness of the teachers of their children.[22] Central to Young's message throughout was the theme that not enough was being done to educate blacks in the South, and he called upon the teachers to do more for themselves. Emphasizing a self-help philosophy, he called for an educational awakening in Alabama and the South equal to that of New England sixty-five years earlier. He urged teachers to build school buildings and not depend on using churches and lodge halls. In urging the black teachers to accept his self-help philosophy, Young gave examples of teachers who had persuaded their communities to build schoolhouses, and he urged teachers to encourage their black communities to support their schools as unselfishly as they supported their churches and lodges. This emphasis on self-help was stronger in Young in 1897 than it had ever been before, and thus it represents some indication of the influence Washington and Tuskegee had had on him during his period there.[23]

Finally, while urging greater self-sufficiency to his Alabama colleagues, Young still saw the need for the efforts of white friends of black education. White friends from the North and local church groups were encouraged to go out into the rural areas where the greatest need existed, and they were also encouraged to go into higher education rather than into competition with the expanding public school system in the urban centers of the South, thus "extending" common schools and providing the teachers for such schools. Young then proposed a plan very similar to the later Rosenwald Fund's matching fund concept for encouraging the building of proper schoolhouses. An interested foundation would offer to meet half the cost of building a new schoolhouse if the surrounding community itself furnished the other half of the needed funds. Thus, he envisioned philanthropy and self-help working together, strengthening both sides without making one dependent on the other.[24]

22. *B. T. W. Papers,* vol. 3, 217–19, 234–36.
23. Young, *Common School Extension,* 7–9.
24. Ibid., 9–11. For a clear explanation of the work of the great foundations in the area of black education including the Rosenwald Fund, see

After giving his 1897 speech, Young returned to Georgia State Industrial College to promote the training of black teachers of the common schools. He hoped to extend the common school learning to the widest possible range in Georgia, but he discovered that white Southerners were deliberately making an effort in Georgia and throughout the Deep South to halt the extension of black public schools. Whites felt that their schools should forge ahead even at the expense of black education. It became public policy in the Deep South that educational funds should be diverted from the black schools in order to perfect white schools. Public schools for blacks became, Young said, "merely educational gestures." Of course, there were always a few notable exceptions. In most cases, however, dual educational systems were in place, not only in terms of organization and physical equipment but also in "standards and ideals." Blacks were "educational wards." They were to be "trained" rather than educated. Young saw this as a new slavery.[25]

Just before Young left Georgia State Industrial College, he was approached by D. W. Culp and asked to write an article on the question: "Is It Time for the Negro Colleges in the South to be Put into the Hands of Negro Teachers?" Young agreed to write the article. In this article, he addressed a question that was being debated nationally as black educators were demanding control of their institutions of higher learning, especially those under the control of white churches and missionary groups such as the American Missionary Association. Young's earlier philosophy, expressed so strongly in his speech to the Alabama Teachers' Association, that the job of educating the black masses out of poverty and vice left over from the

---

Charles W. Dabney, *Universal Education in the South,* vol. 2, 432–83, and Anderson, *The Education of Blacks in the South.*

25. Range, *Rise and Progress,* 90, 95–96, 189–92, 232. The standards of Georgia State Industrial College were purposely kept down by a reactionary board. Young felt this Southern effort was so widespread that it was not until after the first quarter of the twentieth century that black public schools became meaningful. The private colleges of Georgia, especially those in Atlanta, fared much better under enlightened management. Of course, by modern standards all black colleges were low, but so were the standards of most white colleges. Between 1902 and 1914 the General Board of Education surveyed seven hundred institutions in the United States that claimed to be colleges and universities. It found only a few worthy colleges, and some were not even good secondary schools. Young, "The Quest," 37–39.

heritage of slavery was a huge job and that there was enough educating to be done for all who were deeply concerned and interested
to be involved, was clearly stated again.[26]

In answering the question proposed to him by Culp, Young said
"No" to the idea of black schools being serviced and managed totally by black teachers. He added, though, that black teachers should
have a much greater hand in the managing of these schools as soon
as their education and talents made them capable of doing so. Of
course, Young was probably addressing himself mainly to the private schools, because at Georgia State there was a conservative,
white board that advocated the teaching of industrial education
only. It is unlikely that he would want that kind of management of
the black schools to continue. Indeed, Young understood that the
white state governments of the South at that time had no inclina-
tion to surrender the management of black public colleges to
blacks, and his experiences at Georgia State, where the president
and faculty were all black but the dictatorial board of commissioners was all white, simply confirmed this perception.

In justifying and qualifying his initial "No," Young said that black
teachers should not take over these institutions for two reasons: financial and intellectual. In support of his conclusion that blacks
were not ready financially to take over their institutions, he pointed
out that most of the institutions of higher education were supported by contributions of whites, and he suggested that the withdrawal of white teachers and boards of trustees would probably
mean the withdrawal of white contributions as well. Young felt that
white contributors gave money to black institutions only when
they knew that the money would be administered by whites, and
he noted that blacks had had only limited experiences in the financial world and thus were not fully ready to accept the responsibilities of handling such funds. Booker T. Washington, Young said, was
the only black he knew who was capable of getting the "white
man's money" to support black institutions, and he added that all
the black schools in question were still too poor and feeble to depend totally on the limited wealth of the black race.

26. Nathan B. Young, "Is It Time for the Negro Colleges in the South to
be put into the Hands of Negro Teachers?" in D. W. Culp, editor, *Twentieth
Century Negro Literature*, 125.

In discussing the intellectual unreadiness of blacks, Young noted the inadequate supply of properly trained black professors in 1901. As he had noted throughout his career, he felt that in intellectual background black professors should be the equal of the white professors in the best universities.[27] He pointed out that there were no black universities and less than half a dozen real black colleges, and that not enough of the graduates of these schools realized that they needed additional training "before becoming anxious candidates for professorships and college presidencies." The race was not "far enough removed from slavery," said Young, "to have the intellectual and moral background" needed to develop fully competent professors and presidents. It had "taken the white race many generations to develop an Eliot, a Dwight, a Hadley and an Angell, not to say anything about the Butlers, the Harrises, and the Wheelers."[28] Thus Young asked black teachers who were poorly trained to "bend themselves with renewed energy to hard study, laying aside all bogus degrees, and meaningless titles, and acknowledge the fact that they are yet intellectual pygmies."

Young insisted, however, that black teachers and trustees should gradually take over the responsibilities of their institutions so that they would not "remain permanently under white tutelage and management." The outstanding graduates of these institutions, after further training, should be offered positions, and as white teachers aged and retired, they could be replaced with black teachers. That way the white donors would stay and so would the black patrons.

Young ended by warning certain black churches not to assume a hostile attitude toward other groups that might follow different educational policies. "There cannot be too much educational activity among Negroes for Negroes," he concluded, and in many ways this statement encapsulated his whole philosophy of black education at this time.[29]

In 1901, Young again made a significant statement of his educational values and philosophy. This statement shows how consistent were his educational beliefs from Tuskegee through Georgia State

27. Ibid., 126.
28. Ibid., 127.
29. Ibid., 127–28.

College. The statement is contained in a letter to Booker T. Washington. It shows Young's continued interest in training teachers. On April 25, 1901, he wrote Washington seeking a recommendation for a new educational movement made up of a group of wealthy individuals under the leadership of Robert C. Ogden who were deliberating on ways to improve the common schools of the South:

> During all the years of my teaching career, I have steadily kept in view the idea of keeping in close touch with the rank and file of my fellow teachers in the "highways and hedges," and of helping them as best I can. If the plan of the above party shall embrace a mission of this kind, I would regard it a high privilege to place myself at their service . . .
>
> I hope I shall not be charged with egotism when I say that I have carefully and sympathetically studied the Southern rural school problem especially in Georgia and Alabama, and I have a definite idea of the *situation* not only, but also a remedy therefore—of *a* remedy if not *the* remedy . . . I am influenced in this matter by no other motive than a desire to get into the place of greatest usefulness to my day and generation. My present position is pleasant, and, in a measure, throws me into the work I desire—the training of teachers and institute work.[30]

Here on the eve of his departure from Georgia State Industrial College, Young expressed the same interest in teacher training that he exhibited in his 1897 speech on "Common School Extension" before the Alabama State Teachers' Association. It is with this educational philosophy and outlook that Young would assume the presidency of Florida Agricultural and Mechanical College in August of 1901.

30. Young to Washington, April 25, 1901, Booker T. Washington Papers.

CHAPTER 4

Young at Florida Agricultural and Mechanical College (1901–1923)

I n 1901, after four years at Georgia State College, Young was elected president of the State Normal School for Negroes in Florida. Young never knew why he was elected. In fact, he was surprised that he was chosen in light of the history of the school.[1] Florida Normal and Industrial School was established in 1887 as the "Colored School," a normal institution; but it was referred to by all as the "State Normal College for Colored Students." The school had come into existence through the efforts of Thomas V. Gibbs, a black representative in the Florida legislature, whose father, Jonathan C. Gibbs, had served as secretary of state from 1868 to 1873 and as superintendent of public instruction from 1873 to 1874 during the Reconstruction period in Florida. The Florida Constitutional Convention of 1885 had provided for a school for blacks, and Thomas Gibbs took advantage of this provision-sponsored legislation to establish the Normal and Industrial School.[2]

The first president of the school was Thomas de Saille Tucker, a lawyer in Pensacola at the time of his appointment. Born in Sherbro, Sierre Leone, West Africa, and brought to the United States by a missionary, Tucker enrolled in Oberlin College's preparatory

1. Young, "The Quest," 66–67.
2. Leedel W. Neyland and John W. Riley, *The History of Florida Agricultural and Mechanical University,* 6–7. Thomas Gibbs was born in New York but lived in Washington, D.C., and attended Howard University. He was appointed to West Point but quit and attended Oberlin from 1873 to 1875.

school from 1858 to 1860. Then in 1860, he enrolled in Oberlin College, from which he earned a bachelor of arts in classical studies in 1865 and a master of arts in 1891. Tucker also earned a bachelor of law degree in 1882 from Straight University in New Orleans. Emphasizing a curriculum that was classical in nature, Tucker began the development of the Florida school in 1887. In 1890 the school's growth and development were greatly aided by funding under the second Morrill Act. One year later, Tucker moved the school to the outskirts of Tallahassee and the more spacious surroundings of a place called "Highwood."[3]

The Congress which provided the Morrill Land grant money stipulated that the funds were to be used for industrial and agricultural instruction, but Tucker considered the main mission of the school to be teacher training. Toward this goal he built up the natural sciences area and employed teachers such as Thomas W. Talley, a Fisk University–trained chemist. By 1893 there was a faculty of nine, including Thomas V. Gibbs as first assistant and mathematics teacher. In fact, Gibbs was almost a copresident and was responsible for organizing many of the school's activities.

In October 1898, Gibbs died, and without Gibbs's aid Tucker seemed to have difficulty running the school smoothly. Moreover, there was an increasing call by local white leaders for blacks to be trained in agricultural and industrial pursuits. It was inevitable that Tucker's bias for classical studies would be met with disapproval, and it was not long before Tucker and the state superintendent of schools, William N. Sheats, came into conflict. In June 1901, Sheats presented sixteen charges against Tucker. Claiming that Tucker was not an efficient administrator and that he was ignoring the development and growth of the school's agriculture and industrial programs, Sheats asked that Tucker not be reappointed president.

Tucker, who was very sick at the time and who would die within a couple of years, tried without success to defend his literary program. He began to call the school "Florida State Normal and Industrial College" in order to appease his critics.[4] He did not, however,

---

3. Ibid., 5, 7, 12–13, 20. *Oberlin General Catalogue of 1908* (Oberlin: Oberlin College Press, 1909), 993.

4. Neyland and Riley, *History of Florida A&M*, 24–27, 40–47. Thomas W. Talley was offered the presidency of Florida State Normal and Industrial College. By 1900 he was not only head of science but vice president. How-

change the emphasis of the school and even seemed to downgrade its agricultural and industrial training. In his report to Superintendent Sheats for the school year 1899–1900, in fact, he stressed the accomplishments of the Literary Department and noted, "the faculty are conscious that their primary obligation is to prepare teachers for our public schools." If they found a student who was incapable of making it through the literary curriculum, then that student would be "provided with some other means of acquiring an honest livelihood." For these students there was the program of "incidental industries."[5]

Events moved swiftly against Tucker in the summer of 1901. On June 24, Superintendent Sheats nominated Young for Tucker's position of president. Sheats believed that Young would remedy many of the school's problems and "surround the institution with a different spirit from that which seems to have taken possession of it." Two days later, Sheats was authorized to invite Young to submit a plan of reorganization and to visit the school. On August 6, Young arrived without a written plan and met the State Board of Education. The following day, the board elected him president of Florida State Normal and Industrial School. Three days later, Tucker was informed of the board's decision. He resigned, vacated the president's house, and left the campus within the two weeks allowed him.[6]

The selection of Young to replace Tucker was interesting and ironic in view of the fact that both Tucker and Young shared relatively the same philosophical values and the same Oberlin liberal arts training. Young's selection seems to have been totally the work of William N. Sheats, and the reasons for this choice probably died with Sheats in 1922. Sheats was an interesting man. Although in many ways he was an average white Southerner of the day in terms

---

ever, Talley wanted to be a teacher and not an administrator. He eventually went back to his undergraduate school, Fisk University, and taught chemistry for many years. The chemistry building at Fisk bears his name. Interview with Mrs. Thomasina Talley Greene in Jefferson City, Missouri, August 1982.

5. Biennial Report of the Superintendent of Public Instruction of the State of Florida (1902) (Tallahassee: State of Florida), 201–6. Hereafter referred to as Biennial Report of the Superintendent. See also General Catalogue for Florida State Normal and Industrial College, 1900–01, Florida A&M Black Archives, Tallahassee.

6. Neyland and Riley, *History of Florida A&M,* 47–49.

of his beliefs and prejudices, who accepted and advocated the separation of the races, he was nevertheless described by W. E. B. Du Bois as "an unusually *broadminded* man." Du Bois's description of him stemmed from Sheats's concern for quality education in general and quality black education in particular.[7]

Sheats had participated in the 1885 State Constitutional Convention, which authorized black schooling, and he also took an interest in improving the quality of black public schools. In 1885 and 1886 he taught black teachers at a two-month normal school in Gainesville, and he was responsible for making it mandatory for all public school teachers to pass a uniform state examination for certification.[8] By so doing, Sheats went against those who thought it was unfair to give white and black teachers the same examination. At the same time, however, this action created the opportunity and reason to improve the quality of the black teaching force. Thus the normal schools became more important because of these law and licensing procedures.

Sheats also encouraged the development of the first teacher institutes at the white and black normal schools. These institutes soon became summer sessions, which increased the enrollment and the state funding of the normal schools. Teachers who attended these summer schools were able to improve the grade of their certification and earn credit toward a degree. At the same time, the normal schools, both black and white, could improve their faculties, curricula, and teaching methods with the increased funding. This was all due to Sheats's efforts.[9]

There is really no way of knowing how Sheats became aware of

7. Biennial Report of the Superintendent (1920–1922), 3, 5. Nathan B. Young, Excerpts from unpublished "Notes of Nathan B. Young, Sr.," 1, Florida A&M Black Archives. W. E. B. Du Bois, *The Common School and the Negro American,* 70, 72. The underlining in the quoted passages is in original text. There was a campaign going on in Florida, like in most of the South, to reduce the funding for black education in public schools on the ground that they paid less taxes than whites. Even black militants such as Du Bois differentiated between moderate white racists like Sheats and extreme racists like Tillman, Vardaman, and Thomas Dixon. George M. Fredrickson, *The Black Image in the White Mind,* 283–84; and Du Bois, *The Souls of Black Folk,* 176.

8. Nita K. Pyburn, *The History of the Development of a Single System of Education in Florida, 1922–1903,* 137–38, 146–47.

9. Ibid., 148–50.

Young or why he was responsible for his selection to be president. It could be that Sheats had contacted Booker T. Washington, a man whose philosophy he greatly admired and whom he would invite to speak in Florida a few years later despite much local opposition. Perhaps Washington had mentioned Young and his abilities. Another possible source might have been Richard R. Wright, Sr., the best-known black educator in Georgia and the president of Georgia State Industrial College. Then, too, Young frequently traveled throughout Georgia encouraging teacher training, and he could well have come to Sheats's attention through these educational activities. At any rate, Sheats was the man who selected Young, and the two of them over the next twenty years "labored together in an educational way, through 'thick and thin' and sometimes through 'hell and high-water.'"[10]

It is easy to understand why Young would be interested in such a position. As he had made clear at Tuskegee and in his writings at Georgia State, Young was deeply interested in developing a strong academic institution for black students in the South. He had tried to stress academics at Tuskegee, only to be told by Booker T. Washington that that was not going to be Tuskegee's major emphasis. At Georgia State he had worked in a more intellectually congenial atmosphere where initially he not only had his concepts reinforced but also was given the opportunity, as director of the Department of Pedagogy, to develop more fully his administrative skills. Thus, when he was called to Florida, he was ready for the opportunity to give the black citizens of Florida "a well rounded preparation for professional as well as for industrial pursuits."[11]

Since Florida Normal and Industrial School was the only tax-supported institution of higher education for blacks in Florida, Young felt that it should provide all the "educational opportunities that white citizens could get at their institutions of higher learning." By 1903, Young had given the school a threefold mission—a normal school, an agricultural program, and a mechanical program. Young said that he intended to send into the black schools "properly trained teachers; to the farms and shops well-equipped artisans and

10. Even though Young and Washington disagreed on educational methods, they maintained a friendly relationship until Washington's death in 1915. Young, "Excerpts from Unpublished Notes," 1.
11. Young, "The Quest," 66–67.

to the state-at-large intelligent, law-abiding and thrifty citizens." Indeed, as Young noted in his 1903 report to the state superintendent of schools, he wanted the school to be "placed in the front rank with similar institutions in the other Southern states." Accordingly, he "labored hard" to develop his school "into an efficient educational agency."[12]

Of equal importance to Young was the involvement of as many black students as possible in his modern, "multifaceted" education program. In the creation of farmer institutes he attempted to reach out to local and regional black farmers. In his concern over upgrading the summer institutes, he wanted to encourage the enrollment of black teachers across the state. This expansion of programs at Florida State Normal and Industrial School led to a concern for more dormitory space. But Young was faced with a state board that appropriated the funds for Florida education and that apparently did not want Florida State Normal and Industrial School to expand. Therefore, the funds were never provided to construct the dormitories and, thereby, make significant expansion possible.[13]

Having witnessed the efforts of the Board of Commissioners at Georgia State to retard its growth, Young tried to move slowly during his first years in Florida. Indeed, from 1901 to 1909, when the State Control Board changed the school's name to Florida Agricultural and Mechanical College, Young referred to it as the "State Normal and Industrial School," in contrast to Tucker's "State Normal and Industrial College." It is possible that Young was trying to appease the local white powers, and most probably the white leaders of Tallahassee felt more relaxed toward the institution when it was called a "school" rather than a "college." Young also realized that his institution was only a secondary school and not a college, but he set about slowly and carefully building it into the college that he aspired to offer the black citizens of Florida.[14]

Young's initial thrust was to develop the agricultural and me-

12. Young, "Excerpts from Unpublished Notes," 1. Biennial Report of the Superintendent (1903), 208–11.

13. Biennial Report of the Superintendent (1903), 208–11.

14. W. E. B. Du Bois, "Nathan B. Young," *Crisis* (September 1923): 226–27. Du Bois wrote Young and asked him about the events at Florida A&M and published Young's response verbatim. Raymond Wolters, *The New Negro on Campus,* 194.

chanical areas that Tucker had chosen to ignore, but he did not plan to overlook the normal, academic areas either. Thus he gave the school the threefold mission, and he set about developing and strengthening each of the components of his "multifaceted" school. By 1902 he had built new buildings, expanded the campus, and added new equipment to the agriculture department. He had also added numerous courses to the industrial curriculum (millinery, tailoring, blacksmithing, wheelwrighting, laundry, and painting), and had made the academic courses more intensive. That summer he ran special sessions for teachers, so that they could return to their schools in the fall and improve the standards of their own curricula. He established a series of farmer institutes modeled after those he had seen developed at Tuskegee and Georgia State. He also began a military training program, which was one of the requirements of the Morrill Land Grant Act.[15]

Young traveled throughout the state to sell his school's program, appearing before church groups of all faiths, teachers' meetings, and business and civic groups. These efforts brought immediate results. By 1904, enrollment had increased nearly 100 percent, up to 255 students from 33 Florida counties.[16]

The industrial program grew rapidly. By 1904, Young had added two more industrial courses (shoe making and brick laying), bringing the total of industrial courses up to sixteen. And, in that same year, he initiated several significant requests for building construction: for an auditorium capable of holding one thousand students, for a dairy building and barn, for an industrial building, for improvements of the campus water and sewer facilities, and, most impressively, for a hospital and nurses' training school.[17]

On the last day of December 1905, the school suffered a setback. Duvall Hall—which housed the library, administrative offices, and cafeteria—burned down. The most serious loss was the destruction of the library. Young immediately asked leaders of the school's

15. Biennial Report of the Superintendent (1903), 208–11. Neyland and Riley, *History of Florida A&M*, 52, 56. *College Arms* (October 1910): 15, Florida A&M Black Archives. This was the school's magazine. It was for students and alumni, and Young headed the editorial staff.
16. Biennial Report of the Superintendent (1904), 205–7. Neyland and Riley, *History of Florida A&M*, 54–56.
17. Neyland and Riley, *History of Florida A&M*, 54–56.

alumni association to contact the agents of Andrew Carnegie, the great philanthropist, and Carnegie agreed to contribute up to half of the needed ten thousand dollars if the school's friends and patrons could raise the other half. The school failed to achieve its half of the bargain, but Carnegie was so impressed by its efforts that he gave the full ten thousand, and a two-story brick veneer building was constructed. Florida Agricultural and Mechanical College thus became the first black college to receive a Carnegie library. Other black college presidents wrote to ask Young how he had accomplished this. Young responded that Carnegie's only condition was that the library be stocked with books and magazines. Alumni and friends donated two hundred dollars in cash for books, and the library was opened in February 1908. By 1913 it had eight thousand volumes, thirty-four periodicals, ten daily newspapers, and many weeklies.[18]

Young's aspirations were still being fulfilled fairly well. By 1906 the school's enrollment has increased to 280 students (coming from 36 Florida counties). Of these students, 136 enrolled in the Preparatory Department and 144 in the Normal Department. The Normal School graduated a record 40 students, thanks in part to the increased enrollment in the summer school. In 1907 and 1908 campus enrollment figures continued to climb. In 1907 there were 175 grammar school students, 105 high school students, and 14 "Senior" school (Normal School) students, for a total enrollment of 294. In 1908 there were 162 grammar school students, 116 high school students, and 29 "Senior" school students, for a total of 307.[19] Dormitory space was obviously becoming an even greater problem.

In his 1907 budget request, Young again made his perennial request for dormitory space. He also renewed his request for a dairy barn and agricultural building, and auditorium, a mechanical arts building, and a hospital and nurse training school. To his surprise, and probably as a result of his success with the Carnegie library and

18. Ibid., 57–59.
19. Ibid., 56–57. Biennial Report of the Superintendent (1907–1908), 191–93. In his report dated October 8, 1908, Young called his school "Florida State Normal and Industrial School (The Colored Normal School)." Young chose to emphasize the school's original name. It is more than likely that he intended to build and upgrade in importance the normal school's activities. He was adding liberal arts courses in the name of the school's mission. He could have been trying to lessen whites' hostility toward the school.

at increasing the school's enrollment, the Board of Control responded positively to some of these building requests. The board recommended $5,000 for educational expenses, $5,000 for an infirmary, and $10,000 for the agriculture building and dairy barn.[20]

During this same year, the Board of Control recommended to the legislature that the school's name be changed from the "Colored Normal School" to "Florida Agricultural and Mechanical College for Negroes." The board called "the present name misleading," and explained that the school did have a Normal Department, but that the main reason for which the school was created was to provide agricultural education in compliance with the Morrill Act of 1862. This new name, in the board's opinion, "would more accurately describe the character of the institution." On May 22, 1909, the state legislature approved the recommendation.[21]

Understandably, Young reacted with delight to the name change. In the June 1909 issue of the school's magazine, *College Arms,* Young proudly proclaimed the change in his "Notes from the President," and he told the students that they were a college in name as well as in fact.[22] He also told them that the college would now be offering three new courses—a course in modern business, in stenography, and in bookkeeping and typewriting. These new courses were added to the new Department of Mechanical and Domestic Arts. Young considered these courses to be meaningful industrial courses, because they were in the fields opening up in the modern business world and a student with these skills in 1909 could find employment. In the new college structure the Department of Agriculture offered a course in such modern farming fields as dairying, truck farming, poultry rising, husbandry, and agronomy. Young also noted that the Academic Department was offering new courses in English, science, and vocal and instrumental music.[23]

Although the school was now called a college, the physical plant did not change, and the college remained very poorly housed. There were no solid brick buildings, and most of the wood structures were

20. Neyland and Riley, *History of Florida A&M,* 59–60.
21. Ibid.
22. *College Arms* (June 1909), Florida A&M Black Archives.
23. Ibid., and Neyland and Riley, *History of Florida A&M,* 60–61. As part of the military training at Florida A&M, a marching band was established, but the students had to provide their own band instruments.

in disrepair. Adding to the poor housing problems, the school was extremely overcrowded. Young's efforts to sell the college had worked too well for what the Board of Control was willing to provide in buildings. In 1910, Young reported that at the close of school in July 1909 there were 289 students. By July 1910 the total student population had dropped to 242. Young explained that the decrease in enrollment was due to lack of sufficient housing. Dormitories built for 150 residents had more than 200 students packed into them. The health of the students was so seriously affected by the overcrowding that many were sent home. Young pointed out that with adequate dormitories enrollment could be increased by "at least a hundred percent" within two years.[24] Young did not get the necessary dormitory space to support this expansion.

Despite failure to procure funds for expansion, Florida Agricultural and Mechanical College offered its first Bachelor of Science degree in 1909. The four-year course of study leading to this degree included advanced geometry, algebra, trigonometry, physics, and two years of German. With the addition of English, history, biology, and a few other college courses, the degree requirements still totaled only seventy-two hours. Although the state recognized the degree, the Division of Higher Education of the Bureau of Education of the Department of Interior in 1912 reclassified the college as a "normal school." Young wrote the chief of the division, K. C. Babcock, to complain about the reclassification, adding that the school was "fast approaching your standard of requirements for admission to your regular college list." He also pointed out that the program in science at Florida Agricultural and Mechanical College was equal to the program for the degree at the average agricultural and mechanical college of the South.[25]

But Young was fighting a losing battle. An earlier communication from the chief of the Division of Higher Education showed an unwillingness to consider black institutions as capable of college work. Similarly, the federal division chief said that in 1912 all black agricultural and mechanical schools such as Florida Agricultural and Mechanical College had been removed from the regular list of

24. Biennial Report of the Superintendent (1908–1910), 202–6.
25. Neyland and Riley, *History of Florida A&M*, 61–63. It was not until the 1920–1921 school year that Florida A&M offered a 120-hour bachelor of science degree.

"Colleges, Universities, and Technological Schools." Further, he held that in determining the classification of a school, college work did not "necessarily mean liberal arts work." He then proceeded to set forth his reasons for reclassifying Florida Agricultural and Mechanical College as a normal school.

First, there was an English Normal course in the school's catalog, and, second, half of the advanced students were registered in this course. For similar reasons other black agricultural and mechanical colleges had been reduced to normal schools. In this opinion, such education was best suited for blacks:

> At the time of my visit to Tallahassee last year I got the impression that you were very wisely and properly emphasizing the mechanical arts, agriculture, household science, and normal courses, and that such advanced work as you attempted was really done with a few individuals rather than under the elaborate course. I note also that the total registration in the scientific course of the "Seniors School" was 11, as against 9 in the English normal course.[26]

To this federal official, sub-college-level work was appropriate for Florida Agricultural and Mechanical College. However, he also said that what was offered was not college-level work. Even though he may have been a racist, there was no arguing with his conclusion. Young had to realize that outside of Florida the institution was not recognized as a college.

With this change from college to normal school, Young saw the progress he had hoped to make further retarded. His budget request of 1910 included funds for an administration building (which he had been requesting since 1902), the often-requested auditorium, and more academic classrooms, but none of these requests was approved. What the legislature did provide, however, were funds to improve the agricultural and mechanical arts facilities; from this point on, it became clear that these were the areas that would

26. Quoted in ibid., 285–86. By the 1920s, Young recognized federal vocational agents as part of a "well-defined movement" to lower the standards of black state-supported colleges and to turn them "solely or mainly to vocational training." See Young, "These Colored United States," *Messenger* 5 (November 1923): 866–96.

receive funding. The federal funds provided by the Morrill Act would pay the full salaries of Young and of all teachers in the agricultural, mechanical arts, home economics, biology, and library areas, and half of the salaries of the professors of English and history, but without funds from the state other areas would suffer. The Florida legislature appropriated funds for less than 20 percent of the operating cost of Florida Agricultural and Mechanical College. For example, in 1912, the total budget for the school shows $721.24 from the Institutional Fund (i.e., from the sales of products), $23,081.70 from the federal Morrill Fund, and only $5,087.25 from the state. This was fairly typical of most of the budgets during Young's tenure at Florida Agricultural and Mechanical College.[27]

In spite of this clear indication of the state's attitude, Young continued to work toward the growth and development of the college. In 1910 he obtained a grant of five hundred dollars from the Slater Fund to maintain the infirmary and nursing program; he managed to increase enrollment to 321, with students now beginning to reside in selected homes in Tallahassee; and he increased dramatically the number of teachers enrolled in the summer session.[28]

Young, however, recognized the political and economic realities with which he had to contend. In his 1910–1912 *Biennial Report* he made no reference to the work of the academic department and normal courses or the summer teacher-training program. Instead, he indicated that the purpose of the college was "to make itself helpful to the rank and file of the Negro citizens of the state by stressing the manual and industrial arts and agriculture," and this to "become an agent of real usefulness to the state at large."[29]

This pattern of limited progress continued during the next several years. Young managed to phase out the grammar school and to get a model training school constructed for observation and practice teaching. He accomplished the latter only by agreeing that if the state would construct the building, he would find outside fund-

27. Biennial Report of the Superintendent (1910–1912), 193–95, 394, 400; Biennial Report of the Superintendent (1913–1914), 312–13, 358–60.
28. Neyland and Riley, *History of Florida A&M,* 64. Biennial Report of the Superintendent (1909–1910), 205, 374–82. The maximum funding that Florida A&M received under the Morrill Act was twenty-five thousand dollars.
29. Biennial Report of the Superintendent (1910–1912), 400.

ing to maintain the program, just as he had done with the infirmary and nursing program. He did manage to develop midwinter institutes in the agriculture department to complement the existing farmers' institutes. He did not, however, receive funding for any of the other construction needs. He also failed to get support for scholarships (like those provided at Tuskegee and Hampton) for students in agriculture and mechanical arts.[30]

During the next few years, additional funding came from the federal government. By 1914, the Congress passed the Smith-Lever Act, which increasingly involved the college in agricultural and home economics extension work. Each state established in connection with its agriculture college an extension division along with its agricultural experiment station, which directed all farm and home demonstration projects for various boys' and girls' clubs established in each county. By 1918, these activities in Florida had expanded to a Negro Extension Division, employing several persons and centered at Florida Agricultural and Mechanical College. In 1917, Congress passed the Smith-Hughes Act to encourage training in agricultural, industrial, and commercial subjects and the teaching of vocational subjects. This act provided additional funding for Florida Agricultural and Mechanical College in these areas. Under the Smith-Hughes Act a federal grant-in-aid matched by state funds provided for two professors. There was also a four-year course leading to a bachelor's degree in agriculture, mechanical arts, or home economics. Students were also allowed in a two-year teacher training certification program. A proportion of the amount allotted to each of the Southern states by the Smith-Hughes Act was expended for blacks. These two acts were clearly so helpful because the state funding was so limited. So limited had things become, in fact, that Young's 1915 address before the National Association of Teachers of Colored Schools was really quite pessimistic about the chances for the appropriation of state or public funds for acceptable colleges for blacks in the South.[31]

30. Biennial Report of the Board of Control of State Institutions of Higher Learning (1910–1912) (Tallahassee: State Printer, 1912), 143–49. Hereafter referred to as Biennial Report of the Board of Control.

31. Ibid. Neyland and Riley, *History of Florida A&M*, 66–71. Biennial Report of the Board of Control (1910–1912), 145–49. In Young's 1915 presidential address before the National Association of Teachers of Colored

Under Young's leadership, Florida Agricultural and Mechanical College sought to provide its students with a broad education, comparable, as far as possible, to that being offered by Southern colleges. Students were exposed to outstanding black men and women, who served as role models for them to follow. Through the years they were brought into contact with educated blacks, particularly around January 1 each year during the commemoration of the Emancipation Proclamation. Among the noted speakers brought to the campus were Channing Tobias, Kelly Miller, George E. Haynes, John Hope, Benjamin Brawly, Alain Locke, and, on several occasions, Booker T. Washington. When outside speakers were unavailable, Young would often give lectures on timely topics himself. In 1915, for example, he delivered the pre-baccalaureate meditation entitled "Militant Citizenship," which, because of his criticism of racial inequality, probably did not endear him to white state officials, but which he obviously felt that his students needed to hear if they were going to be educated.[32]

Students were also encouraged to compete with other students beyond the borders of the state. For example, in 1915 Young established the Tri-State Debating Tournament, which included the black

---

Schools, he called for the establishment of a black graduate school in the Deep South to be funded by private foundations. Copies of the speech can be found in the Talladega College Archives and the Moorland-Spingarn Collection at Howard University in Washington, D.C. Young regularly attended national education meetings and occasionally served as one of the main speakers. In October 1908, for example, he spoke to the annual session of the American Missionary Association on "Vantage Ground for Teachers." In 1909 he attended the Tuskegee Negro Conference. Young to E. J. Scott, Tuskegee, Alabama, February 1908, Washington to Young, February, 1908, Booker T. Washington Papers. In April 1910 Young attended education meetings at Talladega, and in November 1912 the *College Arms* reported that he spent most of the previous summer traveling over a four-state area of the Deep South, where he attended at least one education meeting in each state. See also Neyland and Riley, *History of Florida A&M*, 66–67; *College Arms* (November 1908, December 1908, October 1915). The speech was published in full in the January 1909 issue of the *College Arms*. The speech emphasized that even above book learning, it was the teachers' duty to morally uplift and encourage good citizenship in their students.

32. Neyland and Riley, *History of Florida A&M*, 66–67, 71–72; *College Arms* (March 1912, April 1914, December 1915). This is a very strong speech advocating good citizenship and active involvement in the society. Young is very blunt in his criticism of the system of racial caste.

colleges of Georgia, Alabama, and Florida. He also involved his students in oratorical contests, literary societies, and drama organizations. Talented music students represented Florida A. and M. at national conferences, which not only brought national attention to the college but also won many friends at home. Likewise, in 1901, the development and growth of intramural sports and intercollegiate athletics began. Since Young felt that colleges should not play high schools, Florida's varsity football team traveled, in 1906, to Tuskegee and Alabama State College for games. Out of these contacts came, in 1913, the Southern Intercollegiate Athletic Conference, with Florida A&M as a charter member.[33]

At Florida Agricultural and Mechanical, Young's answer to the close supervision and control of the faculty, which Washington had desired at Tuskegee, became faculty involvement. Young established faculty committees to direct all aspects of college life, and these committees administered virtually all the programs of the school. The most powerful was the Prudential Committee, which was the executive committee of the faculty and which was made up of all the department heads. The president was a member of this committee, and, in his absence, the committee administered the school and made all the necessary decisions. General teachers' meetings were held the first Monday of each month, and teachers were encouraged to make suggestions freely on improving the school, which, of course, they did.[34]

But this involvement went beyond the committee assignments and teachers' meetings. Besides the many committees to which they were assigned, faculty members were assigned as advisers to classes, with Young usually taking the juniors and seniors himself. Beyond these commitments, Young also expected his teachers to lecture the students once a week on something useful that was outside of the teachers' discipline. For example, a history teacher might lecture on the stock market. Furthermore, teachers were also asked to cooperate in winning friends for the school by visiting the homes of friends and patrons. Faculty members were also expected to set

33. Neyland and Riley, *History of Florida A&M,* 25–26, 73, 120, 123–24; *College Arms* (March 1912, April 1914, December 1915).
34. "Minutes of the Weekly General Faculty Meeting and Prudential Committee," Florida A&M Black Archives. Minutes were kept from 1901 to 1911, but fire destroyed the years 1901–1905.

good examples for the students, and this generally meant refraining from drinking, smoking, and card playing. And, as with the students, faculty members were asked to be active in visiting and belonging to local churches, an activity that was especially crucial at times when the school was trying to "sell" a special program such as the Farmers' Conference to county residents.[35] In short, Young expected almost as much from his teachers as he demanded of himself, both in academic and nonacademic areas; this of course was one reason why Florida Agricultural and Mechanical College was able to make the limited progress that it made.

The progress that Young made at Florida Agricultural and Mechanical College, though limited, could not have been made without some forces at work to aid him. In the private sector, there was Andrew Carnegie and his major help with the school's library; there was, as well, the Slater Fund with its support of the nursing program. Less directly, there were organizations like those representing white teachers in white institutions which, in 1911 and 1912, had petitioned the state legislature for more adequate funding of teacher training and which, in the process, had resulted in additional funding for teacher training at Florida A&M as well.[36]

Perhaps some help had even come unwittingly. It is interesting to note the 1908–1910 *Biennial Report* of Edward Bradford Eppes, county superintendent of public instruction for Leon County, in which Tallahassee is located. Under a section entitled "The Educational Needs of the Colored Race," Eppes gave the opinion that the main obstacle to the county's agricultural well-being was the "disposition on the part of the young Negroes to leave the farm." The county lacked agricultural workers, and Eppes felt that through the proper kind of education, these black youths could be induced to stay home. Through a special fund, then, Eppes had employed an industrial and agricultural organizer, and he even wanted to get public school reading textbooks that positively emphasized the agricultural and country life.[37] It is quite probable that Eppes and

35. Ibid.
36. Biennial Report of the Superintendent (1910–1912), 406–9. Neyland and Riley, *History of Florida A&M*, 65.
37. Biennial Report of the Superintendent (1908–1910), 100–101. Leon County's population was more than 50 percent black, and more than 70 percent of the black population lived in the rural areas.

the economic conditions of Leon County had a great influence on the board's decision to upgrade the Normal School to "Florida Agricultural and Mechanical College for Negroes."

After World War I another historical factor that Young believed he had on his side was the debt that he and others believed the nation owed to blacks for their contributions to the war effort. Indeed, because of racial bias in the Selective Service system in Florida, Blacks had been drafted at a greater rate than had whites: despite the fact that blacks represented less than 40 percent of Florida's population, black draftees from Florida outnumbered whites by 12,904 to 12,769.[38] Young was hopeful that educational facilities for blacks in Florida, and at Florida Agricultural and Mechanical College in particular, would be expanded to accommodate the young blacks who had been drafted. Although some progress had been made during his first seventeen years, Young's aspirations for the growth and development of Florida A&M remained pretty much the same.

He continued to call for dormitory construction because he wanted to be able to serve a higher percentage of Florida's black population. In his 1918–1920 Biennial Report he noted that his present teaching faculty was capable of instructing four hundred students, but the school's plant presently only allowed for about three hundred.[39] Moreover, Young suggested that with the national emphasis then being placed on increased educational opportunities, within a few years Florida A&M should be enlarged to accommodate a full five hundred students. Young then noted, probably intending to be ironic, that if the state was not willing to let Florida A&M expand, the state should establish a separate normal school for the training of black teachers. This would allow Florida A&M to function solely as an agricultural and mechanical college, and to devote all of its funds and facilities to becoming a center for all black vocational training. Of course, Young knew that if the State Board of Control was unwilling to recommend adequate funding for the college as it was presently constituted, the board was hardly going to recommend the establishment of a second black college. Still, the suggestion made his point dramatically clear, and he closed his report, as

38. Neyland and Riley, *History of Florida A&M*, 73–74.
39. Biennial Report of the Board of Control (1918–1920), 300.

expected, by requesting ample funding for his school for the next two years.[40]

Besides his continual desire for physical expansion, Young also hoped to build a true college. The time had come, he thought, for the college to devote itself solely to higher education. Thus, just as he had recommended and achieved the elimination of Florida Agricultural and Mechanical College's grammar school in 1912, he now recommended the discontinuance of all high school courses as well. In place of the semi-college, Young proposed an organizational structure based on college-level courses only.[41]

On December 20, 1920, Young submitted to State Superintendent of Public Instruction Sheats his outline for a modern college organization. Instructional activities of the college were organized under five departments: academic, agriculture, mechanical arts, home economics, and health, which included the nurses' training school. Under the administration area were the boarding, fiscal affairs, and disciplinary departments. Each instructional department was under a dean, and the faculty, offices, and classes of the different departments were housed in separate buildings. The school auditor headed both the Boarding Department and the Fiscal Affairs office, and there were deans of men and women who supervised the Disciplinary Department. The heads of all the departments made up the Prudential Committee, with Young as its chairman. This was the executive committee of the college, and it met weekly, while all the teachers and administrators met monthly. The college had a total of thirty-nine faculty and staff members that included six administrative officers, eighteen instructors of vocational subjects, and ten full-time and five part-time academic instructors.[42]

The Nurses Training Program received special emphasis. This program was completely reorganized, and its standards were raised to

40. Ibid., 300–301.

41. Ibid.

42. Biennial Report of the Superintendent, 287–93. Young modeled Florida A&M after Oberlin College. There the Prudential Committee ran the college. Oberlin was from its very start a faculty-run college. See chap. 1. Interview with Dr. John F. Matheus, former auditor, May 1982, Tallahassee, Florida. He claims that Young was just the opposite of the stereotypical view that most black college presidents were plantation bosses. Dr. Matheus also claimed that Superintendent William N. Sheats supported Young's efforts to upgrade the school.

prepare Registered Nurses capable of passing the state licensing examination. After 1918, all nursing students had to have a high school diploma, and the curriculum went from a two-year to a three-year program. Prospective student nurses had to be between the ages of eighteen and thirty, and have good health and morals. To encourage women to enter the medical health field, Young provided scholarships—covering board, lodging, uniforms, and laundry service—to all nursing students. There was, however, a three-month probationary period for students. Furthermore, once this program became settled and successful, Young planned to establish a visiting nursing program as well.[43]

Unfortunately, several factors continually worked against Young's hope of developing Florida A&M into a standard college. First among these factors was the continuing refusal of state officials to fund anything other than the agricultural and mechanical arts program. In June 1909, for example, Young replied to an earlier inquiry from Booker T. Washington about Florida's State Senator Cone. The senator had made some anti–black education remarks that had been printed by the Associated Press, and Washington was concerned. After giving him a breakdown of the state appropriations for higher education and of that for Florida Agricultural and Mechanical School, Young told Washington that Cone had made a "strenuous effort to defeat the appropriations for summer schools for teachers because it provided for Negro teachers." In Cone's speech to the state senate, in fact, he fiercely assailed Florida's superintendent of public education for fathering the bill, and he nearly defeated it. Young thought, however, that Cone was seeking political power and was "hoping to ride into politics on the back of the Negro."

43. Biennial Report of the Board of Control (1918–1920), 299–305. At this time the board demanded a detailed breakdown of the finances of the Boarding Department. This was probably motivated by the facts that the department was bringing in large sums of money and that Young was using these funds to give scholarships in some areas such as nursing and deferring other students' expenses. In 1918 Thomas J. Jones in his survey on black education also recommended that the boarding funds be taken out of the president's hands and be more tightly controlled. Although these funds became a source of trouble between Young and the Board of Control, the dispute was over how Young used them and not regarding any wrongdoing. Neyland and Riley, *History of Florida A&M*, 70–71. See Hines, *Black Women in White*, on nursing programs at Florida A&M and other black colleges during this time period.

Young went on to say that the speech would have no effects on the "policy of this school, whose Board of Control is composed of five high-tone gentlemen who manage all the institutions of higher learning in the state." Young ended by saying, "I am optimistic still and feel sure that such blatant-mouthed demagogues are making a losing fight in the South."[44]

Young's optimistic nature was well placed so long as the Board of Control was made up of "five high-tone gentlemen." But these gentlemen had to be reappointed every four years by the governor, and the political climate of Florida was changing. Evidence of this change came a few years later, when on July 12, 1911, P. K. Yonge, a member of the Board of Control, wrote Dr. A. A. Murphee, president of the all-white University of Florida at Gainesville, concerning the curriculum at Florida Agricultural and Mechanical College. The board wished to make the curriculum at Florida A&M more agricultural and vocational, and Yonge was seeking Murphee's advice as to the most practical way to carry out this policy. Three months later, Yonge again wrote Murphee and sent along a communication he had received from the Bureau of Education in Washington, stating that federal officials also favored an emphasis on agricultural and industrial arts training at the black college. Yonge again asked for Murphee's suggestions for changing both Florida Agricultural and Mechanical College's curriculum and catalog. Receiving no reply, Yonge wrote to Murphee again and reminded him of his earlier letters. Finally, Murphee responded and agreed that agricultural and mechanical curricula were best suited to the educational needs of Florida's black youths.[45]

44. Young to Washington, June 17, 1909, Booker T. Washington Papers.
45. P. K. Yonge to D. A. A. Murphee, September 21, 1911, Gainesville, Florida, University of Florida Archives. P. K. Yonge at the same time also made efforts to get engineering equipment, an agricultural building, and a dining hall for the University of Florida. Yonge, of Pensacola, was the manager of the Southern States Lumber Company. He would be reappointed to the board in 1921 as chairman and in 1923 he would be a key person in Young's dismissal from the presidency of Florida A&M. This and other letters between Yonge and Murphee suggest that efforts to emphasize vocational training at Florida A&M had been underway for at least a decade before Young was dismissed. Yonge to Murphee, February 9, 1912, University of Florida Archives. Ironically, while Yonge and Murphee were trying to restrict or eliminate the college and liberal arts courses at Florida A&M, they were trying to build a history and language building for the Univer-

In December 1919, the General Education Board provided Florida with the money to employ its first state supervisor of Negro education. J. H. Brinson, a Southern-born white man and former superintendent of public education in Marion County, Florida, was appointed to this position. Brinson's main job was to promote the training of black agricultural and industrial teachers. To prepare for this, he was sent to visit Louisiana and Alabama to observe the training of black teachers in those states, and he also attended the annual farmers' conference at Tuskegee Institute. As a result of the latter visit, Brinson became interested in promoting the type of agricultural and vocational education that Tuskegee offered, and he secured six hundred dollars from the General Education Board to send twenty black teachers to Tuskegee for the summer of 1920. Subsequently, Brinson claimed that Florida Agricultural and Mechanical College, the state-established teacher training school, was too far away for blacks to attend its summer sessions. He was given another five hundred dollars from the General Board of Education, which he used to set up a competing summer school at Ocala in Marion County. Brinson even encouraged officials in other counties to establish their own teacher training sessions rather than send their black teachers to Florida Agricultural and Mechanical College.[46]

Young also had to contend with the increasingly hostile racial climate that developed after World War I, partially as a result of economic hard times and job competition. Young and Florida Agricultural and Mechanical College were caught up in a period of intolerance. In Florida, the Ku Klux Klan made a strong revival and carried on an often-violent campaign to eliminate the black vote. In 1920 a major race riot, which lasted three days, occurred in Ocoee over the efforts of blacks to vote, and in 1923 a white mob in

---

sity of Florida at Gainesville. Funding was held up by the death of a state official, and Yonge admitted that the funding would "depend to some extent as to who will be appointed to this position." Yonge to Murphee, February 15, 1912, University of Florida Archives. When Young had trouble in 1920 there is some evidence that local white businessmen wanting the beef and other contracts at the school were involved as well as those wanting the school to devote itself to agriculture and mechanical arts. Despite Yonge's business connection to a lumber company, he seems to have been motivated by a desire to change the curriculum at Florida A&M. Interview with John Matheus, May 1982, Tallahassee.

46. Biennial Report of the Superintendent (1918–1920), 259–64.

Rosewood ran through the black community and burned six houses and a church, leaving five blacks and two whites dead. In that same year, four thousand blacks in Jacksonville stood in line from 8 a.m. to 5 p.m. without a single one being permitted to vote.[47] Besides the denial of the vote, Florida's blacks were also victimized by a widespread forced-labor system. Under a state law of 1919, which was similar to the Black Codes of 1866, anyone who promised or contracted labor and then refused to work after receiving an advance was guilty of a misdemeanor. During the 1920s, most of the men sentenced under this law were recruited through misrepresentation and fraud, then were forced to work under inhumane and intolerable conditions.

In the lumber and turpentine industries there was extensive abuse of this forced-labor system. In 1923, Tallahassee became the center of national attention when a man was whipped to death in a lumber camp after having been assigned to it for failure to pay a fine for hopping a freight car. The camp doctor tried to cover up the cause of death by reporting that the man had died from malaria. Further investigation revealed that the local sheriff routinely rounded up hoboes for the payment of twenty dollars a head from the lumber company.[48]

In response to the increased racial violence and degradation of blacks in Florida and the rest of the South, the NAACP organized a campaign to establish Southern branches. In 1916 former Florida resident James Weldon Johnson became the NAACP's Southern agent; he made several trips into the South to organize new branches, beginning in his home state. His first trip to the Southern Atlantic states resulted in the establishment of thirteen new branches and 639 additional members. By 1920 there were 42,000 NAACP members in the South, as a result of the efforts of Johnson, W. E. B. Du Bois, Walter White, and others.[49]

Young, who had many times spoken up for black civil and politi-

47. George B. Tindall, *The Emergence of the New South, 1913–1945,* 154–55, 165–66, 192. On Rosewood see Michael D'Orso, *Like Judgment Day.*
48. Ibid., 212–13. The campaign of several Florida newspapers caused a rise in public indignation and a legislative investigation. Eventually, the convict leasing was for the most part eliminated and new penitentiaries were built.
49. Eugene Levy, *James Weldon Johnson,* 187; James Weldon Johnson, *Along This Way,* 314–16.

cal rights, could not ignore this responsibility. He had already gained some national attention for bold stands on black voting rights; he now began sending letters to the NAACP regarding the Klan's efforts to prevent blacks from voting in Florida. At first, Young sent these letters through his friend, Judge Robert H. Terrell in Washington, D.C., but he later began sending them directly to the NAACP's headquarters in New York City. In these letters he described beatings and floggings, the murders of black voters, and the dynamiting of the homes of black leaders. Young also enclosed Florida newspaper clippings, as well as a letter from the grand master of Florida's Klan, which warned whites against encouraging blacks to assert their political rights. Young even took on the dangerous role of investigating racial incidents and providing the NAACP with factual evidence concerning them.[50]

One of these cases concerned a Dr. W. S. Stevens of Quincy, who was beaten and forced to leave town for trying to vote. In January 1921, Walter White asked Young to secure an affidavit from Stevens. He asked Young to mail the letter to Stevens from a Tallahassee mailbox since White thought it "unwise" for Stevens to receive mail from New York City. White explained that the NAACP had experienced their mail being opened in small Southern communities, and he expressed his appreciation of Young's "splendid cooperation" in this matter. Young sent additional information to White and informed him that he would have a conference with Stevens instead of mailing him the affidavit because Stevens was "living in a 'hell-of-a-place.'"[51]

50. Neyland and Riley, *History of Florida A&M,* 72–73; Young to R. H. Terrell, May 7, 1923, Robert H. Terrell Papers, Manuscript Room, Library of Congress. Young often visited with Terrell when in Washington, D.C. Mrs. Mary Church Terrell and Young were both Oberlin graduates, and they were on campus together during the year 1885. Young to Walter White, January 2 and January 5, 1921. With these letters are undated newspaper clippings from Florida newspapers referring to the murders of blacks and particularly to the case of Dr. W. S. Stevens of Quincy, who was beaten and forced to leave town for trying to vote. "Grand master Florida Ku Klucks" to W. R. O'Neal and Judge Jno. N. Cheney, October 28 (1920), NAACP Papers, 1921, Manuscript Room, Library of Congress, hereafter cited as LC. Walter White to Young, January 13, 1921; Young to Dr. W. S. Stevens, January 17, 1921, NAACP Papers, 1921, LC.

51. Walter White to Young, January 13, 1921, and January 17, 1921, NAACP Papers, 1921, LC.

Later that month Young wrote White that he had gotten Stevens to agree to tell his story to W. E. B. Du Bois. Young included some of the particulars in his letter. Besides Stevens's beating, several other black men were beaten and run out of town, and the voting places were "guarded with armed men in order to keep Negroes from voting." Much of this was taking place not only out of racial bigotry but also because of political unrest in the area and the fact that blacks were presently registering at a rate that was six times greater than that of white voters. The only positive thing that Young could mention was the fact that "a number of decent-minded white men" in Quincy had kept Stevens from being killed.[52]

When Walter White was being denounced as a "deliberate prevaricator," he wrote to Young and asked if he could publish parts of Young's letters to prove that he was telling the truth about events in Florida. Despite his strong personal commitment to the effort and the personal risks that he had taken, Young suggested that it would be "inadvisable" to authorize publication. First, it might result in further harm to Dr. Stevens, because there was a "Reign of Terror" going on in Gadsden and Liberty Counties. Secondly, Young was fearful that his actions might prove harmful to Florida Agricultural and Mechanical College. In this regard, he noted that Congressman Frank Clark, who was attacking White's truthfulness, was a demagogue who was ambitious to become a senator and was therefore trying "to become popular with the back-woodsmen, hence his wild raving." Even so, Young noted, Clark had influences that could harm Florida Agricultural and Mechanical College's efforts "to secure a substantial appropriation from the legislature convening next April, by jumping on the president as being in 'cahoots' with the terrible N.A.A.C.P." Thus, Young felt that the letters would do more harm to the college than they would do good for the NAACP.

Noting that he was not really concerned with his own personal ambitions at Florida Agricultural and Mechanical College but was simply concerned about the institution's own financial well-being, Young suggested that when Du Bois lectured at the college the next month, he would "have a chance to get first-hand information as to the whole Florida situation." In this way the cause of justice

52. Young to Walter White, January 27, 1921, NAACP Papers, 1921, LC.

would be served without unnecessary risk to Florida's only college for blacks.[53]

This, then, was the situation that blacks in general and Florida Agricultural and Mechanical College in particular had to live with during Young's last five years at the college, and there is no question that this atmosphere deeply affected the school's condition. In fact, it is probably safe to say that despite Young's circumspect approach to the publication of his letter regarding Dr. Stevens, his various bold actions on behalf of black civil rights earned him and his school enemies in the white community and contributed to the controversies that eventually began to influence events at Florida Agricultural and Mechanical College.

In addition to the state legislature and educational governing boards and in addition to the racial climate in Florida, Young also faced opposition from internal forces as well. On June 30, 1918, W. H. A. Howard, the director of Mechanical Arts, reported to Young on the department's progress during the years 1917–1918. He said that the past year had been the "most strenuous" the department had faced, with many handicaps to overcome. The area lacked instructors, and it was difficult to induce new faculty to enter the field. Student enrollment also fell off, and the department was only marking time. On the other hand, Howard hoped that "the signs of the times indicated that the industrial phase" would receive a large place in the future, so he was setting himself the task of preparing for future conditions so that the industrial work would be ready to "fit into the new scheme when the time is ripe." With this in mind, Howard complained that a number of recent recommendations for upgrading the work of his program had not been acted upon by Young.[54]

Four years later, Howard wrote a very similar letter. The department had never experienced greater handicaps and disadvantages in previous years, he claimed, and it suffered from lack of adequate funding, instructors, and students. While the college itself had a large number of students enrolled, he noted, very few were in his department, and this falling enrollment was undermining

---

53. Young to Walter White, January 10, 1921, NAACP Papers, 1921, LC.
54. W. H. A. Howard to N. B. Young, June 30, 1918, Florida A&M Black Archives.

the department. Hence, he called for the reorganization of mechanical arts and the hiring of additional teachers, claiming that during the past year students and teachers without experience had conducted much of the teaching in the department. In short, the program was demoralized, and Howard urged the "immediate and sympathetic help of the President."

In recommending several ways to deal with this situation, Howard showed that he was an ambitious man interested in establishing himself at the head of a greatly expanded department and bureaucracy. Furthermore, acceptance of Howard's recommendation would have completely undermined the carefully balanced curriculum that Young had developed over the years, and the liberal arts program would have been all but destroyed. For example, he urged that every student in the freshman class be regularly assigned to take teacher training courses in mechanical arts, despite the fact that heretofore there had never been an assignment of a whole class to a course like this in the college.[55]

When Young did not accommodate him, Howard soon found an ally in A. A. Turner, the supervisor of the Smith-Hughes program in vocational education. Turner was convinced that the one or two hours of vocational instruction which the high school students received was not enough, and most of the college students devoted themselves to their academic subjects and took no trade courses. This situation, Turner believed, violated the college's land grant mission, and he came, one day, to Young's office with "a proposition that would practically scrap the program in progress, by changing the objective of the school—making it purely a vocational enterprise." Young "vigorously opposed the scheme."[56]

Having failed to sell the idea to Young, Turner then went to the Board of Control and tried to secure their approval. There was considerable deliberation by the board, but Young was able to win the battle, at least temporarily. Next Turner turned to the State Board of Education, a group that was made up of the chief elected officials of the state, with the governor acting as chairman.[57]

This was a propitious time for Turner in that a new governor was

---

55. W. H. A. Howard to N. B. Young, June 20, 1922, Florida A&M Black Archives.
56. Young, "The Quest," 66.
57. Ibid., 66–67.

about to enter office, and he agreed that the purpose and direction of the college should be changed toward vocational education. It was not surprising that the governor-elect, Cary Hardee, would be willing to undo Young's balanced program which had been more than twenty years in the making, because Young was an independent Republican and Hardee was a Democrat. During his campaign, in fact, Hardee had played upon the fears of white voters regarding the large-scale emigration of black farm workers from West Florida, and, like many other whites, Hardee believed that academic higher education for blacks would ruin them as field hands and make them dissatisfied with their inferior status in society. Hardee's election meant that Young would soon be forced out as president and that Florida Agricultural and Mechanical College would be reorganized along vocational lines.[58]

With more than twenty years of labor at stake, Young refused to compromise with Howard, Turner, and Hardee. Moreover, it was not likely that any compromise on his part would have resolved the situation anyway. Thus, as a result of the 1920 elections, P. K. Yonge was appointed to the Board of Control; eventually he was made chairman. When Yonge had been on the board earlier (1909–1913), he had worked with the president of the University of Florida at Gainesville to make the curriculum at Florida Agricultural and Mechanical College entirely vocational, so there was little doubt about what his plans were now.

The newly appointed Board of Control began to exercise tighter control over the course of study at Florida Agricultural and Mechanical College. On July 11, 1921, for example, the board passed a motion stipulating that in the future it would request that a list of the graduates of Florida Agricultural and Mechanical College be submitted to the board for its approval before the awarding of diplomas and degrees; in that same meeting, the board ordered that Young confer with its members on the progress of a building currently under construction at the college.[59]

Furthermore, the new members of the board did not wish to reappoint Young as president, but the scheduled period of reelection came before they could build a sufficient case against him.

58. Wolters, *The New Negro on Campus,* 195–96.
59. "Minutes of the Board of Control," July 11, 1921, 32–35.

Thus the campaign to reelect Young in 1921 was successfully waged by his old ally William N. Sheats, the superintendent of public instruction, who was able to get a majority of the State Board of Education to back Young's reelection at the July 29 meeting.[60]

Even so, the forces against Young on the board were able to adopt a resolution aimed at making the college more vocational. The statement claimed that, after a careful investigation, it had been found that a "large proportion of the instruction offered" at the college was "along general Academic and Classical branches," and it noted that the purpose of Florida Agricultural and Mechanical College was for training black youth in agriculture, mechanical arts, homemaking, and teacher training. Indeed, it further noted that the "needs and opportunities of the Negro youth of the state are largely in the fields of agriculture, industry and home making," and it thus resolved that the Board of Control "inaugurate and prescribe such a course of instruction" at Florida Agricultural and Mechanical College. More specifically, the college was now to require each student to select one of the vocational trades, at which he needed to spend four hours in each eight-hour school day. The board then ordered that a copy of this resolution be sent to Young with instructions that he prepare a curriculum for Florida Agricultural and Mechanical College along these lines by the next regular meeting of the board.[61]

This was not all. The board also ordered Young to prepare a list of all vouchers that were paid in July from the new appropriations, a list of all bills approved to that date for goods and services prior to July 1, 1921, and a list of all bills still owed by the college made prior to July 1. Young was then to deduct the entire amount from the resources of the college, prepare a new budget for 1921–1922, and submit several copies to the board for use during their next monthly meeting. Finally, Young was to prepare and submit a list of all the outstanding bills against the college, including its boarding fund.[62] The purge was obviously on its way.

That next month the board ordered its secretary to find out and report the entire circumstances of the boarding fund, and in Octo-

60. Ibid., August 8, 1921, 46.
61. Ibid.
62. Ibid.

ber board members passed a motion that showed that their real intent was to stop the entire growth of the college. They ordered Young to cease advertising the college and to make no further expenditures beyond those that were absolutely necessary to keep the school open. By January 1922, the board had adopted a new curriculum that greatly increased the role of vocational training, and in the following month Chairman Yonge recommended that the board authorize publication of a catalog for 1922–1923 that incorporated this new curriculum as the official course of study for the college.[63]

Now that the college had been undermined as a seat of higher education for Florida's blacks, the board turned its attention to students and to Young. In February 1922, Young came before the board and explained at length the status of the boarding fund. As soon as he had left the room, however, the board ordered that Young be instructed to notify all students and their parents that the accounts of all students must be paid in full no later than March 1, 1922. Young was to report to the board the status of all such accounts at its March 13 meeting, and at this meeting the board would "take direct action" if such accounts were not paid. Furthermore, to discourage enrollment of out-of-state students, these students were to be "charged an annual tuition of $20.00 payable in advance." This was a fivefold tuition increase. Later, the board would refuse Young's request to allow students from other states to attend Florida Agricultural and Mechanical College tuition-free when they came from states that did not charge Florida's students tuition.[64]

At this last meeting, the board unanimously adopted a resolution aimed at further restricting the enrollment at Florida A&M by restricting Young's use of the boarding fund. Heretofore, Young had

63. Ibid., September 12, 1921, 67. There actually was a bank loan in Young's name associated with the boarding fund. Up to this time, the boarding fund was entirely Young's responsibility and had there been a shortage in the fund, he was expected to absorb the loss personally. The secretary of the board did not report any improper activity regarding the note. Ibid., October 11, 1921, 74; February 13, 1922, 109–10.

64. Ibid., 112–13. Evidently, the number of out-of-state students had become an issue at Florida A&M. Because of the school's high standing in the Lower South, enrollment was constantly increasing. Young reported twenty-eight out-of-state students in 1916, forty-eight in 1918, and forty-four in 1919. After 1919 their numbers are not reported.

allowed students to work off their debts to the college over the course of the year. By giving these students employment on the campus and allowing them deferred payments of the boarding fees, Young was underwriting the education of many poor black youths. Over a biennial period, Young could do this and have his books balance at the end. Now, however, the board was forcing him to have his books balanced at the end of each month, as their resolution at this meeting now ordered Young to furnish monthly statements showing the exact status of the boarding fund.[65]

Not surprisingly, at the next monthly meeting the board unanimously adopted a resolution instructing Young to dismiss all students in arrears as of April 1 on any account incurred before March 1; as though convinced that Young would not enforce this first resolution, the board also passed a second resolution which required Young to provide the board, within one week of receiving the first resolution, six copies of a list of all students who were in arrears on March 1, 1922, noting the amount due and the reason for that debt.

There was one last piece of business dealing with the college during this meeting. That was the instruction to the secretary of the board that he should notify Young "that the Board does not consider it advisable to send his name to the State Board of Education for reappointment." Over the course of the next year, there were several skirmishes in the same vein and over the same issues, but they were all essentially repeats of these earlier events. Florida Agricultural and Mechanical College was meant to be simply vocational, its student body was to be kept minimal, and Young was certainly not fit to be its president.

There were several clashes between Young and the board over money matters as well as the direction of the college. Much of this conflict centered around the boarding fund, but there were other areas of conflict. First, the board increasingly excluded Young from having any say in awarding supply, repair, and construction contracts. For example, in May 1922 the board paid for the building of the Tobacco Experiment Station, which was contracted without any input from Young. Secondly, Young was prevented from

65. Ibid. Interview with John Matheus, May 1982, Tallahassee. Dr. Matheus said that Young had a few political allies such as William N. Sheats. Sheats died in 1922.

putting private foundation money in the school's general account, as he had always done in the past. These monies were now placed in a special account under the control of the secretary of the board rather than of Young. Thirdly, the board moved to restrict Young's ability to transfer funds from one account to another. In August 1922 he was ordered to make sure that all registration and music fees collected were deposited in the incidental fund. While the board had the right to demand tighter control of the school's monies, it seems apparent that the board objected most to Young's taking money from cash accounts to support underfunded programs and students. Finally, the board often changed or rejected the budgets submitted by Young. On at least one occasion, none of the other state schools had their budgets disapproved except Florida A&M College. Later, the University of Florida's president turned in an incomplete budget, yet the board accepted and approved of his general plan unconditionally, while rejecting Young's budget. Much of the board unhappiness with the budgets of Florida A&M had to do with their general complaint that the school was putting too much emphasis on liberal arts and not enough on agriculture, mechanical arts, and home economics. This complaint was put forth also by the chief federal vocational education agent in Florida to the governor and the board in a special meeting. However, most of Young's conflict with the board had to do with the boarding fund, and in the end this issue would be his undoing. After more than a year of continuous conflict, he gave the board the excuse they needed to fire him when he failed to submit a special report on the boarding department's indebtedness. On May 14, 1923, Young was ordered to make this report at the board's May 29 meeting. For some unknown reason, Young did not make the report, giving the board a solid reason for removing him from the presidency.[66]

66. "Minutes of the Board of Control," February 22, 1922, 113; March 13, 1922, 125, 130; April 14, 1922, 135–36, 136–40; May 8, 1922, 145–46; June 10, 1922, 152; July 10, 1922, 165–68; August 14, 1922, 178–79, 182, 184–85; October 9, 1922, 195–96; January 8, 1923, 200, 223; April 9, 1923, 251; May 12, 1923, 252; N. B. Young to P. K. Yonge, November 16, 1922, letter and budget exhibits, 2, Young to Yonge, April 21, 1923, letter and budget exhibits, 6, Florida A&M Black Archives. Young was turned down by the Board of Control when he sought a general increase in salaries for faculty and staff. Young did not see these salary increases during his remaining tenure at Florida A&M, but within four years of Young's leaving

On June 11, 1923, the board dismissed Young. In his place it appointed W. H. A. Howard. Accordingly, the secretary of the board was instructed to notify Young that "he has not been re-elected for the next year and to turn over to Dean W. H. A. Howard . . . all property and funds belonging to the college."[67]

Young's dismissal did not bring peace to the college. The alumni and students were on their guard that Howard's appointment meant changes in policies and curriculum. Immediately upon Howard's election, the Board of Control asked him to present them with a new "list of faculty nominations and other employees" for the school year 1923–1924. In July he was instructed to make sure that all students paid board and tuition in advance. At the same meeting, Chairman Yonge presented a letter from the Alumni Association of Florida Agricultural and Mechanical College questioning the failure of the board to reelect Young, but the board "did not consider it wise to reopen the matter."[68]

But the alumni and students would not let the matter die, and soon a petition, signed by a number of students, protesting the appointment of Howard as acting president was sent to the Board of Control. At its October 8, 1923, meeting, however, the board received the petition and simply ordered it to be filed. Moreover, it also instructed its secretary to notify Howard "to permit no insubordination or 'striking' by the students . . . even if he had to expel the entire student body."[69]

The students considered Howard, who only had a normal school diploma from Georgia State Industrial College, to be unqualified to replace Young as head of the school, and they were disturbed by Howard's carrying out of the board's mandate to emphasize the vo-

---

the increases were approved by the Board of Control and the state legislature. When Young came to Lincoln University in 1923, it was falsely rumored that he left Florida because he had asked for a salary of four thousand dollars a year and the governor of the state said that "no nigger was worth that much money." Neyland and Riley, *History of Florida A&M*, 75; Interviews with Professor James D. Parks and Mrs. Harriet Robinson, August 1981, Jefferson City, Missouri.

67. "Minutes of the Board of Control," June 11, 1923, 281.

68. "Minutes of the Board of Control," June 11, 1923, 282; July 11, 1923, 292, 294–95.

69. Ibid., October 8, 1923, 323; Neyland and Riley, *History of Florida A&M*, 78–79.

cational aspects of the college's program. Many faculty members were equally disturbed, and this brought about several resignations. To the students, Howard was especially unpopular for enforcing the board's rule that all board and tuition had to be paid in advance, and many students, alumni, and faculty believed that Howard was behind Young's dismissal.[70]

Eventually the students began boycotting classes in protest of Howard's appointment and the changes in the college's program. In the midst of this student unrest, Duvall Hall, a classroom building, mysteriously burned. Howard made matters worse by calling on the local sheriff and his deputies to restore order. The white deputies soon came into conflict with the black students. Even when the secretary of the board came to the campus and threatened to close the school if order was not restored, the students did not return to their classes.[71]

Despite all of Howard's and the board's attempts at restoring order, the campus remained in turmoil into the next year. Meanwhile, Howard expelled fourteen students for playing a leading role in the students' strike, and his actions were fully endorsed by the board.[72] Even though the strike was broken, peace had not returned to the campus.

Soon Dr. A. J. Kershaw, the head of the college's Alumni Association, responded to students' complaints and made an open appeal to Howard to step down for the good of the college. He claimed that white politicians who were determined to dictate the kind of education best suited for blacks had put Howard in office. Accordingly, if Howard stayed, Kershaw warned, he would be regarded as an "Uncle Tom" by the black population of Florida.[73]

70. Neyland and Riley, *History of Florida A&M*, 79.

71. Wolters, *The New Negro on Campus*, 199–201. *Tallahassee Daily Democrat*, October 13 and 15, 1923; N. B. Young to *Tallahassee Daily Democrat*, October 19, 1923. Howard reported to the Board of Control that Dean Thomas left the campus the day before without "permission" and that his position was vacant. Since Thomas was not listed as one of the teachers recommended for rehire, Howard planned to get rid of him somehow. "Minutes of the Board of Control," November 13, 326; August 13, 1923, 304.

72. Neyland and Riley, *History of Florida A&M*, 80, says eleven students were dismissed, but the board's minutes list the names of ten boys and three girls. See "Minutes of the Board of Control," November 13, 1923, 326.

73. Wolters, *The New Negro on Campus*, 199; *Savannah Tribune*, November 15, 1922.

In January 1924 the campus was disrupted by a fire that destroyed Gibbs Hall, the main women's dormitory. Arson was suspected, and three young men were expelled from the college. Many
girls lost all their clothes, and the black community of Leon County
had to hold a special relief rally. Many students were forced to leave
the campus. Three months later the mechanical arts building burned
down, and once more arson was suspected. The Board of Control
was so sure of this, in fact, that it employed a detective to investi-
gate the matter, offering him ten dollars per day, plus expenses up to
one thousand dollars, to find the guilty parties.[74]

Meanwhile, Howard continued to be an object of scorn in Florida's black community. At the end of the 1924 school year Chairman
Yonge admitted that Howard had been an unfortunate selection and
that the college had experienced "a very unsatisfactory year." Likewise, State Supervisor of Negro Education Brinson reported that "a
condition of rebellion bordering on anarchy" had developed at the
college under Howard. Consequently, in May 1924 the board notified Howard that he had not been reappointed for the coming year.
By then Young had been at Lincoln University in Missouri for a full
year, seeking once more to establish a high-quality college for blacks.

As a final assessment of Young's presidency at Florida Agricultural
and Mechanical College, it might be useful to analyze both the environment in which he labored and the specific actions which that
environment eventually mounted against him.

Young's assessment of the general environment at Florida Agricultural and Mechanical College can be found in an article he wrote
in November 1923, entitled "These 'Colored' United States."[75]
Young noted that the racial tensions and prejudices that found
wide expression in the 1920s were not new to Florida, but had been
there for most of his first twenty years as president of Florida Agricultural and Mechanical College. Florida, Young said, had long
"lost the racial catholicity of Spain" and had "found the racial prejudice of these United States." Like the rest of the country, Florida
was "hostile to Afro-America," and the Florida black, as elsewhere,

74. Neyland and Riley, *History of Florida A&M*, 80; *Tallahassee Daily Democrat*, January 23, 1924. "Minutes of the Board of Control," March 13,
1924, 366; May 12, 1924, 389–79; *Savannah Tribune*, November 11, 1923;
Neyland and Riley, *History of Florida A&M*, 80–112.
75. Nathan B. Young, "These 'Colored' United States," *Messenger* 5 (November 1923): 896.

was "maltreated and cheated, cajoled and paroled with occasional justice." By 1923, Young pointed out, Florida was "making strenuous efforts to win the pennant in the lynching league," so that, by the first of that year, Florida was ahead of Georgia and Texas in the number of blacks lynched. Young saw this as an "exhibit" of Florida's "full Americanization."

Politically, the black man, according to Young, was a "nonentity" throughout the state. Educational opportunities for Florida's population were "negligible," and in "all matters of citizenship a sort of *ward* relationship to his white fellow-citizens, who [were] his self appointed guardians," existed. The white Southerner's control of the black man was as complete as that of the slave master over the slave. The *"unthinking* Negro has not yet discerned that he is the white man's ward, but little removed from that of slave," Young claimed.

Educationally, the lot of blacks was substandard. While there were a few serious efforts south of Jacksonville, "practically nothing was being done in West Florida." This neglect was particularly true for the rural districts, where the public education policy of the state toward blacks was especially tragic and shortsighted. On a statewide basis, Young felt, Florida was surpassed in her "niggardly educational policy only by Georgia, the most sinning of all the Southern states in its educational neglect of its Negroes."

Florida had been, he continued, "unwittingly led . . . into making a real effort at the *higher* education of the Negro." When this was discovered, however, by federal vocational agents, "there was a sharp reaction against such an educational program." There were frantic attempts to put Florida Agricultural and Mechanical College "into reverse gear, to 'soft-pedal' *cultural* education as being undesirable for Negroes." The white political leadership of Florida had "a low-browed conception of the mission of education to the Negro."

Young also saw what he considered "a well defined movement" throughout the South, aided by federal vocational agents, "to *substandardize* the few state supported colleges for Negroes by devoting them solely or mainly to vocational training." The purpose of these activities was to make the black man a permanent peon to the white man in the South, with no regard for the welfare of blacks. In short, the attempt was "to educate him narrowly as a Negro, not *broadly* as a man and a citizen."[76]

76. Ibid., 866, 896 (italics in original).

In a public letter to W. E. B. Du Bois in September 1923, Young became much more specific and personal in assessing his years in Florida. In explaining his forced retirement from Florida Agricultural and Mechanical College "after twenty-two golden years of service . . . for an appreciative people," Young noted that he was not leaving on his "own initiative, but upon the initiative of the 'power that rule' to whom I have become a *'persona non grata,'* because, forsooth, I refused to sneeze when the local federal vocational agents took snuff." Young went on to say, "I refused to endorse their programs for this college. They, assisted by the governor of the state, undertook to redirect the activities of the college to give it a more industrial trend."[77]

When "it came to a showdown," however, "this policy could not be legally carried out." And the academic status of the college could not be changed by a "resolution of the State Board of Education." Having foreseen this possibility, Young had always kept the growth of the school within the legal limits. Even so, when the politicians "failed to accomplish their purpose by direct methods," they sought to secure someone for the presidency whom they could control. Despite the apparent success of this move, Young said that he still had hopes for the school because "the alumni and patrons of the college are on guard to see that the college suffers no detriment by any change in the presidency."[78]

Considerably later in his life, Young looked back on the experience and noted that he might have avoided the controversy at Florida Agricultural and Mechanical College if he had used more "political finesse." Instead, he observed, he had adopted "an undiplomatic attitude," and had "the *courage,* rather than the caution of his educational convictions." Being the kind of man he was, all Young could do was face the situation without bended knee and take "the results on the chin standing up."[79]

This, then, was the man that Lincoln University and the State of Missouri named in 1923 as the president of the state's only black institution of higher learning.

77. Quoted in W. E. B. Du Bois, "Nathan B. Young," 226.
78. Ibid., 226–27.
79. Young, "The Quest," 67 (italics in original). W. E. B. Du Bois, "Nathan B. Young," 227.

107

Nathan B. Young, president of Florida A&M University, 1901–
1923. Black Archives Collection, Florida A&M University.

Booker T. Washington. Photograph by Frances Benjamin Johnston
in 1906. Library of Congress.

Graduating class of 1904, Florida A&M. Black Archives Collection, Florida A&M University.

Florida A&M varsity football squad, 1904.

Carnegie Library, Florida A&M. Black Archives Collection, Florida A&M University.

Old Memorial Hall, Lincoln University. The building was destroyed in 1972. Inman E. Page Library, Lincoln University.

Graduating class of 1927, Lincoln University, with President Nathan B. Young, center. Inman E. Page Library, Lincoln University.

Map showing Lincoln's three-hundred-mile-radius service area drawn by Young. Inman E. Page Library, Lincoln University.

College Hall, built in 1930, later renamed Nathan B. Young Hall. Inman E. Page Library, Lincoln University.

W. E. B. Du Bois speaking at Lincoln University. Photograph by Edward L. Patterson. Inman E. Page Library, Lincoln University.

Nathan B. Young near the end of his career at Lincoln University.
Inman E. Page Library, Lincoln University.

CHAPTER 5

Transforming an Institution

The Lincoln Years

L incoln University, the school that Nathan B. Young came to head in 1923, was the first of many black educational institutions founded during the first decade after the Civil War. The history of Lincoln down to 1923 had been both inspiring and troubled. It was the only such institution established through the efforts and sacrifices of black soldiers. By 1923, Lincoln had been developed to about the level of a secondary industrial and normal school, and it was troubled by internal strife. Young came with the dream of building the school into a standard four-year college, and he set about to bring this dream into reality.[1]

During the Civil War, the Western Sanitary Commission, a benevolent association, began organizing classes for black soldiers at Benton Barracks in St. Louis. The classes, mostly in reading and writing, continued in the black regiments, as the former slaves were taught

---

1. Curtis, "Nathan B. Young, A Sketch," 107–10; Young, "The Quest," 68. It was nationally known that Lincoln was so involved in state politics that every time the governor changed so would the president of Lincoln. In fact, Lincoln's presidents changed even more frequently, some lasting less than twenty-four hours. In 1894, W. E. B. Du Bois refused to accept a higher-paying position at Lincoln because he feared that state politicians would prevent him from doing honest research and telling the truth. *St. Louis American*, April 7, 1938; W. E. B. Du Bois, *Dusk to Dawn*, 49, and W. E. B. Du Bois, "Future of the Negro State University," address delivered at Lincoln University, January 12, 1941, Lincoln University Archives.

around the campfires by their white officers. Some of these officers were college-educated men who were inspired by a sense of mission to help uplift their black brothers. As the war continued, members of the black regiments became increasingly aware of the lack of educational opportunities for them in Missouri.

Lincoln was born of two of the seven black Civil War regiments from Missouri—the 62nd and 65th U.S. Colored Infantry Regiments. In January 1866 at Fort McIntosh, Texas, members of the 62nd began mustering out of the service, and a conversation between Lieutenant Richard B. Foster and a fellow officer centered on the tragic absence of a school in Missouri where the soldiers could continue their education. Foster was asked if he would establish such a school if the regiment raised the money. Foster agreed, and a movement began which resulted in Foster and the men of the 62nd raising $5,000. The 65th Colored Infantry Regiment, a brother unit, soon raised another $1,379.50.[2] These soldiers also recognized the need for a school back in Missouri, and they also contributed generously toward the establishment of one. One Private Samuel Sexton gave one hundred dollars, despite his earning only thirteen dollars a month.

At Fort McIntosh, Texas, a committee was formed, composed of Surgeon C. Allen, Captain Henry R. Parson, Captain Harrison DuBois, First Lieutenant A. M. Adamson, and First Lieutenant Richard Baxter Foster. This group was empowered by the soldiers to add other members that might be needed to make the school for blacks in Missouri a reality. The work that had begun at Fort McIntosh was continued in St. Louis. The committee's members agreed to add two or three influential persons from St. Louis to their ranks. There were several locally important people interested in promoting education for blacks. James E. Yeatman and J. W. McIntyre agreed to join the committee and to help raise funds for the project. In February 1866, the committee was supplanted by a Board of Trustees. Included among the members of this new board were James E. Yeatman, J. W. McIntyre, Richard B. Foster, Henry Brown, Harrison Dubois, W. R. Parsons, C. Allen, and A. M. Adamson. Later, Governor Thomas C. Fletcher, Judge Arnold Krekel, Superintendent of

2. In 1900, W. E. B. Du Bois said that Lincoln Institute "had perhaps the most romantic beginnings" of all the black colleges. Du Bois, ed., *The College-Bred Negro,* 12. In 1847 Missouri had passed a very restrictive law against teaching blacks how to read or write.

Public Schools T. A. Parker, William Bishop, Emory S. Foster, and R. F. Wingate would join the board, replacing some other original members. Governor Fletcher served as chairman of the board. When Joseph W. McClurg replaced Fletcher as governor, he also became a member of the board and was made its president. McClurg was followed on the board by Governor Silas Woodson and B. Gratz Brown, and Brown was followed by the last governor to serve on the board, John Phelps.

With more than six thousand dollars in hand, Foster attempted to establish a school in St. Louis in 1866; when that failed, Foster moved on to Jefferson City. There, in September 1866, the school was opened with two pupils in an abandoned public schoolhouse on "Hobo Hill." Lincoln Institute, as it was called, operated as a private school for a number of years. The school's first major building was constructed in 1871. Foster and black political leaders felt that blacks were due a share of funding provided to Missouri by the 1862 Morrill Act, and by 1870 they had persuaded the state to give five thousand dollars annually toward the support of the school for training black teachers for the public schools.[3]

In the beginning Lincoln was managed by principals, a position that changed hands about every two years as a result of the board's domination of the school and its extreme sensitivity to political pressures. Foster first served as principal. During 1870–1871, W. H. Payne, a black man, became principal, with his salary being paid by the American Missionary Association. In the 1871–1872 school year Foster returned as principal, but was not reappointed because board members voted against him for failing to support Governor McClurg. Next came the Reverend Henry Smith, an Oberlin graduate, who was appointed from 1872 to 1874, only to not be reappointed in 1875. Between 1875 and 1878, Samuel T. Mitchell, a Wilberforce graduate, was the second Negro to serve as principal; in 1878, Reverend Henry Smith returned for a year, but he was replaced by A. C. Clayton in 1879.[4]

---

3. Richard B. Foster, *Historical Sketch of Lincoln Institute,* July 4, 1871; Sherman W. Savage, *A History of Lincoln University,* 7–10, and Albert P. Marshall, *Soldier's Dream,* 3–34. On Foster's dismissal it was claimed that he had voted against Governor McClurg.
4. Marshall, *Soldier's Dream,* 3–34. Young felt that Foster's leaving helped account for the school's hectic history. He said if Foster had stayed to his

In 1879 the state superintendent of schools recommended that the state should help support the operation of Lincoln Institute. As early as 1873 attempts had been made by Foster and black political leaders to make Lincoln a state school. These early attempts had failed, but in 1879 the legislature granted Lincoln fifteen thousand dollars to help reduce the school's indebtedness. It was found that this grant of fifteen thousand dollars was unconstitutional, since the state could not give money to private organizations or corporations. Governor John Phelps, who was also the president of Lincoln's Board of Trustees, held up such legislation until the board could deed the school buildings and lands to the state. The grant was thus legal, and Governor Phelps signed the legislation. In this manner Lincoln Institute became a state-supported school.

Lincoln became the state normal school for Negroes. Under the law, the state's normal schools were governed by a Board of Regents whose members were drawn from the local district. Since Lincoln was the state's normal school for blacks, its board members were drawn from throughout the state. When a Board of Regents was substituted for the Board of Trustees, state law prevented the governor or any other state officials, except the state superintendent of schools, from serving as a member. Since the normal schools were considered a part of the public school system, the state superintendent of schools was an ex-officio member of all boards.[5] The state superintendent of schools would often be the only member of Lincoln's Board of Regents who had any background in education, and thus he exercised a considerable amount of influence through the years.

The next year, 1880, Inman E. Page, a twenty-six-year-old black man, was appointed Lincoln Institute's first president. He came to Lincoln in 1878, first as the assistant to Principal Henry M. Smith and then to Principal A. C. Clayton. Page was born in slavery in

---

death as head of the school its history would have been calmer. After Foster, most presidents only stayed for a few years. None was allowed to die in office or resign. The school became a totally board-managed school. Young, "A Fifty Year Jaunt." Savage, *History of Lincoln,* 19–149. See especially 34–36 on the establishment of Lincoln as a state school, and 40–59 on I. E. Page's presidency. Page resigned to become president of the new Langston University of Oklahoma.

5. Savage, *History of Lincoln,* 48.

Virginia and was the son of a livery stable operator who had been able to purchase his own and his family's freedom. Page entered school in Washington, D.C., and later studied at Howard University. He transferred to Brown University and graduated in 1877, with his classmates electing him class orator. After a year teaching at the Natchez Seminary in Mississippi, Page came to Lincoln. Serving as president from 1880 to 1898 and later from 1922 to 1923, he brought a period of stability to the school. Some financial stability was achieved in 1891, when Lincoln became a land-grant institution under the second Morrill Act of 1890. Later ten thousand dollars was appropriated by the state legislature for the erection of an industrial arts building. An additional nine thousand dollars was provided for the purchase of tools and machinery. Besides the school's operating budget and the Morrill Land Grant funds, the legislature appropriated one thousand dollars to build a residence for the president.

Page added the first significant college work to the curriculum and greatly built up the school's physical plant. Even so, before Page resigned in 1898, he was the target of two unsuccessful efforts to remove him. In 1889 the board tried to remove him on the grounds that he ruled the school in an arbitrary manner and good teachers would not stay with him, but local pressure forced the board to rescind its action. Again in 1892 the teachers complained of mismanagement of the school's affairs and threatened to resign three weeks before the end of the school term. The board resolved this crisis by firing all the teachers at the end of the school year. These two attempts at removing Page seemed to be motivated by the ambitions of his assistants and unrest among the faculty. In the first attempt, the presidency was immediately offered to and accepted by Page's first assistant. The outcry in the local press forced the board to reconsider its decision within a week. In the second case, Page's vice-president was a leading force.[6]

After Page's resignation in 1898, there followed still another period during which the presidency changed hands many times. Indeed, there were so many presidents between 1898 and 1902 that Lincoln's historian, W. Sherman Savage, called it "the period of presidents." In 1898, John H. Jackson, a teacher at the Kentucky

6. Ibid., 50–78.

State School, was appointed president. Jackson succeeded in dropping the lower grades from the curriculum and in establishing a series of lectures by outstanding, nationally known black educators. But Jackson was replaced by J. H. Garnett as acting president in 1901, and on that same day Garnett was replaced by John W. Damel, who, it was thought, would give greater emphasis to the mechanical arts and agriculture. But apparently Damel fell from favor with the board within six months, and the next year he was replaced by Edward A. Clarke of Wilberforce, who in turn served only six months before he was replaced by Benjamin F. Allen.[7]

Allen served as president from 1902 to 1918, but there really was not much tranquility during his sixteen-year tenure. He had to spend much of his time protecting his position. Allen emphasized teacher education. He had been educated in the liberal arts, but tried not to reveal his bias by balancing the liberal arts curriculum with an industrial arts curriculum. Nevertheless, after 1910 Allen began receiving opposition from certain members of the Board of Regents, though in 1913 he was reappointed for a two-year term. First of all, he was tied to the old faction on the board and in the community, and a younger group was coming into power. Secondly, he continued to emphasize teacher education, at the expense of agricultural and mechanical arts, while there was increasing demand for industrial education from state officials.[8]

7. Ibid., 273–78, 278–84. Clarke wrote a very critical report to the all-white board of regents. He claimed the school was in poor shape and needed better students and teachers. Clarke said that the staff at the school was undisciplined and ready to burst into insubordination. He claimed that board members had janitors, matrons, teachers, and students reporting on the president's administration with the aim of thwarting his plans. He complained that positions were filled at the school by the way a man voted and potential faculty circulated petitions among shopkeepers and passersby on the streets. He insisted the board repudiated such methods. He also recommended that the president be appointed for two years to eliminate "annual unrest," and that the election of faculty members be upon the recommendation of the president. He also wanted an upgrading of mechanical arts by hiring a trained teacher instead of a blacksmith and put more emphasis on teacher training. Clarke was dismissed at the next meeting of the board. Black students and citizens protested in vain. Alumni called for the appointment of at least one black member of the board. Their request went unanswered.

8. "Minutes of the Lincoln Institute Board of Regents," February 23, 1913, Lincoln University President's Office. Allen was a graduate of Atlanta University.

Even as he was being reappointed, political interference was in process. At the same meeting in which the board reappointed Allen, for example, a new board member recommended the appointment of R. A. West as both secretary to the president and superintendent of buildings and grounds at a higher salary than any member of the faculty, $125 per month. Also at that meeting, two members of the state legislature appeared before the board to recommend their choice for superintendent of farms and instructor of agriculture. Lincoln's students even began to take their grievances against the administration directly to members of the state legislature.[9]

Besides increased interference by politicians in the affairs of the school, President Allen also had to deal with the racial hostility of Jefferson City citizens. One controversy centered around a white tenant farmer who supervised the school's farm and whom some members of the board thought was stealing from the school. These members suggested that the farm be placed under the control of the black instructor of agriculture. In response to this, however, several prominent Jefferson City residents opposed the farm's supervision by that instructor. The farm was located on the main street in a residential part of the city, and various whites objected to having a black teacher living there. The board was initially divided on this issue, but eventually the sentiments of the Jefferson City petitioners prevailed.[10]

The board was also divided over purchasing procedures. Purchases were normally taken care of by the three-member Executive Committee, which was appointed by the president of the board. After an investigation into overcharging on the bills for the elementary teacher training program, a majority of the board passed a motion which provided that after January 1, 1913, all purchases were to be made by a newly created "purchasing agent," who was to be "a white male without connection or interest in any store, firm, or corporation handling materials, products or labor that may be used by the school."[11]

Even though the full board chose not to trust its Executive

9. Ibid. The two members of the legislature were Mr. Houston of Lincoln County and Mr. Carrington of Maries County.
10. "Minutes of the Lincoln Institute Board of Regents," November 23, 1912, January 18, 1913, February 25, 1913, and June 10, 1913.
11. Ibid., November 23, 1912. The board did not hire a purchasing agent until after 1920.

Committee in this instance, the real power at Lincoln at this time remained with the Executive Committee of the Board. Its members directed all affairs of the school when the full board was not in session, and the full board met only about three times a year. The Executive Committee authorized and paid all bills, and it hired and fired all staff members. If a shoemaker needed to be hired or equipment purchased, the Executive Committee handled it. The board was politically secure and seemed unruffled even when criticism came from state officials and agencies. In 1913, for example, the state auditor's office charged the board with overstepping its authority in allowing certain additional costs for plumbing, construction work, and electrical wiring. The auditor did stir some action, and the board voted that its president and the Executive Board could approve no account for payment until those accounts had been examined by the full board. The board, however, soon went back to business as usual, and the Executive Committee was again given authority to manage the school's affairs. Not long afterward, in fact, at the 1914 annual meeting to approve faculty appointments, one board member, Superintendent of Public Instruction William P. Evans, objected that two members of the staff without degrees were being paid too much, at which point it was made clear that both of these people had views which were politically sympathetic to the views of the majority of the board. The board was not even upset at the charge that one school employee was being paid a double salary. Understandably, then, President Allen had very little real authority beyond recommending faculty appointments.[12]

On the recommendation of a prominent Jefferson City banker, Allen was reappointed in February 1915 to another two-year term. By this time, board members were increasingly involved in making appointments on the basis of the political preference of candidates, and a good deal of Allen's time was spent making compromises in order to retain his position. During this period the board called upon influential blacks from Jefferson City and the major centers

12. Ibid., June 11 and 12, 1913; June 5, 1914. These were both staff positions and obviously political appointments. The superintendent of public instruction probably objected most to one of the political appointees without degrees being paid more than any of the teachers. Later, the board would solve this problem by conferring an honorary master's degree on this staff person. Ibid., February 18, 1915.

like St. Joseph, Kansas City, and St. Louis to speak before the student body and to receive honorary degrees from Lincoln. In some cases these "degrees" then "qualified" persons to retain or receive appointments there. Most received master of arts degrees, and the very influential J. R. A. Crossland of St. Joseph was awarded a Doctor of Law degree.[13]

At the annual meeting on June 14, 1917, Allen was renominated as president, though Uel Lampkin, state superintendent of schools and a new member of the board, made the motion that the position be vacated. As a result, a special meeting was held in the law office of board member T. S. Mosby, where Allen was reappointed for another year on a 4–3 vote. It was also decided, however, that Allen would not be reappointed thereafter. The board then moved to establish a committee of three to review applications for the presidency.[14] Eventually it appointed J. R. E. Lee, the principal of Lincoln High School in Kansas City, to succeed Allen. Lee had not filed a formal application, but it was explained by Superintendent Lampkin that he had expressed a willingness to serve. Lee was thereupon elected president for a one-year term. He refused the position, however, probably because of the low salary. As a result, on June 12, 1918, Clement Richardson, a faculty member at Tuskegee Institute, appeared before the board at its request and gave a history of his life and work as a teacher. He was appointed president the same day.

Clement Richardson was born on June 23, 1878, in Halifax County, Virginia. He received his secondary education at Mount Hermon, Massachusetts, between 1898 and 1902. He attended Brown University from 1902 to 1905 and Harvard College from 1905 to 1907. In 1907 he received the bachelor of arts degree from Harvard. Richardson earned the master of arts from the University of Kansas in 1923. Before coming to Lincoln, he had headed the English department at Morehouse from 1907 to 1908 and at Tuskegee Institute from 1908 to 1918. Richardson was the author of a booklet entitled *Extension Work at Tuskegee*, published in 1912, and of the

13. Savage, *History of Lincoln,* 142–49. "Minutes of the Lincoln Institute Board of Regents," June 8, 1916.

14. "Minutes of the Lincoln Institute Board of Regents," June 14 and 29, 1917. There had been several applications for the position, including those of I. E. Page and William Pickens. Ibid., February 28, 1918.

Cyclopedia of the Colored Race. The latter work, published in 1917, contains a number of biographies of influential black Missourians. In the course of gathering the information for his book, Richardson may have made the contacts that led to his being called to Lincoln Institute in 1918.[15]

Richardson was thought a suitable man for the presidency because the board was interested in promoting industrial education at Lincoln, and Richardson's background at Tuskegee seemed to point in that direction. Because of his Tuskegee background, the board hoped that Richardson would bring additional money to Lincoln through the Smith-Hughes Act. State Superintendent of Schools Lampkin, in fact, had requested that Professor J. D. Elliff of the University of Missouri at Columbia make a survey of Lincoln with this goal in mind, since up to this time, Lincoln had been mainly interested in teacher education. In his 1917 report on Negro education, for example, Thomas J. Jones had pointed out that industrial features were subordinated to academics at Lincoln, and his report said that agricultural activities were negligible.[16]

Richardson tried to improve the school's industrial and agricultural program, but he was hindered by the managing board. Like Allen, he had to spend a good deal of his time trying to retain his position, largely because the board's executive committee was making all the decisions. The board still picked the faculty, purchased all materials, and paid all the bills. It was also responsible for letting out the lucrative coal, food, repair, and construction contracts. All of this did not make Richardson's attempts to develop a new agricultural program any easier. Richardson's efforts in this area were also frustrated by the fact that the white tenant on the farmland

15. Ibid., March 16, 1918, April 2, 1918, June 12, 1918. For biographical information on Richardson see Joseph J. Boris, ed., *Who's Who in Colored America,* 167. Young was one of the editors of the *Cyclopedia of the Colored Race* and Richardson was the general editor.

16. "Minutes of Lincoln Institute Board of Regents," March 16, 1918. Thomas J. Jones, *Negro Education,* 381–83. It is obvious that Lincoln was not receiving anywhere near the federal funds of schools such as Florida Agricultural and Mechanical College in the Deep South. This was because the black population was smaller and the state was unwilling to give the black school a larger share. Lincoln received a sixteenth of the funding for Missouri, with the remaining funds going to the University of Missouri and the Missouri School of Mines.

reported directly to the board, thus Richardson was not involved in decisions about agriculture. In addition, extensive nepotism created internal conflicts on campus. In 1919, at Richardson's request, the board established a policy that no relatives of present faculty members would be hired on a regular basis.[17]

In 1920 Richardson was reappointed as president on a motion by Sam Baker, who was now state superintendent of schools and a member of the board. Richardson soon had to deal with a shortage of funds because the governor held back several thousand dollars in the areas of teacher's salaries, support, and repairs.[18]

Richardson also had to deal with political interference in the affairs of the school. Midway through 1920, the president of the Board of Regents called Richardson and asked that he include a request for more land in his 1921 budget. The board's president, T. S. Mosby, informed Richardson that he was privy to information that the legislature was willing to approve $30,000 for Lincoln to acquire new land for an athletic field. In fact, Mosby had already signed an option with Jefferson City businessman W. M. Ruwart to buy the land for $27,000, and Ruwart had hired an influential Jefferson City businessman to act as his agent in selling the land, promising the agent everything that he got over $18,000. The agent was a former officer of Lincoln's Board of Regents and a business associate of T. S. Mosby. As a result, Mosby agreed to pay $27,000 for the $18,000 piece of land, allowing the agent to get $9,000 for himself. This was just "business as usual" on the Lincoln campus once more, carried out this time by Democratic politicians.

When Republican Governor Arthur M. Hyde took office in 1921, he called the deal a fraud and ordered an investigation by the attorney general and a legislative committee. Ultimately an investigation was held. In the process, it was learned that the land was generally valued at $500 an acre by experts, that Ruwart valued it at $1,000 an acre, and that the state had paid $1,500 an acre. Nothing came of the investigation, however, because the board was then

17. Interview with Dr. Milton Hardiman, former Lincoln Institute student, Jefferson City, Missouri, August 1981. Savage, *History of Lincoln,* 158–59; "Minutes of Lincoln Institute Board of Regents," June 12, 1918, February 17, 1919, July 11, 1919, February 28, 1919.

18. "Minutes of Lincoln Institute Board of Regents," July 11, 1919, and May 27, 1920.

asked to reaffirm its approval of the original deal, and characteristically, it did just that. Apparently accepting the validity of the testimony of a Republican official, Sam Baker, that the board's actions were valid and being influenced by editorials in the Democratic *Jefferson City Missouri Democrat* claiming that Governor Hyde was raising the issue simply "to make trouble for some Democrats in Jefferson City," the attorney general failed to win the case.[19]

Meanwhile, a more positive event, which was to have a great impact on the future of Lincoln, occurred in St. Louis. In 1920 Missouri's first black state representative, Walthall Moore, was elected by black St. Louisans. Moore's backers were interested in expanding the educational opportunities available to the black youth within the state. They wanted their state-supported institutions improved. These black Missourians also wanted Lincoln converted from a secondary normal and industrial school into a standard college. Moore was fully in accord with these aspirations. He was well prepared for the job. He was "a diplomatic and polished gentleman" with a "knowledge of state affairs" that soon made him one of the most important members of the Missouri House of Representatives. Moore was born in Marion, Alabama, on May 1, 1881. He attended the public schools in Alabama, St. Louis schools, and Howard University in Washington, D.C. In 1896 he settled in St. Louis and worked as a clerk for the U.S. Post Office and the Railway Mail Service. He helped to establish the first black steam laundry business in Missouri, and he was studying law at the time he was elected to the General Assembly.

In 1921 Missouri's blacks got the state legislature to change the name of Lincoln Institute to Lincoln University and to change its status to that of a four-year college. Moore introduced the bill, which provided for the reorganization. This bill established a new Board of Curators, which was to consist of the state superintendent of public schools, ex-officio, and eight members, at least four of

19. Savage, *History of Lincoln,* 167; "Minutes of Board of Curators," April 30, 1921; *St. Louis Globe Democrat,* August 6, 1921; *Kansas City Star,* August 11, 1921; *Kansas City Journal,* August 21, 1921. It also appeared in numerous other newspapers. Walthall Moore also called for an investigation of the land deal. *Jefferson City Missouri Democrat,* September 16, 1921. *House Committee Report in Extra Session on Lincoln University Land Deal.* Lincoln held the land since the state could not recover its money and it is today a running field for the university. The official report of the committee plus actual statements of all witnesses are in the Arthur M. Hyde Papers.

whom should be black. There were no restrictions of the residence of board members, other than that they had to be citizens of Missouri and live in the state. The board was authorized and required to reorganize Lincoln Institute so that it afforded black Missourians the same opportunities furnished white youth at the University of Missouri at Columbia.

Unfortunately, the Board of Curators of Lincoln was not constituted in a way corresponding to the boards of the University of Missouri and the other white schools in the state. The governor was charged to appoint four curators for Lincoln whose terms expired in 1923 and four whose terms would run to January 1, 1925. Moreover, all of Lincoln's curators could belong to the same political party. In contrast, at the white institutions, each curator's or regent's term ran for six years, so that every two years no more than a third of the board members would change, while at Lincoln half of the members would change every two years. At the other schools, membership in political parties was to be balanced among the members of the boards. Another unusual feature of Lincoln University's new Board of Curators was that it maintained a spot on the board for the state superintendent of public schools. While this state officer was an ex-officio member of the boards of all the state normal schools, he was not a member of the board of the University of Missouri, which served as a model for the organization of Lincoln's board. A related practice that continued was the placing of a faculty member or official of one of the white state normal schools or of the University of Missouri on Lincoln's managing board. Thus the way by which Lincoln University's board was constituted allowed for further instability over the next several years.[20]

The 1921 law also provided that until Lincoln University was fully developed, the Board of Curators was authorized to arrange for the instruction of black students of the state at any university, in any adjacent state, where courses were offered that were taught at the University of Missouri but not at Lincoln University. The last provision of the 1921 act appropriated an extra five hundred

20. "Missouri's First Negro Representatives," *Missouri Historical Review* 44, no. 3 (April, 1950): 340. *Laws of Missouri,* 1921, 51 General Assemby, 86; Extra Session, 75; *Revised Statutes of Missouri,* 1929, vol. 2, sec. 9616–17. Bill repeal Article 17, chap. 102 of the Revised Statutes of Missouri, 1919; Savage, *History of Lincoln,* 168–69.

thousand dollars from unappropriated school funds in order to carry out the act. These funds, however, would not be forthcoming. There were no unappropriated school funds at the end of the year. Even so, the 1921 act itself, and especially the mandatory inclusion of black curators on the board, was a major step forward for the school. And the passage of this act was a major reason why Nathan B. Young chose to come to Lincoln two years later.[21]

The new Board of Curators decided not to reappoint President Richardson. He was offered a hearing if he so desired. A delegation of students had already appeared before the board to ask that Richardson be retained. The student's appeal, however, had no effect on the board's actions because Governor Hyde and the board were already against Richardson. Even though at one point Hyde had valued Richardson's views, he and the board had turned against Richardson because of his role in the land deal. Many in the local community thought that Richardson had been treated unfairly, since he had only done so in order to hold on to his position in a very political environment.[22] Hyde, however, was serious in his desire to improve Lincoln, and he had been influential in getting the reorganization act through the legislature.

On May 8, the board directed its secretary to contact former Lincoln president Inman Page of Oklahoma City about accepting the presidency of the school. This whole matter of appointing a president to succeed Richardson was put into the hands of Professor George R. Crissman, chairman of the Teachers' Committee of the Board of Curators, and on July 25, 1922, upon recommendation of the committee, the board met and appointed Page president. One week later Page appeared before the board in Jefferson City to exchange ideas and expectations. Because of the delay in changing

21. Savage, *History of Lincoln,* 169–70, 172–74. In the period between the abolishing of the regents of Lincoln Institute and the appointment of curators of Lincoln University by August 1, no teachers or staff were paid. It was not until September 1, 1921, that they were paid. *Jefferson City Daily Democrat,* May 2 and 13, 1922.

22. Savage, *History of Lincoln,* 175. "Minutes of the Lincoln University Board of Curators," April 25, 1922, April 26, 1922. T. N. Ormiston to Clement Richardson, December 10, 1920; Clement Richardson to T. N. Ormiston, December 14, 1920; Clement Richardson to T. N. Ormiston, December 8, 1920. Richardson explained that all bills and financial records were kept by the board's secretary. T. N. Ormiston to Clement Richardson, December 22, 1920, Hyde Papers. Interview with Dr. Milton Hardiman, August 1981.

the president, anxiety prevailed about the reappointment of teachers. Moreover, there was considerable opposition to the reappointment of the seventy-year-old Page, with the local newspaper critical of his age and claiming that he had been trying to be reappointed president for some time. Furthermore, Page was accused of having conferences with Governor Hyde and actively campaigning for the Republican Party in a recent election. It was also said that Page was the choice of the black Republican secretary of the board, Rufus Logan, and St. Louis State Representative Walthall Moore. The newspaper charged that Moore was now controlling affairs at the school. Consequently, there was a storm of opposition to Page and to some of his supporters on the board, but in spite of all of this, he was appointed.[23]

Page had a hectic year as president. First of all, there was opposition to him from the white community and from some local black citizens as well. Second, because of the spending of the previous board, salary funds for the school ran out, and the board had to borrow money to pay the teachers and staff. Third, the students went on strike for better food and more social freedom. Worse still, Page personally broke up a student protest over the lack of social freedom by pulling a gun when students tried to mob him. Eventually Governor Hyde had to call out the sheriff and prison guards to restore order to the campus.[24]

23. Savage, *History of Lincoln*, 176–77; "Minutes of the Lincoln University Board of Curators," June 14, July 25, and July 31, 1922; *Jefferson City Daily Democrat Tribune*, July 26, 1922; Rufus L. Logan to A. M. Hyde, January 21, 1923; A. M. Hyde to Rufus L. Logan, January 22, 1923; C. H. Kirshner to A. M. Hyde, May 8, 1923; C. H. Kirshner to A. M. Hyde, May 18, 1923; A. M. Hyde to C. G. Williams, May 22, 1923; Rufus L. Logan to A. M. Hyde, May 21, 1923; A. M. Hyde to Rufus L. Logan, May 22, 1923; and A. M. Hyde to C. H. Kirshner, May 22, 1923, Hyde Papers. Kirshner was the president of Banker's Mortgage Company of Kansas City. Rufus L. Logan was a Kansas City real estate dealer and Standard Life Insurance Company agent. Many Jefferson City businessmen also objected to Logan, because they were accustomed to charging the school more than retail for all purchases. Logan would not go along with this practice. Earlier in his career Logan edited *The Professional World of Columbia*. Politicians attacked Logan's moral character and saw that his reappointment failed. There is no evidence that there was any truth to the attacks on Logan's character. During this period it was common to question the personal character of one's political enemies.

24. Savage, *History of Lincoln*, 178. Interview with Dr. Sidney Reedy, August 1981. Dr. Reedy witnessed the mob scene from the window of a nearby building; *Daily Democrat Tribune*, January 19, 1923.

Apparently, the elderly Page was too restrictive for the student body. During his first term most of Lincoln's students had come from the small towns of mid- and out-state Missouri. This time, however, Page found a number of students from St. Louis and Kansas City. The highly intelligent black students from the urban areas of Missouri had previously been urged by their principals, such as Frank Williams of St. Louis, to go out-of-state for their college work.[25] Now these better-prepared urban students were coming to Lincoln in increasing numbers.

Unable to cope with all of this opposition to his administration, Page decided to resign and accept a position in the Oklahoma City schools. There was a rush of applicants for the vacated position. Since it was known that blacks were considered for the presidency of Lincoln on the basis of their political views, Hyde now received volumes of letters of recommendation for candidates for the presidency. In order to manage all of this, Hyde depended on the advice of C. H. Kirshner, president of the board, and Hyde's personal adviser regarding Lincoln. Kirshner reiterated to Hyde his opposition to former president Richardson and noted that, if nothing else, Page had probably served as an adequate buffer between Richardson and a new man to be appointed in Page's place. Page, Kirshner thought, was a man of "fine character," but he was too old. Kirshner hoped that the board would find a "much younger man with character and ability."[26]

Events soon moved along even faster than Kirshner had anticipated, for in the very week that he wrote to Hyde that no president had been decided upon, the executive committee selected "N. B.

25. Interview with Dr. Milton Hardiman, August 1981; "Minutes of Lincoln Institute Board of Regents," passim; Interviews with Professor James D. Parks and Dr. Sidney Reedy, August 1981.

26. Savage, *History of Lincoln,* 178. Page tendered his resignation on August 8, 1923. C. H. Kirshner to A. M. Hyde, July 19, 1923; B. F. Bowles to A. M. Hyde, January 1, 1923; Edward W. Foristel to A. M. Hyde, June 5, 1924; Aaron E. Malone to A. M. Hyde, June 25, 1924; B. F. Bowles to A. M. Hyde, July 24, 1923; C. H. Kirshner to A. M. Hyde, July 10, 1923; A. M. Hyde to C. H. Kirshner, July 11, 1923, Hyde Papers. Kirshner was a classmate of Young's at Oberlin and Hyde later was at Oberlin, but Kirshner gave no indication of the possible election of Young even less than a week before the election. Kirshner was also a graduate of the law school at the University of Cincinnati and a practicing attorney for a number of years before becoming president of Banker's Mortgage Company of Kansas City. He was also a trustee of Oberlin.

Young of the A and M College, Tallahassee, Florida."[27] The force behind the recommendation and appointment of Young seems to have been Mrs. Julia Child Curtis. She was a progressive educator who served on the school board at St. Louis, where the black high school was rated among the finest in the country. Her husband was from Alabama, and his family there was probably acquainted with Young. Moreover, Young knew some of Mrs. Curtis's family in Alabama and Chicago. Also, in addition to Kirshner, who was a classmate of Young's at Oberlin and who probably supported Mrs. Curtis's recommendation, there were other graduates of Oberlin in the St. Louis area who knew Young. These were people who were interested in upgrading Lincoln to a standard four-year college. Young's reputation led them to believe that he was the kind of educator they were interested in having run Lincoln.[28]

Young was formally elected president on August 10, 1923, and from the very beginning he set forth his goals for Lincoln University. He hoped to make Lincoln a standard, fully accredited liberal arts college: a "First-class Institution of Higher Learning in the Middle West."[29] Upon Young's arrival, Lincoln was an unaccredited and poorly organized institution, where politics and personalities held sway. Lincoln was not recognized as a quality institution of higher learning. Lincoln's graduates were not accepted as teachers in the high schools of Kansas City and St. Louis, and its students risked having their credits reduced by 25 percent if they attempted to transfer to an accredited college. Lincoln's name had been changed, but little else had been done.

In 1923, Lincoln was a college only in name. The school lacked adequate facilities. The limited curriculum was taught largely on

27. George R. Crissman to B. F. Bowles, July 16, 1923, Hyde Papers. Bowles had sought the presidency for himself.
28. Interview with Judge Nathan B. Young, Jr., July 1981; Interview with J. D. Parks, August 1981. Both Judge Young and Professor Parks identify Mrs. Curtis as playing a role in Young's election, but neither were aware of C. H. Kirshner's connection with Young. Likely the two formed an alliance to elect Young. Mrs. Curtis was also from Alabama, and earned a bachelor's degree from Atlanta University and did graduate work at the University of Chicago. She began a teaching career at Sumner High School in St. Louis and later became a social worker. She married Dr. W. P. Curtis, who was a leader in the St. Louis branch of the NAACP.
29. "Minutes of the Lincoln University Board of Curators," August 10, 1923. Nathan B. Young to W. E. B. Du Bois, quoted in "Nathan B. Young," 226–27.

the secondary level, and usually not by subject-matter experts. The vast majority of Lincoln's students were in the high school department, and most of these students were from rural Missouri communities with inadequate educational standards. The faculty was largely unqualified, and this was the school's greatest obstacle to obtaining the status of an accredited, standard college.

Lincoln's lack of adequate facilities was a serious shortcoming, and eventually would have to be improved if Young was to get Lincoln fully accredited. When Young arrived, Lincoln's physical facilities consisted of one "Main Building," three dormitories, a Mechanical Arts building, a training school, and a power plant under construction. The "Main Building" had been erected in 1895 and contained twenty-one classrooms, the office of the administration, the music department, a large auditorium, a library, storerooms, and a large reading room. All classroom instruction, except in the trades, home economics, and training school classes, occurred in this three-story-plus-basement brick and stone building. All three of the dormitories were of brick construction, with two for women and one for men. The men's dormitory had just been completed at a cost of one hundred thousand dollars. The training school was a frame building of one story and a basement. The Mechanical Arts building was a two-story structure that housed all the trades: machine shop, auto mechanics, blacksmithing, carpentry, woodworking, tailoring, and shoemaking. The home economics department was housed in the basement of one of the women's dormitories. The campus occupied forty acres, and the school had sixty acres of farmland and a variety of farm animals.

The curriculum at Lincoln was limited. For example, there were only four English courses: composition and rhetoric, English literature, Shakespeare, and English poetry. The main teacher had a bachelor of arts from an unidentified college. The second teacher in English had a bachelor of pedagogy (a sixty-hour diploma) and a third English teacher graduated from Atlanta University's normal school in 1894. Some of the teachers taught in very diverse areas. For example, Frank E. Bowles, with a bachelor of arts in the social sciences, taught history and chemistry. Frances E. Terry, with a sixty-hour normal school diploma, taught both music and geography, and Arthur Richardson, a 1907 sixty-hour graduate of Tuskegee, taught music and tailoring. W. Sherman Savage, who earned a bachelor of arts from Howard University in 1917, taught practically all of the social sciences. He was required to teach history, government, sociology, and economics. While Savage was a recent college graduate and had taken summer graduate courses at the University of Kansas in 1921 and 1922, his limitations and the resulting effects on the curriculum was obvious. He could only offer three college courses in economics. In sociology, he could only offer the principles of sociology, and in American government only one college course was offered. Savage and Frank E. Bowles divided up the history offerings. While there were seven college courses offered, the history curriculum was rather uneven, with only European history, modern European history, the American Revolution, pre–Civil War, the Ancient World, the Reformation, and Hebrew history.

The largest number of students at Lincoln in 1923 were in the high school department. This meant that many of the teachers spent most of their time teaching high school students. During the 1922–1923 school year there were only 88 students in the college department and 317 in the high school. There were 62 students in the sixth through the eight grades. Lincoln also had 51 elementary grade students in the model school. There were 10 special students, who neither met the entrance requirements of sixteen high school units from an accredited high school nor could pass Lincoln's entrance examination. In addition, there were 102 college summer school students, who were for the most part public school teachers trying to upgrade their state certificates. In total, Lincoln had 630 students, with fewer then 100 in the college department. There were only two college seniors and three juniors, but the number of college students was already growing. There were 29 in the sophomore year and 54 in the freshman year. More than the student population, it was the lack of qualifications among the faculty that held back the school's development.[30]

While there had been some progress by 1923, the faculty at Lincoln was not up to the standards of a four-year college. Further, faculty morale was low because of poor pay and political interference in the school. The former Lincoln Institute was considered "a 'pie counter' for selfish politicians." A hotbed of dissension and intrigue

30. *Bulletin of Lincoln University, Annual Catalog, 1921–22, 1923–24; Lincoln University Record,* August 1924.

had been created among the faculty by "personal favors, to some and injustices to others." Some of the faculty, such as Mary Allen, held their positions because of sentiment and were not well-trained in their teaching areas. The most serious problem, however, was the low salaries. Because the salaries were so inadequate, Lincoln could not attract the best-qualified teachers. There was a resulting high turnover of teachers, and some of the faculty had to be taken from the school's most recent graduates. When Young came to Lincoln, the maximum salary paid any teacher was $160 a month, and that amount had only been reached that year. The year before the highest salary had been $130 a month. The year previous to that teachers were paid such varying amounts as $65, $85, and $90 a month.

These low salaries made it difficult to attract faculty members who had bachelor degrees and graduate work. Lincoln had a difficult time competing with public schools in urban areas such as St. Louis. The highest-paid teachers in the St. Louis high schools were paid salaries equal to that of Lincoln's president; in 1922, the high school principals were paid $2,000 a year more than Lincoln's president. When Young arrived there were seven faculty members with bachelor of arts and science degrees listed in the catalog. There were four faculty members with bachelors of pedagogy, and two with bachelors of didactic science. Only two faculty members had earned master's degrees. William Jason, who taught chemistry and physics, had a master of arts, and J. W. Damel, who taught botany and chemistry, had a master of philosophy. The remainder of the faculty had not earned bachelors' degrees. Several, such as Mary Allen, who taught Latin and English, had earned a normal school diploma. There were a number of teachers of the industrial and mechanical trades also on the faculty, as to be expected at land grant institutions, but none had an earned bachelor's degree, and, judging from the catalog course descriptions, these trades were taught on an elementary basis and had very few students and graduates. In 1922–1923 there were three graduates of auto-mechanics, two in tailoring, and one in shoemaking, whereas there were fifty-five graduates of the high school, and fifty-six graduates of the various postsecondary teacher training diploma programs.

When Young assumed the presidency of Lincoln, only about half the faculty that had served under Inman Page returned. Young had to fill out the remainder of the faculty on about a month's notice.

Fifteen former Lincoln faculty members returned in 1923. Of this number, nine were normal school graduates, four of whom had graduated from Lincoln within the previous three years. These four teachers' duties were about equally divided between the trades and academic areas. Young required that the entire faculty give evidence of all their college-level and graduate studies, and he insisted on knowing when and where the studies were completed. Interestingly, some Lincoln faculty consequently "lost" degrees that they had previously claimed. In 1922 T. Parker Smith of the commercial department had claimed a master of arts. In 1923 he was listed as having earned a bachelor of arts in 1888 from Lincoln University in Pennsylvania and as having attended several commercial schools. Young assigned him to the high school. Likewise, Letitia E. Williams, instructor of art, claimed to have earned a bachelor of fine arts degree from Columbia University in 1912. Evidently, she fooled Young, for she was credited with the degree in the 1923–1924 school catalog. In the 1925–1926 catalog, however, she was listed as only having a two-year teacher's diploma, and she was forced to attend summer school in 1926. In the 1927–1928 school year she was replaced by James D. Parks, who had earned a bachelor's degree. Of course, all faculty members who had earlier claimed bachelors of pedagogy or bachelors of didactic science turned out to have earned only sixty-hour normal school diplomas from Lincoln. Representative of this group was Carrie V. Simpson, instructor of English. Her bachelor of pedagogy turned out to be a sixty-hour diploma from Lincoln in 1921. She attended summer school in 1924 at the University of Chicago, but was not listed in the 1925–1926 catalog. Also falling in this category was Virgil E. Williams. Under Page he was listed in the catalog as having a bachelor of didactic science. He was in charge of buildings and grounds, a position that traditionally had been given to political appointees. In 1923 he earned a ninety-hour diploma and was teaching mathematics. In 1924 he earned a bachelor of arts from Lincoln. In 1925–1926, he was dropped from the faculty. Williams returned to Lincoln in 1927–1928 as registrar and president of the General Alumni Association. In 1929–1930 he left the school.[31]

Of course, Lincoln could not become a standard college with

31. Savage, *History of Lincoln,* 181–99; *Lincoln University Record,* August, October, December 1924 and March 1925; Interview with Judge Nathan B. Young, Jr., July 1981; Robert Brigham, "Negro Education in Missouri," 205, 208; *Bulletin of Lincoln University, Annual Catalog, 1921–22, 1923–24, 1925–*

such an academically weak faculty. Young wanted Lincoln University to become more than a university in name. He wanted to make it a university that was on such a demonstrably high level of achievement that it would be recognized and respected as such across the country. This, of course, required accreditation. From the beginning Young wanted to upgrade Lincoln in several areas, because each improvement would be an important step toward making Lincoln that "First-class Institution." First of all, he needed to improve the quality of the faculty. There were no academic teaching ranks, and, of course, there were no professional criteria by which to establish such ranks. Young established clear academic rank, and he set up related salary scales to establish distinctions in rank. Accordingly, under Young's new organization, an instructor received $180 per month, an assistant professor $200 per month, a professor $250 per month, and a professor with a Ph.D. $275 per month. Second, Young found that he needed to organize the school into departments. There were no clearly distinguished and organized departments. A third major concern was the need to upgrade facilities, especially in the area of the sciences.

Young's first priority was to upgrade the faculty. To begin with he separated the high school faculty from the college faculty and eliminated the elementary grades altogether. The high school was now to be handled by a principal, and, by 1925, all new high school teachers were required to have at least a bachelor's degree from an accredited college. On the college level, new teachers were expected to have at least a master's degree from an accredited graduate school. Those teachers on the college level who were already at Lincoln when Young arrived but who had not yet earned their master's were required to complete at least eight semester hours of graduate work at an accredited university each summer. Young recommended those who completed this summer graduate work for increases in salary. Historian W. Sherman Savage and others received their master's degrees in this manner. Later, under a program recommended by Young, the heads of departments were given sabbatical leaves with half pay in order to study for and complete their doctorates.[32]

26, 1927–28, 1929–30, 1931–32. In 1921 there were only four teachers with bachelor's degrees and two with master's degrees.

32. Savage, *History of Lincoln*, 181–99; *Lincoln University Record*, August 1924; interview with Professor James D. Parks, August 1981.

Several highly competent faculty members—many from Florida Agricultural and Mechanical College—came to Lincoln with Young to join the high school and college faculties and staff. All of these newcomers had either bachelor of arts or bachelor of science degrees, and many of them had degrees from institutions such as the University of Pittsburgh, Ohio University, Kansas State, and the Massachusetts Institute of Technology. Among the new teachers added to the faculty was French instructor Gaynell D. Wright, a graduate of the University of Pittsburgh. She was formerly an instructor of French in the high school at Cumberland, Maryland. Gertrude E. Lawless, graduated from Talladega College, was the supervisor of the training school and assistant in education. She was formerly an instructor in the American Missionary Association schools at Fessenden, Florida, and New Orleans. Those coming from Florida A&M included Vergil Watkins, instructor of English, a graduate of Ohio University, and formerly an instructor of English at Florida A&M; Bessie Hawkins, domestic science teacher, a graduate from the Mechanics' Institute in Rochester, New York, with completed graduate work at Columbia and formerly an instructor in the Kansas City high schools and at Florida A&M; and Charles Anderson, English instructor, with a bachelor of arts and bachelor of oratory from Geneva College in Beaver Falls, Pennsylvania and a former instructor of English at Florida A&M. From Jacksonville, Florida, were A. Theora Edmondson, the assistant registrar, with a number of years of experiences as assistant auditor at Florida A&M; Noah Griffin, a graduate from Fisk University, instructor of Latin and dean of men; and George Williams, with a bachelor of science from Florida A&M, the instructor of auto-mechanics and engineering. Harry B. Thornton was a graduate of Howard University and an instructor of mathematics. W. P. Terrell, bachelor of science in mechanical engineering, was a graduate of the Kansas State Agricultural College and the Massachusetts Institute of Technology. Terrell was the director of mechanic arts. He was formerly director of mechanic arts at Prairie View College, Texas, and had also served at different times as architectural engineer of the Service Engineering and Construction Company in Atlanta and Windham Brothers Company in Birmingham. C. Eugenia Sullivan, bachelor of science in commerce, was the private secretary to the president. She was a graduate of Temple University and had been a private secretary with the Windham Brothers Construction Company in Birmingham. Anna L. Porter came to Lincoln as an instructor of chemistry and had a bachelor of science degree from the University of Pennsylvania.[33]

Young also recruited educators qualified to teach on the college level with masters and doctorate degrees from such universities as Harvard, the University of Chicago, and Boston University. Sterling Brown, who was employed to teach literature, for example, had attended Williams College with an academic scholarship and graduated in 1922 with Phi Beta Kappa honors and went on to Harvard on a Clark fellowship in literature and earned a master of arts. While literature was already being taught at Lincoln, Brown was the best-trained teacher up to that time, and he did much to establish a strong program. In addition to Sterling Brown, Young also hired a first-rate educator in Langston Bate. Bate graduated from Kentucky Normal at Frankfort in 1917, then attended Illinois Normal College, earning a bachelor of education degree. He was awarded the master's degree in 1923 and the doctorate in chemistry in 1926 at the University of Chicago. Bate taught at Kentucky Normal for two years before coming to Lincoln in 1926. Bate was the first black Ph.D. at Lincoln, where he set chemistry off as a separate department and encouraged a great interest in the sciences. Among the others attracted to the Lincoln faculty by Young and his program in the next few years were Norval Barksdale, who held degrees from the University of Kansas and Dijon University in France, to teach modern foreign languages; Lucien Simington Curtis, with degrees from Harvard College and Columbia University in economics; Thomas Miles, a graduate of Lincoln University in Pennsylvania and the University of Pennsylvania, in mathematics; Eunice V. Pepsico, with both the bachelor of science and master of arts from Ohio State University in home economics; James Dallas Parks, a graduate of Bradley Polytechnic Institute, in art; and Henry S. Blackiston, who earned the doctor of philosophy degree at the University of Pennsylvania, in German and Latin. Coming from some of the better New England universities were Albert A. Kildare, with a bachelor's and master's degree from Boston University in physics,

33. Savage, *History of Lincoln*, 181–99; *Lincoln University Record*, December 1923 and August 1925; *St. Louis Argus*, April 17, 1925.

and Cecil A. Blue, with a bachelor of arts from Harvard College in 1925 and a master of arts the following year from Harvard University in English. From schools in other parts of the country came Everett B. Jones, bachelor of arts, Colgate, 1905, master of science, University of Iowa, 1927, William W. Dowdy, bachelor of arts, State University of Iowa, 1923, master of science, Cornell University, 1928, biology, and U. S. Maxwell, bachelor of arts, University of Colorado, 1921, master of science, University of Chicago, 1928, chemistry. Sidney J. Reedy, an alumnus of Lincoln who received the bachelor of science in 1926 and went on to earn his master of arts from the University of Iowa in 1928, returned as principal of the high school and teacher of Latin. In a remarkably short time Young had raised the quality of the college and high school faculties. Under Young the number of faculty members with graduate degrees increased fourfold. Gone were the political appointees of the past, and in their places were competent, college-trained educators.[34]

In the area of curriculum development and professional administration, he made major contributions by organizing departments and establishing stronger degree programs. Departments were organized in the fields of art, education, English, French, music, agriculture, chemistry, mathematics, and physics. New courses were added in most areas. Likewise, for the first time in Lincoln's history the bachelor of arts and the bachelor of science degree programs, taught largely by faculty members with graduate degrees, were implemented.

Before Young's arrival, Lincoln offered a bachelor of arts, a bachelor of science, and a bachelor of science in education. There was also a program leading to diplomas granted to those students who completed the required number of hours in the specific course of study. First there was a sixty-hour diploma, which granted a life certificate to teach in the state elementary schools. It was based on four years of high school and two years of college-level work.

---

34. Interview with Sterling Brown, July 1981. Brown also stated that Young had known his father from Oberlin and Fisk University and felt his training was such to make an excellent teacher. *Lincoln University Record,* December, 1923, 6–7. *Bulletin of Lincoln University, Annual Catalog, 1921–22, 1923–24, 1925–26, 1927–28, 1929–30, 1931–32.* After leaving Lincoln, Richard Kenneth Fox, bachelor of arts, Ohio University, 1923 and assistant professor of education in 1927–1928, wrote to newly elected Governor Caulfield stating that Lincoln's greatest problem was the political activities of members of the board of curators.

Secondly, there was the ninety-hour diploma, which granted a life certificate to teach in high schools and elementary schools of the state. It was based on four years of high school and three years of college work. Finally, there was the thirty-hour diploma, which gave a certificate valid for two years of teaching in the state's elementary schools. This diploma was based on four years of high school and one year in academic and professional education courses at the college level.

The requirements for the degrees of bachelor of arts and science were the completion of at least one year in residence and 120 semester hours of work. This included physical education, a major of at least 20 hours in one department, and a minor of 15 hours from a department allied to the major department. The remainder of the hours had to be distributed among the fields of English, foreign language, biological science, physical science, social science, mathematics, philosophy, and psychology. The curriculum was divided into four areas: language and literature (including foreign language, art, and music), natural science, social science, and mathematics and philosophy. On paper Lincoln's bachelors of arts and science were similar to degree programs at other colleges. Because of the weaknesses of the teaching faculty, however, the nonstandard natures of Lincoln's degrees were painfully obvious. During the junior and senior years twenty-eight to thirty-two semester hours of electives were to be taken each year, but there were not enough college-level courses offered at Lincoln to properly meet these requirements.

Additionally, Lincoln offered a two-year premedical program, started in 1921 by board member J. E. Perry of Kansas City. Perry was an 1895 graduate of Meharry Medical College. At this time the science facilities at Lincoln were only satisfactory for a one-year course each in high school physics, chemistry, and biology. There was one small general laboratory available for experiments in all the sciences. Perry worked with Professor W. B. Jason, and, beginning with one thousand dollars, tried to improve the science department to a level that met the standards of the Council on Medical Education of the American Medical Association. While these efforts were praiseworthy, Lincoln's science instruction was substandard until Young hired Langston Bate and others, and the sciences were separated into individual departments, with adequate laboratory facilities. The two-year program in home economics required students to take six hours of English and some science courses plus several hours of home economics and professional education. The two-year elementary teachers program required students to take six hours each in English, biology, and history, three hours in social science, and the remaining thirty-nine hours in education. Those who had completed this last program could go on for a bachelor of education by taking additional professional education courses and fulfilling major and minor requirements.

The major reason for Lincoln's inability to offer the standard bachelor's degree was the poor qualifications of the faculty. Before Young arrived, most of the college-level courses were offered by faculty members who had not gone beyond the bachelor's degree. Many members of the college faculty lacked even that qualification. Particularly weak was the bachelor of science in education, which consisted largely of professional education courses taught by one teacher and an assistant. This teacher, Sylvester F. Collins, had earned a bachelor of arts degree in 1909 from unaccredited Livingston College and had done some additional study at Boston University in 1915. Since most of the students coming to Lincoln at the college level wanted to teach, Collins's courses were popular. He had been a member of the faculty at the old Lincoln Institute. While Young favored the traditional subject matter courses in the arts and sciences over the professional education courses, he apparently did not disturb Collins's program during his first year as head of Lincoln. During the 1923–1924 school year, Young mainly experimented with the degree programs.

At this time bachelor's degrees were instituted in a variety of areas: agriculture, commerce and business administration, home economics, mechanic arts, and music. These experimental degree programs proved to be a failure, because of lack of student enrollment. In the 1925–1926 school year Young returned to the three bachelor's degrees formerly offered in the arts, science, and education. Young discouraged students seeking certification as high school teachers from taking the bachelor of science in education. Instead these students were advised to take the course of study leading to a bachelor of arts and then elect fifteen hours in education. By 1927, Young had established the policy that only experienced, able teachers expecting to become elementary and high school principals would be admitted to the bachelor of science in education program. Inexperienced students hoping to earn certification were advised to take a bachelor of arts or a bachelor of science degree and eighteen additional hours of professional education courses and practice teaching. Young further reinforced this approach by requiring that all students working toward the bachelor of science in education had to meet all the requirements for graduation under the bachelor of arts and bachelor of science programs. While these changes probably did not meet with the approval of S. F. Collins and other faculty holdovers from the old Lincoln Institute, they fitted Young's concept of a well-educated teacher.

Under Richardson and Page, Lincoln's administrative organization was weak. The school's central administration had consisted of the president, registrar, supervisor of buildings and grounds, manager of the boarding department, and girls' matron. There were no standing faculty committees. By 1925, Young had reorganized the administrative structure. Several changes were made in the hope of bringing the school closer to accreditation as an institution of higher learning. A College of Liberal Arts was organized, and William B. Jason was appointed its dean. Student life was better organized in a single department and placed under a dean of women and dean of men. A freshman orientation program was established. A University Council, made up of administrators and faculty members, was organized to handle students' disciplinary problems, and a Business Committee, whose membership included the chief administrative officers and faculty representatives, was established to handle business affairs. In addition, other faculty committees were organized to assist in carrying on the work of the college. The library was moved to larger quarters, a trained librarian was placed in charge, and a successful effort was started to increase the number of books and periodicals from five thousand to thirteen thousand. To increase the pride of the students, faculty, and alumni, the school's buildings were named in honor of those who had rendered distinguished service to the institution, and a Founders' Day was established to perpetuate the memory of the 62nd and 65th Regiments. Finally, a system of classification was instituted where students were ranked according to the number of hours of college work they had successfully completed. All students were now required to obtain a C average in 75 percent of their course work to remain at Lincoln. The grading standards were tightened and made more uniform by establishing a quality grade point average system and implementing criteria for graduating with honors.

When Young arrived at Lincoln, a large number of student activities were already established. Especially important were the school's religious activities. Every student was required to attend daily chapel exercises and the weekly services of one of the five black churches in Jefferson City. In addition, there were religion associations such as the YMCA and YWCA. Lincoln also had four literary societies: Pierian, Phyllis Wheatley, the Senate, and Little Women Clubs. These organizations met once a week and presented public programs. There were several musical organizations: an orchestra, a band, a choral society, an all-male mandolin orchestra, and a glee club. Debating clubs for the college men and the male high school seniors were active. Athletics were important at Lincoln, and interclass and departmental games were encouraged. Lincoln also took part in the Missouri Valley Inter-Scholastic meets and events. The most popular sports at the school were football, baseball, basketball, tennis, and track. In 1923 Lincoln's football team played against the Boonville High Tigers, Bartlett Agricultural High School, George R. Smith College, Western College, Sumner High School, Douglass High School, and Western University. Young retained nearly all of these activities, but he reorganized them to provide closer faculty supervision. Several clubs were also opened to female as well as male students. Young made some other changes in extracurricular activities for students. He employed a full-time coach for athletics and eliminated high schools from the football schedule, replacing them with such colleges as Wilberforce, Fisk, and West Virginia State. Young also arranged to have current feature films shown on campus. This gave students and faculty an alternative to the segregated theaters in Jefferson City.[35]

Young knew that the changes he was making would require greater funding from the Missouri legislature. If he was going to attract and retain the best teachers, he would need to offer them adequate salaries. When he arrived at Lincoln, teachers' salaries were extremely low and turnover was extremely high. In order to remedy this situation, Young began to campaign throughout the state for increased appropriations, and he was rewarded in 1925 with an

35. Savage, *History of Lincoln*, 181–99; *Lincoln University Record*, August 1924; Interview with Professor James D. Parks, August 1981; *Bulletin of Lincoln University, Annual Catalog*, 1921–22, 1923–24, 1925–26, 1927–28, 1929–30, 1931–32; J. E. Perry, *Forty Cords of Wood*, 424; Boris, ed., *Who's Who in Colored America*, 155.

appropriation of four hundred thousand dollars, which was nearly double Lincoln's previous biennial funding.[36]

In order to secure more funding, Young began to organize appeals to those whom he considered the patrons of Lincoln. Thus he established the *Lincoln University Record* to keep in touch with Lincoln's alumni, and he encouraged the establishment of alumni chapters throughout the state. Although a Lincoln alumni organization had been established earlier, it was a loosely organized body and was not very effective. Young gave special attention to building up the alumni chapters in St. Louis and Kansas City, the two centers in the state with the largest black populations. In these activities, he was drawing on his experiences in Florida, where a powerful alumni group had saved the program at Florida Agricultural and Mechanical College from complete destruction.

Young kept the alumni informed of the school's need, and he was fortunate to find black newspapers headed by progressive editors in the two large urban centers: C. A. Franklin of the *Kansas City Call,* and J. E. Mitchell of the *St. Louis Argus.* Both men supported Young's efforts to upgrade Lincoln University, and this was a great help to him in his attempts to get adequate appropriations from the state legislature.

In 1924, Young established a Department of Public Information and issued a weekly news release that stressed the progress being made and itemized Lincoln's needs. With the help of these releases, his newly organized alumni chapters, and the *Kansas City Call* and *St. Louis Argus,* Young soon had the active support of much of the state's black community. Black newspapers made it a matter of racial pride for the black citizens and voters to support Lincoln University, and the idea that black Missourians had to take the education of their young into their own hands was now a constant theme. The *St. Louis Argus* arranged for a special train for those from St. Louis who wished to attend Young's inauguration and exhorted its readers that the black people of Missouri had to make Lincoln "what it ought to be."[37]

36. Savage, *History of Lincoln,* 181–99; *Lincoln University Record,* August 1925; *St. Louis Argus,* April 17, 1925.

37. Savage, *History of Lincoln,* 181–99; *Lincoln University Record,* August, October, December 1924 and March 1925; Interview with Judge Nathan B. Young, Jr., July 1981; Robert Brigham, "Negro Education in Missouri," 205, 208; *Lincoln University Record,* April 1924; "Minutes of the Lincoln Univer-

Young's program for full accreditation of Lincoln received endorsements from black religious, social, and professional organizations throughout the state. The Missouri State Association of Negro Teachers' annual convention, meeting in St. Louis in 1925, strongly endorsed his plan. Young was very active at this convention, and he took every opportunity to make known his hopes for Lincoln. Significantly, the president of the association, W. H. Harrison, devoted the end of his main address to a statement favoring the program at Lincoln. The black citizens of the state, like the black soldiers of the past, he said, should give "their last and their all." Lincoln, Harrison stated, should be lifted from the "quagmire" of politics and placed upon a plane of higher intellectual standing. The committee on the presidential address thought that Harrison's "impassioned appeal" for Lincoln was "manly and courageous." It was, perhaps, because of Harrison's address that Young was elected the next president of the association.[38]

Young was also active with interracial groups such as the Missouri Conference for Social Welfare. Speaking before this group, he complained that "several hundred Negro youths" attended college outside of Missouri "who would be attending Lincoln University if it were a full-fledged institution of higher learning." He called on Missouri's educators, lawmakers, and "forward looking citizens of both races to provide Black youth with equal educational opportunities . . . in the spirit of true democracy and American fair play."[39]

Young's ultimate goal was to have Lincoln accredited as a standard, four-year liberal arts college. In the first year of his administration, he asked for an inspection by the Association of Colleges for Negro Youth, an organization founded in 1913 that only admitted institutions to membership that were doing college-level work. It had

---

sity Board of Curators," November 3, 1923; *St. Louis Argus,* January 4, 1924, May 8, 1925; *Kansas City Call,* May 30, 1924, January 23 and April 17, 1925. A special train also came from Kansas City filled with well-wishers to Young's inauguration. President John Hope of Morehouse College was the main speaker.

38. "Program of the Missouri State Association of Negro Teachers," 1925 Meeting, St. Louis, 37–39, Lincoln University Archives. Many of the resolutions have the influence of Young on them. Young likely introduced the idea of appealing to the foundations for funds, which had not been done in Missouri up to this time, and the ideas of promoting black history and of lowering the number of children needed for establishing a school. Ibid., 33, 40.

39. Quoted in Brigham, "Negro Education in Missouri," 207, 208.

higher standards of admission than any of the other black educational associations, but Young viewed gaining admission to it as only the first step. What he really desired was membership in the North Central Association of Secondary Schools and Colleges. Even at that time, the North Central Association applied the same standards for membership to black and white institutions. Young felt that the recognition of membership in the North Central would help him to bring the education offered at Lincoln up to the level of that offered by any other college, black or white.[40]

The Association of Colleges for Negro Youth authorized an inspection of Lincoln, but the evaluator did not think that Lincoln was adequately equipped in laboratory sciences. Young met with the board in early January 1925 and discussed the question of getting the school accredited. The board established a committee led by board member Crissman, a professor on the education faculty at Central Missouri State Teachers College, and Young conferred with Dr. J. D. Elliff about steps that should be taken to get Lincoln into the North Central Association.[41] Elliff was a professor of high school administration at the University of Missouri at Columbia and a very active member of the North Central Association, generally handling the accrediting of high schools in Missouri for the association.

At the end of January 1925 Elliff met with the executive committee of Lincoln's board and offered suggestions for getting the school approved. He urged the board to make a bachelor's degree the minimum qualification for Lincoln's high school teaching faculty and a master's degree the minimum for the college faculty. The board decided at this meeting that Lincoln would try to get its high school department accredited by the North Central Association in 1925 and its teacher training curriculum accredited the following year.[42]

Before Lincoln's high school division could be considered for accreditation by North Central, it first had to be accredited by the Missouri State Department of Education. This process had never

40. Savage, *History of Lincoln,* 181; "Minutes of the Lincoln University Board of Curators," November 3, 1923. Young had also suggested, at this same time, that a new building be formally dedicated and be named for an individual who had contributed to the welfare of the school, and that there be a formal inauguration of the university's president. All were approved.

41. Savage, *History of Lincoln,* 181–91. "Minutes of the Lincoln University Board of Curators," January 13, 1925.

42. "Minutes of the Lincoln University Board of Curators," January 31, 1925.

had been attempted before, despite the fact that the state superintendent of public schools had been a member of Lincoln's board for many years. When Young came to Lincoln, he eliminated the elementary grades and reorganized the high school. He placed the high school under the direction of a principal, raised admission standards, and reorganized the course of study. Previously the high school had offered four courses of study: college preparatory, home economics, commercial courses, and mechanical arts. Students in home economics and in commercial and mechanical arts did not have to take any social sciences or foreign languages. The number of courses was very limited and mainly confined to the introductory level. The reorganized course of study had two programs, the classical and the general. Specific courses were now required of all students from the first to the fourth year. The only difference between the two programs was that the general course did not require Latin and modern foreign languages. The number and variety of courses were increased, however, and all high school students were required to take Negro history. By this time, most of the instructors in the high school had bachelor's degrees and those who did not were required to attend summer school. These changes led to state accreditation of Lincoln's high school, and once this accreditation had been received, Dr. Elliff was asked to inspect the high school department for the North Central. Elliff visited the classes and conferred with Young frequently about changes. Finally, he recommended approval of the high school, and in 1925 Lincoln's high school was admitted to the North Central.[43]

With the high school now accredited, Young put his energies into getting the teachers' college division approved. In every issue of the college's *Record*, there was a section called "What Lincoln University Needs to be an Accredited Institution of Higher Learning." Under this heading and over Young's signature was a list of Lincoln's weaknesses. According to Young, Lincoln needed an infirmary, a gymnasium, a commons, a laundry, a home economics

43. Interview with Ruth Allen, daughter of former President Allen. Her mother taught in the high school after her father died and left behind two young daughters. She recalls her mother mentioning that Elliff was always around and visiting her classes. August 1981. In an interview with Professor James D. Parks he recalled Elliff always conferring with President Young. August 1981. *Lincoln University, Annual Catalogue, 1922–23, Bulletin of Lincoln University, Annual Catalogue, 1923–24,* vol. 1, no. 1, passim.

building, a larger men's dormitory, a mechanical arts building, a 50 percent increase in teachers' salaries, a 75 percent increase for support facilities, and a 150 percent increase in repairs and renovation funds. While Young's priorities would change, depending upon his assessment of how critical the need was, these needs were always put forth.[44]

Before Nathan Young arrived at Lincoln, the majority of the school's students were in the high school. In the 1921–1922 regular session, Lincoln's enrollment was 234 high school students and only 54 college students. In 1922–1923 the high school enrollment increased to 317 students, while college enrollment increased only to 88. The following year, 1923–1924, the high school enrollment reached 388 students and the college enrollment increased to 124. After this point, however, the high school enrollment rapidly declined and the college enrollment steadily increased. In 1924–1925, the high school's population dramatically dropped by 174 students to an enrollment of 213, whereas the college student body increased to 139. This trend continued in succeeding years. The significant shift in the enrollment can be partially explained by the increased emphasis placed by Young on the college's development and accreditation. The teachers' college branch of the school was accredited in 1926. In addition, the greatest loss in the high school population came at the time that the standards of the high school were being tightened in order to get it accredited. Also contributing to the decline of the high school was the opening of more secondary schools for black youth in other parts of the state.

The decrease in high school enrollment and the corresponding increase in college enrollment resulted in an increase in the number of bachelor's degree graduates at Lincoln. Several factors influenced these changes. Some of the more obvious factors included

44. *Lincoln University Record,* vol. 1, no. 5, 20; Savage, *History of Lincoln,* 184–85. Young outlined specific improvements that Lincoln University needed in order to become a fully accredited institution of higher learning: "1) An infirmary to safeguard the health of the students; 2) A gymnasium for physical training of the students; 3) A refectory, or commons, for the proper preparation and service of food (to replace an inadequate and outdated operation then in operation); 4) A steam laundry (to replace the makeshift laundry that was for girls' use only); 5) A modernly equipped home economic building; 6) A dairy and a dairy barn, and farmland; 7) An appropriation for the completion of the men's dormitory, which was overflowing; and 8) Enlargement and re-equipment of the mechanics arts building (which was 33 years old)."

higher standards for public school teachers and more emphasis at Lincoln on college-level work. By the school year 1925–1926, there was a much greater interest in Lincoln as a source of the bachelor's degree. This interest on the part of students was matched by Young and many of his faculty members, who were trying to have Lincoln accredited as a teachers' college.

The increased popularity of the bachelor's degree program led to declining interest in the teaching diploma programs. Of the three diploma programs, the ninety-hour program was least affected. This curriculum never had a large enrollment, but the increased emphasis on the bachelor's degree caused this program to stagnate. Between the school years 1921–1922 and 1925–1926, enrollment in this program remained stable with two or three graduates a year. While there was an increase to nine graduates in 1926–1927, this appears to have been related to Lincoln's teachers' college accreditation and was not maintained. Several of the nine returned to complete the bachelor's degree. By 1928–1929 there were only two ninety-hour graduates, and in 1929–1930 there were but four such graduates. The trends noticeable in the ninety-hour diploma were even more visible in the more popular sixty-hour diploma. Again the mid-1920s and the accreditation of the teachers' college seemed to be the turning point against the sixty-hour diploma. Between 1921 and 1927, the sixty-hour diploma program graduated from a low of twenty-six to a high of thirty-four students annually. In 1928–1929, however, there was a sharp decline in the number of sixty-hour graduates to twenty, and this was followed by an even further drop in 1929–1930 to sixteen graduates. The greatest decline in diploma graduates was in the thirty-hour program. Between 1922–1923, when there were twenty-eight graduates, and 1925–1926, when there were thirty-six, the enrollment in this program remained stable. Then, beginning in 1926–1927 there was a sharp and continuous decline in the program. In that year there were only ten graduates, in 1928–1929 there were only three graduates, and the following year there was only one graduate. The increased emphasis on more extensive college work for the state teaching force left this program without much value. In fact, the further away a diploma program was from the bachelor's degree, the more unpopular and unstable it became.

In an effort to make the teacher training program more demanding and in accord with what was actually required of elementary teachers, Young had early in his administration made a cooperative arrangement between Lincoln University and the City School Board for the use of Washington School as a training school. Students who were candidates for the Elementary Life Certificate were required to spend five weeks of observation and six weeks of teaching in the training school under the direction of the school's principal and supervising teachers. The use of the public school as a laboratory for teacher training improved the quality of this program. Other efforts were begun to improve the quality and overall usefulness of Lincoln's program.

In 1926 through an arrangement with the University of Missouri, correspondence courses were offered to nonresident students during the year and credits earned were transferred to Lincoln University. A large number of teachers enrolled in these courses. Extension courses were conducted during the year in Sedalia, Springfield, Mexico, and St. Joseph. Three members of the college faculty traveled to the cities to conduct these courses. With its limited teaching staff it was a difficult undertaking to carry on an extension program without maintaining a teaching load in excess of the North Central's standards. The school needed to add at least two college teachers in order to meet the standards of the North Central.

Young worked through 1925 and 1926 with Dr. Elliff and Superintendent of Schools Charles A. Lee to get the teachers' college division accredited. In May 1925 the board of curators accepted a plan put forth by Lee that called for improving the library and scientific laboratories as well as increasing the number of teachers with graduate degrees. As a result, the teachers' college was admitted to the North Central in 1926. The *St. Louis Argus* said that the friends of Lincoln University throughout the state could rejoice that the school now had an accredited high school and teachers' college division, which it felt was equal to the white high schools and teachers' colleges elsewhere in the state.

By the 1925–1926 school year, Lincoln's enrollment showed that the school had established a steady source of students. This enrollment would continue to show not only a growth in the number of college students over high school but also that Lincoln's students were now coming increasingly from the largest urban centers of the state and from out-of-state. In the school year 1925–1926, of the total college enrollment of 170 students there were 38 from out of state and 39 from St. Louis and Kansas City. In 1927–1928 Lincoln had in its college 186, in the high school 165, in the summer sessions 148, and in the extension program 48, for a total of 547. By the 1928–1929 school year there were 223 students enrolled in the college, 149 in the high school, 102 in the college summer session, 27 in the new high school summer session, and 60 in the extension program, for a total of 561. Including regular and summer sessions in 1929, Lincoln awarded 18 bachelor degrees and graduated 39 students from the high school. The home of record of all the college students enrolled in 1929 showed that out of a total of 223 students, 40 were from out of state and 82 were from St. Louis and Kansas City. The ever-increasing number of out-of-state students indicated that Lincoln was becoming better known in the Midwest and was coming to be considered a regional, if not a national, center of higher education for Negroes. The growth in the college's enrollment from Kansas City and St. Louis indicated that the high school graduates and their parents had begun to look less to out-of-state schools and more to Lincoln for higher education.[45]

The final step of full accreditation as a standard, four-year, Liberal Arts College was still a long way off. While hoping for a quick accreditation in that area, everyone involved realized that it would take more money for additional teachers with graduate degrees, for a new classroom building and scientific equipment, and for laboratories. The alumni and friends of the school were asked to put forth an even greater effort to ensure that the college would be properly funded by the state legislature.[46] Accreditation would indeed be a long way off, but the major stumbling block would not be economics.

45. "Minutes of the Lincoln University Board of Curators," May 4, 1925, Office of the President of Lincoln University, Jefferson City, Missouri; *Lincoln University Record*, vol. 3, no. 1 (September 1926): 8–10; *Bulletin of Lincoln University, 1925–26, 1927–28, 1929–30*.

46. Savage, *History of Lincoln*, 190–91. Young wrote to the newspapers' editors to state that more was needed for accreditation. The papers responded. *Kansas City Call*, August 20, 1926; *St. Louis Argus*, October 29, 1926.

CHAPTER 6

The End of a Career

The Lincoln University that Nathan B. Young left to his successor in 1931 was radically different and a stronger institution than the one he found when he arrived in 1923. Young's role as a builder, however, was not an easy one. From the very beginning, he faced strong opposition to his plans. The elimination of such trades as tailoring and shoemaking, the closing of the elementary school, and the emphasis on degrees for teachers all were opposed by those faculty members who felt threatened by the changes. The first opposition to Young came only two months after his inaugural address, when charges were made that he was bringing in unqualified teachers. The teachers that Young brought from Florida Agricultural and Mechanical College stirred a great deal of opposition, both on and off the campus. These outsiders fed the fire of resentment already burning in such Lincoln faculty members as S. F. Collins and J. W. Damel.[1]

---

1. Savage, *History of Lincoln,* 186–87; Wolters, *The New Negro on Campus,* 209–10. Interview with Professor James D. Parks, August 1981, Jefferson City. Professor Parks particularly remembers J. B. Coleman of Columbia, who would serve on the board after 1929, complaining about the hiring of teachers from Florida and not Missouri. Coleman, like all of these politicians, was a supporter of vocational education rather than liberal arts. Coleman was also active in Negro lodge organizations with J. W. Damel and C. G. Williams. Interview with Judge Nathan B. Young, Jr., July 1981, St. Louis. Young feels that the situation his father faced in Florida was more

Collins was a senior professor in education. He was also a leader in the Missouri Association of Negro Teachers and a highly respected educator in the state. From the beginning, Collins resented Young. He was among those who charged that Young was bringing in unqualified teachers. As a teacher of methods of teaching, Collins also disliked the emphasis Young placed on degrees in subject matter. There were those, however, who believed that Collins personally resented Young for Young's achievement. There is the suggestion that as a leader in the Missouri Association of Negro Teachers, Collins resented Young's election as head of the organization. Collins's main problem, however, seemed to be ambition. He wanted to be president of Lincoln, and he had teachers' meetings at night in his home to promote his candidacy.[2]

By the time Young arrived, Damel, who held a master's degree in religion from Hiram College, had been teaching science at Lincoln for a quarter of a century. Damel was well known in the community and highly influential in local churches and lodge halls. However, Young demoted Damel, placing him in the high school at $1,800 a year while raising the salary of E. B. Jones, a chemistry and biology professor in the college with a bachelor of arts degree from Colgate and recent graduate work at the University of Iowa, to $2,700 a year. Young also appointed W. B. Jason, who held a bachelor of arts and a master of arts from Howard University and the University of Pennsylvania respectively, as dean of the college, principal of the high school, and professor of mathematics and physics at $3,200 per year. It is not surprising that Damel, a former acting president, reacted to this. He felt that he should be on the college faculty as a professor and dean or even president and resented being placed in the high school. The fact that several of Damel's friends without the bachelor's degree were also demoted to the high school only added fuel to the already smoldering fire.[3]

a question of liberal arts versus industrial education. The Lincoln situation he feels was "90 percent political."

2. Wolters, *The New Negro on Campus,* 209. Interview with Mrs. Faye Carter, August 1982, Jefferson City. Mrs. Carter is the daughter of the business manager, I. C. Tull. She got her information from her mother. Her father was fired as business manager when Young was fired the first time. "Minutes of the Lincoln University Board of Curators," May 24, 1925.

3. Savage, *History of Lincoln,* 182, 276–77; "Minutes of the Lincoln University Board of Curators," June 19, 1925.

Perhaps Young demoted Damel because he desired to upgrade Lincoln as a quality four-year institution and did not believe that Damel, who had received his bachelor's and master's of philosophy in 1887 and 1900, was qualified. Damel had spent much of his time at Lincoln teaching industrial education and agriculture.[4] Young probably felt that Damel's knowledge of the modern sciences was limited. Young believed that black youth needed training in the modern sciences, and he knew that strength in this area was important to a first-rate institution. In addition, the accrediting agencies had rated Lincoln's science area as very poor. Thus, when one considers Damel's attachment to industrial education and lack of training in modern science on the one hand and Young's aspirations for Lincoln on the other, conflict between the two was inevitable.

Damel's basic outlook and manner of action can be seen most clearly in a letter he wrote to newly elected Governor Guy B. Parks in 1933, in which he expressed hope that Parks would "remedy conditions" at Lincoln. In the letter, Damel complained that the students were "not given the right ideas and ideals of education for usefulness in life." As a result, they failed "to find any useful work that they are willing to do." Moreover, there was a movement at Lincoln "to discredit mechanical and industrial work" and an "over emphasis" on higher education. The high school, Damel noted, was being discouraged, and those in charge seemed to be trying to work "on the tower before the foundation is laid."

Getting to the heart of his concern, Damel wrote: "they have dethroned reason and common sense . . . and put in their place 'the Doctor's degree.'" Damel had no objection to those students who wished to prepare for the professions having the opportunity to do so, but he did not think it proper "to junk the laundry, throw out the tailor shop, the machine shop, the shoe shop and allow the farm and agricultural work to fall into disuse." What black youths

4. Wolters, *The New Negro on Campus,* 210. Interview with Professor James D. Parks, August 1981, Jefferson City. "Minutes of the Lincoln University Board of Curators," October 19, November 9, 1925. Damel was ordered to take charge of the farm and then later denied permission to hire a worker for the farm. Ibid., June 8, 1926. Damel was allowed to teach physics and general science only if he went to summer school. This shows that while Damel was against Young's policy, he still did not have a great deal of influence over those in charge of the board.

needed, he said, was "the kind of education that will fit them for useful service in life." In conclusion, Damel suggested the name of an educator who had the right kinds of ideas and recommended him for president of Lincoln's board of curators.[5]

Collins and Damel represented the most serious internal opposition to Young, but the most significant opposition came from outside the school. Several prominent Missouri educators and politicians— black and white—opposed Young and the direction he was taking at Lincoln. Among Young's opponents was N. C. Bruce, a well-established mid-Missouri educator. Bruce was an advocate of agricultural and vocational education for black Missourians, rather than liberal and professional education. A graduate of Shaw Normal and Industrial College in Raleigh, North Carolina, Bruce received additional training at several New England colleges and at Hampton and Tuskegee Institutes. In 1907 he established an agricultural and vocational school for black youth in Chariton County, and in 1909 the school was relocated within the county to Dalton and named the Bartlett Vocational School after one of its chief benefactors. Moreover, since as early as 1918, Bruce had sought the presidency of Lincoln. Because of the poor finances of the Bartlett School, Bruce was trying to get Lincoln reorganized as an agricultural and industrial college, with himself at its head. After Young's appointment as president, Bruce met with anti-Young members of the Lincoln faculty to denounce Young's administration and direction. He also traveled throughout the state and wrote to newspapers

5. J. W. Damel to Guy B. Parks, March 13, 1933, Guy B. Parks Papers. At this time the two men running Lincoln were J. D. Elliff and President Charles Florence. Damel does not identify them in his letter. He said he would try to talk to the governor in person on the next Thursday, March 16, 1933. J. W. Damel to Guy B. Park, June 30, 1933, Park Papers. Damel wrote on the stationery of his lodge hall. He was Worshipful Master of Lodge No. 9 of Prince Hall Masons. He addressed Park as "Dear Sir and Friend." He was a believer in vocational education. Also, as previously mentioned, many of his friends lost out with the new academic emphasis. J. W. Damel to Guy B. Parks, May 4, 1934, Park Papers. In an interview in Jefferson City in August 1981 with the son of J. W. Damel, Mr. Carroll Damel, and his wife, both graduates of Lincoln Institute in 1920, they said that there were teachers who had to leave because of the lack of a bachelor degree. These persons were considered good teachers and were well liked by students and the community. Conflict between vocationalists and liberal arts advocates continued at Lincoln for many years. Interview with Professor Cecil Blue and Dr. Lorenzo J. Greene, August 1981, Jefferson City.

promoting practical and industrial education instead of liberal arts training.[6]

Besides Bruce, there were also other black Missourians against Young's efforts at Lincoln. For the most part, these blacks had won the favor of state politicians and had gained power as a result. One such black who worked most effectively against Young and his program was C. G. Williams. Williams was born on a farm about two miles from Frankfort, Missouri, in Pike County. He attended school in Hannibal, Missouri, where he graduated from high school. He later attended Knox College at Galesburg, Illinois, for a time, but did not graduate. With the help of his wife, he taught in Missouri at Fulton and Boonville. He also conducted several summer institutes in the state and was appointed the first inspector of Negro schools for Missouri by State Superintendent of Public Schools Sam A. Baker in 1921. Williams was also active in both political and fraternal organizations, serving several times as chairman of the Negro division of the Republican state committee and at one time as grand secretary and then grand master of the United Brothers of Friendship. As a member of Lincoln's board of curators, Williams could see that Young was a threat to his lodge-centered power base. Even though Williams was influential with white politicians, he saw this power base threatened by the support Young was gaining among

6. "Report of Negro Industrial Commission," Appendix, *House and Senate Journals,* vol. 2 (1919), 4. Bruce was named the first chairman of the Missouri Negro Industrial Commission established in 1918 by Democratic Governor Frederick D. Gardner, and in the 1920s Bruce was appointed Negro Inspector of Schools in Missouri. "History of Dalton School," no pagination. This is a typewritten unauthorized history of the school. Included in the file are some newspaper clippings. Lincoln University Archives. N. C. Bruce to J. D. Elliff, March 9, 1918; J. D. Elliff to N. C. Bruce, March 11, 1918, Elliff Papers. Elliff was a member of the board of trustees of the Bartlett School. W. K. James was the president of the same board and a member of the Lincoln Institute Board. Judge James, a leading white politician from St. Joseph, Missouri, was trying to get Bruce elected president of Lincoln. Bruce wanted Elliff to use his influence on State Superintendent of Schools Sam Baker, also a member of Lincoln's board, in case there was a "deadlock" on the presidency of Lincoln and "the Superintendent seeks to bring in an outsider." Elliff was always a strong supporter of the Bartlett School, if not Bruce. Interviews with Professor James D. Parks and Dr. Joseph Reedy, August 1981, Jefferson City. Wolters, *The New Negro on Campus,* 212; *Kansas City Call,* June 18, 1926; and Bruce quoted in *Chicago Defender,* June 12, 1926.

blacks. Where state appointments for blacks were concerned, Williams was accustomed to having his advice sought. When Governor Arthur M. Hyde sought an acceptable list of appointees for the Negro Industrial Commission in 1921, for example, he wrote to Williams, and Hyde appointed all of those whom Williams recommended. Hyde and other white politicians had been won over in part by Williams's personality, for he was a large, jovial man with whom white politicians of the day seemed to feel quite comfortable.[7]

Williams, then, was used to the old system at Lincoln, where politicians could influence appointments to the staff and even the faculty without regard to merit or training. Naturally, he opposed Young's new hiring practices, which were designed to professionalize Lincoln's faculty. Young had been so successful in raising the standards for employing faculty and staff members that the system whereby Williams and other politicians handed out jobs to friends and supporters had been discontinued. The blacks in the urban areas of St. Louis and Kansas City who were in accord with Young's program were those who traditionally made up part of Williams's power base.[8] Williams felt threatened by Young's position as a black man to whom these urban blacks looked for leadership and direction, albeit in education.

Young might have withstood the efforts of black politicians such as Williams if they had not been allied with white politicians. While the black politicians were mainly interested in keeping a power base and filling jobs on the campus, the white politicians were interested in keeping Lincoln the way it was and in filling the moneymaking contracts that the university regularly let out. Young could not withstand the combined power of these two groups.

7. Brigham, "Negro Education in Missouri," 206. C. G. Williams to A. M. Hyde, May 26, 1921. On Williams wanting to get control of the Negro Industrial Commission for patronage see C. G. Williams to T. N. Ormiston, July 16, 1921, Hyde Papers. For biographical information on Williams see Sherman W. Savage, "Workers of Lincoln University," pt. 1, 60. Interview with Sterling Brown, July 1981, Jefferson City. Brown considered C. G. Williams "a country school teacher and politician." Brown remembered no personal trouble with Williams except for an incident when Williams had told his driver and henchman, named "Kitchen," to get Brown and his wife to start attending church. Brown ignored the order.

8. Interview with Professors James D. Parks and Cecil Blue, August 1981, Jefferson City; interview with Dr. L. S. Curtis, August 1981, St. Louis.

Young's situation was further endangered by the fact that the governor of Missouri could serve only one four-year term, which meant that Governor Hyde had to leave office in early 1925. Hyde had been a supporter of earlier efforts to turn Lincoln into a standard, accredited college. He had strongly supported Young and had even made him a member of the exclusive Constitutional Convention Committee. Indeed, Hyde and Young were both Oberlin graduates, although a few years apart, and this connection seems to have created a friendly relationship between them. As governor, moreover, Hyde had made a concerted effort to cater to the black vote in St. Louis and Kansas City, and this meant supporting Young's goals for Lincoln. Hyde also was motivated by his desire to seek the Republican nomination for U.S. vice president in 1924,[9] a position that he did not win, but one which led him to widen his political base in Missouri as broadly as possible. Naturally, he had an eye toward the traditional Republican black vote. With Hyde out of the governor's mansion, Young's external problems would intensify.

In 1925, Sam A. Baker, an old-style machine politician, moved into the governor's office. Baker had won the 1924 race by a narrow margin of fewer than six thousand votes, and blacks were convinced that his victory would not have been possible without them. They felt that their votes prevented the election from going to the Democratic candidate, Arthur Nelson, who had been endorsed by the Ku Klux Klan. Blacks, therefore, expected Baker to promote their interests through black political appointments and through support of their efforts to make Lincoln a first-rate college.

Baker, however, quickly showed that he had little, if any, interest in the welfare of black Missourians. He provided fewer political

9. "Program of the Constitutional Convention Committee of Missouri," Hyde Papers; *General Catalogue of Oberlin, 1833–1908* (Oberlin: Oberlin College, 1909), 559. Edgard Rombauer to A. M. Hyde, May 26, 1924, Hyde Papers. Rombauer resigned from Lincoln's board because he opposed Hyde becoming vice-president. The black population greatly increased in the state. Between 1910 and late 1920s nearly ninety thousand blacks moved into Missouri from the South. Most of these migrants moved to the large urban centers of St. Louis and Kansas City. Missouri's rural black population also moved to the cities. U.S. Bureau of the Census, *Negro Population: 1790–1915*, 49, 93. Also see Missouri, *Biennial Report of the Missouri Negro Industrial Commission, 1921–1922, 1923–1924, 1925–1926*, passim, and Franklin D. Mitchell, *Embattled Democracy: Missouri Democratic Politics, 1919–1932*, 63.

appointments than his predecessors, and he even suggested that blacks did not need an institution of higher education. To demonstrate further his opposition to the betterment of Lincoln, he refused to reappoint to its board of curators Mrs. Julia Child Curtis of St. Louis, despite the fact that the *St. Louis Argus,* which had supported him, campaigned for her. She was a respected educator and leader in the St. Louis black community, and she had been, of course, in the forefront of the efforts to turn Lincoln into a first-class college.[10]

As stated earlier, political interference at Lincoln by the governor was encouraged, of course, because Lincoln's board of curators was not on the same six-year appointment basis as the boards at the University of Missouri and the other state colleges. Baker used this to his advantage by making appointments to the board that he considered to be politically expedient. He began by placing on the board men who thought as he did about the school. Baker had been a member of the board from 1919 to 1922, and he was used to a less developed Lincoln than Young had now created. Moreover, Baker was familiar with the Lincoln that was mainly a teacher-training institute with vocational and agricultural programs. While Baker was on the board in 1920, in fact, Lincoln had only one student enrolled in the college curriculum, and the school had been little above the level of a high school. This was a situation with which Baker was quite comfortable because it conformed to his views of the type of educational opportunities black Missourians ought to have. Furthermore, Baker had a personality conflict with Young. He did not like Young's sense of independence, and Young, in turn, could not hide the fact that he did not care for Baker.[11]

10. Mitchell, *Embattled Democracy,* 87–88; *St. Louis Argus,* January 23, February 13, 1925. Baker had earlier been the Klan's Republican choice for governor. Baker, however, denied ever being a member of the Klan. Nelson did not make an equivalent denial, and the black vote went to Baker.

11. Brigham, "Negro Education in Missouri," 204. Savage, *History of Lincoln,* 167–68, 191–92, 291; Wolters, *The New Negro on Campus,* 211–13; *Kansas City Call,* June 19, 1925. Interview with L. S. Curtis, August, 1981, St. Louis. Curtis claims that while Baker was superintendent of schools he ran a book-selling company on the side and school officials under his supervision would purchase their school textbooks through Baker's company. Curtis also claimed that all Baker wanted to do was drive his new car upon Lincoln's campus and open the school back up to politics in order to pay off political debts.

In a very short time, then, through reappointments and new appointments, Baker had a majority of the board members under his control. On April 14, 1925, the new board elected its officers, and a Baker appointee, Samuel A. James of Sedalia, was elected president. James, the Republican chairman of Pettis County, was a close political ally of the governor and had carried the vote in his county for Baker in the 1924 election. One of Baker's black appointees, Aaron E. Malone of St. Louis, the husband of wealthy Annie Malone, was elected vice-president. Another Baker appointee, A. A. Speer, who had been on the board of the old Lincoln Institute, was elected treasurer. And C. G. Williams, whom Baker had reappointed, was elected secretary. The results of the election of the officers of the board of curators appeared to have been decided before the election, since all of Baker's new appointees won office. The election of James and Williams gave a clear indication of what was ahead for Young.

Immediately after the first meeting of this board, James announced the members of the executive committee who would run the day-to-day affairs of the school, including the approval and payment of all bills. They were Clifford G. Scruggs, a Jefferson City businessman and a Baker-appointed Democrat, Charles A. Lee, state superintendent of schools, and C. G. Williams. Scruggs was named chairman.[12]

With this new board of curators and officers, Young was in for a struggle. He had only been in office two years when the board was appointed, and he felt that he had only gotten his program started. Yet, despite the progress and the support for Young's program at Lincoln, the board's president indicated that the board was going to seek a new president for the university. James made it clear that Young's integrity and ability were not at issue, but he said that it was simply a matter of a new administration running the state's affairs. This new administration had appointed a new board, and James said that a majority of this new board now desired a president who would carry out their ideas about how Lincoln University ought to be run.[13]

James clearly intended for political consideration to be important

12. "Minutes of the Lincoln University Board of Curators," April 14, 1925.
13. Savage, *History of Lincoln,* 193; Perry, *Forty Cords of Wood.*

in the operation of the school. He again raised the old issue of Young's bringing in a large number of teachers from Florida instead of hiring Missouri personnel. Young tried to defend himself by pointing out that there were only nine teachers from the South, as well as nine from Missouri and seventeen from other parts of the country, but his efforts were in vain. James and others, such as Williams, thought that the school ought to provide jobs for the politically connected. James also wanted to elect Christopher Hubbard, the black head of the Lincoln High School in Sedalia, as president of Lincoln. Hubbard was a graduate of Lincoln's normal program, and James and Hubbard were close political associates. Despite the fact that Hubbard had only a two-year degree and was hardly known outside the state, James let it be known that he considered Hubbard to have better qualifications for Lincoln's presidency than did anyone else in the country.[14]

When the black community learned of the board's intent to replace Young, it began to mobilize in an effort to defend his administration of Lincoln. Letters and telegrams were sent to the board protesting any effort to remove Young, and special delegations from St. Louis and Kansas City came before the board to plead their case. There was so much support from the black community that Young was determined to make a fight to the end. In an effort to save Young, the black press discredited the educational aspirations of Hubbard and accused both James and Governor Baker of putting the school back into politics in order to pay political debts. The press denounced both men as not caring anything about the education of black youth and for only wanting to use the school for the buying and selling of positions.[15]

Despite these protests, Governor Baker and his board were determined to remove Young at the first opportunity. On May 4, 1925, the board met, and the first order of business was the appointment of a president. The motion to reappoint Young resulted in a tie. Then there was a motion to remove Young, and that also resulted in a tie, with Sam James, C. G. Williams, and Clifford Scruggs voting against Young and Dr. J. E. Perry, C. H. Kirshner, and Aaron

14. Savage, *History of Lincoln*, 194. Interviews with Dr. Sidney Reedy, August 1981, Dr. L. S. Curtis, August 1981, Sterling Brown, July 1981.

15. Wolters, *The New Negro on Campus*, 214; *St. Louis Argus*, May 8, April 24, June 12, 1925; *Kansas City Call*, April 17, June 19, 1925, March 5, 1926.

Malone voting for him. Kirshner, of course, was a holdover from the Hyde administration and one of Young's chief supporters. Both Perry and Malone were black curators from Kansas City and St. Louis, respectively, and in both of those metropolitan areas the black community strongly supported Young and his program. Having failed to remove Young, James appointed a committee to receive the applications of candidates for the presidency.[16]

When the board met again on June 9, 1925, it returned to the question of selecting a president. A motion was made that Young be elected for a year's term. There was an effort to defeat this motion by a substitute motion to make Dean W. B. Jason acting president. This maneuver failed, and Young was reappointed by a vote of four to two. Young's reappointment occurred after Clifford Scruggs, a Baker appointee, was called from the meeting because of illness in his family, but the margin of Young's victory was the result of the vote of Charles A. Lee, who had abstained from voting in the May election. Lee was generally thought to be favorable to Young and his program, and it is not known why Lee waited a month before voting for Young. Conceivably, he thought some of the opposition would change their attitude toward Young, and it is likely that Lee got fellow Democrat Scruggs to absent himself from the vote on Young.[17] In any case, Lee eventually voted for Young, and Young would have no trouble getting appointed in 1926, since Governor Baker could not make any new appointments to the board until 1927.

Despite Young's victory, the central opposition to him was still in place. The Baker faction of the board now moved to hinder Young's program of development. Working through the executive committee, the board cut off all advertisements for the school in such periodicals as *School and Community* and the *Crisis*. Young had used these advertisements to spread the word about Lincoln outside the state and attract quality students from other regions. The board also discontinued the *University Record,* which Young had used to

16. Interview with Dr. L. S. Curtis, August 1981. "Minutes of the Meeting of the Lincoln University Board of Curators," May 4, 1925.
17. "Minutes of the Lincoln University Board of Curators," June 9, 1925. In an interview with Professor J. D. Parks in August 1981, he claims that Scruggs, a white businessman, wanted to go along with what blacks wanted. Later, Scruggs provided home loans to faculty members so they would have good housing. He was a long-serving curator and owned a home loan business. In an interview with Dr. L. S. Curtis in August 1981, he said that Lee was generally supportive of Young.

keep the alumni informed about Lincoln's status. Quite obviously, the board intended to cut off Young's support from the outside and thereby undermine his program. James also illegally refused to call any meeting of the full board, which meant that the executive committee, which was dominated by a majority of Baker's appointees, made all decisions about the school. Young was permitted to make very few decisions on his own.[18]

James suggested to a large number of teachers that if they wanted to retain their jobs, they should not support Young and should buy stock in James's company, the Standard Saving and Loan Company of Kansas City. About twenty professors began making monthly payments totaling nearly four hundred dollars in order to purchase stock in James's company. James's activities became so widely known that others began to exploit members of Lincoln's faculty. A white woman claiming to be Mrs. James came to campus and insisted that the female teachers buy their hosiery from her. Fearing for their jobs, many teachers were taken in by this woman's unethical sale techniques.

Because of practices such as these, morale at Lincoln became so low that State Representative Walthall M. Moore called for an investigation by the General Assembly. The investigation was held, but the assembly found that nothing criminal had occurred, although it thought that James's sales activities were unethical and should stop. Despite several demands from the black community to remove James as head of the board, Governor Baker retained him. Moreover, when the terms of board members who had backed Young earlier expired in 1927, Baker replaced them with appointees who were committed to removing Young. This had been feared by Young's supporters in the black community for more than a year, but all of their efforts to prevent it had been of no avail. Now six of the seven board members were Baker appointees, and Young's removal was certain.[19]

18. "Minutes of the Lincoln University Board of Curators' Executive Committee," April 15, October 13, 1925, March 11, April 2, November 23, 1926. Young suggested that Lincoln was located in a "circle of service" to more than two million Negroes within a three-hundred-mile radius of the campus.

19. Savage, *History of Lincoln*, 205. Interview with Professors L. S. Curtis and James D. Parks, August 1981. *Journal of the House*, 54th General Assembly (1927), 1377–78, 1616–17. Professor L. S. Curtis was told that Sam James wanted to see him in the registrar's office. When Curtis reported,

When the board met on April 11, 1927, it voted six to one to re-move Young as president and replaced him with former president Clement Richardson, who was then the president of Western Baptist College in Kansas City. The board meeting during which Young was ousted was held in Governor Baker's office in the State Capitol building in downtown Jefferson City. Following this meeting, the board sent Young a letter informing him that his services would not be needed after June 15, 1927. President-elect Richardson was directed to pick the summer school and fall faculty with the aid of the board, while Young was to bring the regular school year to an end. Young showed up at the board's next meeting on April 26 and offered to assist Richardson in any way he could. Richardson accepted Young's offer. This ended the first administration of Nathan B. Young at Lincoln University.[20]

The board now returned to the practice of using Lincoln as a source of political patronage. It ordered the repair of the abandoned model school and discontinued Young's policy of using Washington School, the public elementary school, in training teachers. When the elementary school had been in operation, it was very

---

James approached him about buying stock in James's loan company. Walthall Moore was kept informed of James's activities by "Citizen Committee of One Thousand," formerly the "Citizen Committee of One Hundred," a St. Louis group watching out for Lincoln's interests. Its members included Mrs. Julia Curtis, J. E. Mitchell, and Homer Phillips. Wolters, *The New Negro on Campus,* 218. For protests in the Negro press see *Kansas City Call,* January 29, 1926, February 25, 1927; *St. Louis Argus,* February 4, 27, March 4, 25, April 15, 1927. Interview with Nathan Sweets, August 1981, St. Louis. Sweets claims that Baker demanded that the appointees agree to remove Young before he would nominate them for board membership. Sweets also claims that he was twice nominated to Lincoln's board, but never sat more than two hours because he did not agree to some political deal. Once he claimed that C. G. Williams and Duke Diggs had a land deal to rob the school that he would not go along with. Later still, Sweets claims he was kept off by Governor Stark for refusing a political deal.

20. "Minutes of the Lincoln University Board of Curators," April 11, 1927. N. B. Young to W. E. B. Du Bois, April 13, 1927; W. E. B. Du Bois to N. B. Young, May 8, 1927; W. E. B. Du Bois to N. B. Young, June 6, 1927, "W. E. B. Du Bois Papers," Schomburg Collection on microfilm, Lincoln University Inman Page Library. Du Bois wrote Young for all the details of his dismissal. "Minutes of the Lincoln University Board of Curators," April, 11, 26, 1927. Other than on this occasion, rarely, if at all, has Lincoln's board meeting been held in the governor's office.

small and did not attract many students. This was one reason why it had been closed. Even though the use of the model school as a laboratory in teacher training was not of major importance to the college, it did provide jobs for teachers with limited academic backgrounds or abilities. So the elementary school was reopened, and two teachers were hired for it.[21]

The board's plans for Lincoln received a setback, however, when on June 2 Richardson wrote James that he was declining the offer of the presidency of Lincoln and staying at Western College. Lincoln was six times larger than Western, but Richardson felt that he could not work under the dictatorial control of the board again. Richardson had visited the campus and attended a board meeting on May 23, and C. G. Williams and other board members had made it clear to him that they wanted to approve all the hiring decisions and to determine who would receive the school's contracts. In addition, the board had fired fifteen faculty members, many of whom had testified in the investigation of James and the sale of his stock to the faculty.[22]

In another meeting in Governor Baker's office, the board accepted Richardson's decision and chose an in-house acting president. This was W. B. Jason, the dean and professor of mathematics, whom the board thought would be an ideal president because he was a likable person who tried to get along with everybody. What the board especially liked about him was his lack of ambition— they thought it unlikely that he would resist the will of the board. To Jason's credit, he upheld Young's standards for the college faculty. Thus, well-trained scholars such as Sterling Brown were retained, and other educators previously recommended for hiring by Young were appointed. Fortunately, in 1925 the board had already established the master's degree as the basic criterion for teaching in the college department, so it generally accepted Jason's recommendations in this area, as it had earlier accepted Young's. Political jobs, therefore, were not filled in the college department. This was not

21. "Minutes of the Lincoln University Board of Curators," April 26, 1927.

22. Brigham, *Negro Education in Missouri,* 211; Savage, *History of Lincoln,* 208–9; Wolters, *The New Negro on Campus,* 218–20. "Minutes of the Lincoln University Board of Curators," June 2, 1927; N. B. Young to W. E. B. Du Bois, June 3, 1927, W. E. B. Du Bois Papers, Lincoln University.

the case, however in filling some of the jobs in the high school, elementary school, and various offices. In these other areas, Jason's efforts at retaining Lincoln's new professional standards were frustrated by dictatorial board members and their backers.[23] In truth, Jason was given very little real power to run the university, and one incident that involved Sterling Brown clearly showed how little power Jason had.

During the summer of 1927, Brown married and was late returning to school. Brown had sent Jason a telegram asking permission to miss the three days of registration and to return on the first day of classes, and Jason had given his approval. When Brown received his first monthly paycheck, however, it was for $150 instead of $300. Angry about losing half a month's salary, Brown confronted Jason, who in turn sent him to Duke Diggs, the newly appointed business manager. Diggs claimed that Brown's paycheck was cut because he had been late, and that Brown would have to see white curator Scruggs in downtown Jefferson City about getting his money back. Brown then went to Scruggs's paint store to demand his money, and he finally convinced Scruggs of the justice of his case. When Brown returned to campus to inform Jason, Jason and Diggs insisted on telephoning Scruggs to confirm his decision. Hearing Scruggs's approval, Diggs then turned to his student helper, Nathaniel Sweets—the future St. Louis newspaper publisher—and ordered him to pay Brown out of the petty cash that was kept in a cigar box under the counter in Diggs's office. Needless to say, this incident amazed Brown and made him wonder who was really president.[24]

The fluidity of administration at Lincoln after Young's removal became apparent in a number of ways. For one thing, the business

23. "Minutes of the Lincoln University Board of Curators," June 2, 1927; Savage, *History of Lincoln,* 209; Brigham, "History of Negro Education," 211; interviews with Professors Blue, Parks, Hardiman, Reedy, and W. W. Dowdy, August 1981, Jefferson City.

24. Interview with Sterling Brown, July 1981, Jefferson City. Brown said that the main building, Old Memorial Hall, was continuously painted: "one semester one half of the building and the second semester the second half of the building, and then, the painters started all over again." There were also large and small round rocks that surrounded the campus's summit. These rocks also were continuously painted with "white paint not whitewash."

manager assumed quite a different role. Diggs wanted to make decisions that should have been made by Jason. This was a different role from that of former Business Manager I. C. Tull. Although hired under Richardson in 1919, Tull had worked cooperatively with Richardson and succeeding presidents Inman Page and Young. Diggs, however, because of his personal association with Williams and with some of the white curators, tried to assume greater control. In November 1927, for example, he wrote a letter to the executive committee of the board suggesting a number of changes in the operation of the school. In order to save the school money, Diggs suggested that classrooms not be used at night as offices and conference rooms, that all electrical appliances be confiscated from students, that the number of student workers be reduced, and that the matrons and teachers be charged room and board. Finally, Diggs requested that the duties of the business manager and the president be clearly set forth, as if they somehow were not clear in Diggs's own mind. For another thing, the progress of the school was hampered by the fact that the board had severely cut back the budget request for the biennial period beginning in 1927. In place of the $625,000 that Young had requested before leaving, the board now suggested that $278,000 would be sufficient. Given this situation, then, nearly all progress toward full accreditation as a four-year liberal arts college suddenly stopped.[25]

The student body reacted strongly against this lack of progress in upgrading the school. The students were aware that Lincoln was being run by white politicians from downtown Jefferson City, and they knew that these politicians were using the school for personal gain. Furthermore, Diggs and the board were now obstructing a number of gains that the students had experienced under Young. Young, for example, had given the students scholarships, a college sports program, and greater social freedom. He had also established a student council in 1924 for the airing of student grievances. Now all of this seemed to be in jeopardy. As a result, a student strike and

25. "Minutes of the Lincoln University Board of Curators," November 10, 1927. White curators thought Duke Diggs was a good role model for blacks; although he did not have more than an "eighth grade education he owned a moving and storage business and several pieces of rental property." Interview with Sterling Brown, July 1981. Brigham, "History of Negro Education," 211.

boycott of classes took place. This strike was soon contained by law enforcement officers after some property damage.[26] The student strike did little more than draw public attention to some of the problems at Lincoln. The solution to Lincoln's problems required more than student demonstrations. It required a different attitude on the part of the state political figures and a different political administration.

After 1925, because of discontent with the Baker administration, black voters had been moving increasingly into the Democratic Party. Disappointment with the Republican state administration and lawmakers was widespread in the black urban centers. Urban blacks held that Republicans had failed to promote black education on three counts. They had failed to support bills aimed at providing all black children a common school education, they had failed to increase appropriations for Lincoln, and they had failed to retain Young as president of Lincoln. During the Baker administration, Democrats showed their interest in black concerns by inserting planks in their 1926 and 1928 party platforms that addressed issues which were vital to the welfare of the black community.[27]

With the Democrats now showing an interest in the black vote, leaders such as C. A. Franklin of the *Call* and J. E. Mitchell of the *Argus* urged a break from the tradition of supporting the Republican Party. Both papers editorialized against the practice of voting for all Republican candidates on the ballot. The firing of Young and the conditions of Lincoln University were made campaign issues in the 1928 election, and black voters were aroused. Seeking the Democratic Party's gubernatorial nomination, State Superintendent of Schools Lee added to his chances by appointing Young to replace N. C. Bruce as state inspector of black schools. Though Lee did not get his party's nomination, many black Missourians voted Democratic for the first time in 1928.[28]

The Republican gubernatorial candidate, Henry Caulfield, was

26. Wolters, *The New Negro on Campus,* 200–221; *Kansas City Call,* October 28, 1927, November 11, 1928; Savage, *History of Lincoln,* 191–99; "Minutes of the Lincoln University Board of Curators," October 1, 1924, November 26, 1926; *St. Louis Argus,* October 14, 1927, February 10, 1928.

27. Mitchell, *Embattled Democracy,* 87–88, 125, 162.

28. Ibid., 125–26; L. S. Curtis, "Nathan B. Young," 109; Wolters, *The New Negro on Campus,* 221–22; *Kansas City Call,* December 2, 1927, November 2, 1928; *St. Louis Argus,* January 13, 1928.

hurt by his association with the Baker administration. Even though Caulfield won against Democratic candidate Francis M. Wilson, the black Republican vote decreased in both St. Louis and Kansas City. As a result of this, Caulfield came into office determined to win back the black community that Baker had alienated. Before taking office, he met with black leaders from across the state to learn their communities' needs. At this meeting, the leaders stressed their interest in legislation and in state monies for expanding common-school education and for the upgrading of Lincoln University. It is significant that in his inaugural address to the Fifty-fifth General Assembly Caulfield outlined the educational needs of the black community. He admitted that the state had failed to provide its black citizens with the equality in education that they deserved. He also admitted that Lincoln was a university only in name, while the University of Missouri was provided with good buildings and equipment and the necessary operating funds.[29]

Before Caulfield made any recommendations for Lincoln or any of the other state colleges, however, he established a State Survey Commission for Higher Education. This commission, composed of distinguished educators and political figures, employed a professional team to conduct studies of all the state colleges. As a result of the findings, the commission recommended that faculty salaries at Lincoln be raised and that more buildings and equipment be provided to improve its ability to educate its students. In keeping with the recommendations of the Survey Commission, Caulfield pushed a $400,000 appropriation for Lincoln through the state legislature for the two-year period beginning in 1929, and another $250,000 was added for a long-promised classroom building.[30]

Governor Caulfield realized, however, that financial support

---

29. Mitchell, *Embattled Democracy,* 126–27. Caulfield also endorsed lowering the fifteen-children limit for establishment of a rural school. In 1929 legislation was passed, with the aid of the Democrats, lowering the figure to eight. Henry S. Caulfield, "Inaugural Address," in *Proclamation and Papers of Governors of Missouri,* vol. 13, 21, 50, 71–72; Larry H. Grothaus, "The Negro in Missouri Politics, 1890–1941," 127.

30. George D. Strayer and N. L. Englehardt, directors, "A Preliminary Report of the Survey of the Public Schools and Higher Institutions of the State of Missouri," Joint Collection–University of Missouri, Western Historical Manuscript Collection and State Historical Society of Missouri; and Grothaus, "The Negro in Missouri Politics, 1890–1941," 128. Strayer and Englehardt, "Report of Public Schools in Missouri," 733–34.

alone would not make Lincoln into a standard university, and that the college also needed to regain the kind of forward-looking leadership that Young had provided during the Hyde administration. As a step in this direction, Caulfield did not reappoint curators James, Williams, and Scruggs when their terms expired in 1929. Moreover, he forced the other Baker appointees off the board as well. In their places Caulfield appointed a new Lincoln Board of Curators. In order to impress the black community with his seriousness about supporting Lincoln, he appointed pro-Young, former Hyde curators to the board. These included Mrs. Curtis, Edgar Rombauer, and Dr. J. E. Perry. Charles Nagel of St. Louis, a former secretary of commerce under William Howard Taft, trustee at Washington University, and an occasional NAACP lawyer, headed the new board. The three other board members were also familiar faces—J. D. Elliff, J. B. Coleman, and Charles A. Lee. Soon Lincoln began to benefit materially and administratively under Governor Caulfield.[31]

The new Caulfield-appointed board immediately got to work cleaning up Lincoln, though they quickly ran into two problems. First of all, the Baker board had awarded—without receiving bids—a number of contracts for repairs, wiring, painting, and building projects.[32] Several of these contracts caused serious problems. When board members discovered that the work contracted for was unnecessary or that it was being done at unreasonably high rates, the contractors merely pointed out that they were only following the contract's specifications, which the board was forced to honor. Indeed, all that the board could do was to make sure that the contracted work was properly and reasonably done before paying the bill.

The second problem area was in personnel. The old board had hired and given contracts of more than a year to certain staff persons. Especially troublesome were Business Manager Diggs and

31. Strayer and Englehardt, "Report of Public Schools in Missouri," 733–34; "Minutes of the Lincoln University Board of Curators," May 30, 1929; interview with Cecil Blue, August 1981.

32. "Minutes of the Lincoln University Board of Curators," December 31, 1928. Once Young was forced out in 1927, the board's executive committee made numerous repair contracts and purchases apparently without the legally required bids being taken. "Minutes of the Lincoln University Board of Curators," June 28, July 13, 28, November, 11, 1927, April 17, December 7, 31, 1928. See also note 24 on Sterling Brown and the painting of the main building.

President Jason. In April 1928, for example, the old board had promoted Jason from acting president to full president, giving him a
two-year contract. When the new board asked Jason to return to his
old position of dean, he said that he preferred to stay with his present contract. In desperation, the board went to the attorney general
of Missouri, who ruled that the board could fire anyone it chose.
With this ruling, the board forced Diggs out of Lincoln and Jason
back to his position as dean.

Now, the board was free to begin its search for a new president,
though there was little doubt that they would once again turn to
Young. Even though he was now nearly seventy years old and his
health was visibly affected by his earlier battles with Missouri's
politicians, Young again accepted the challenge.[33]

He returned to Lincoln in 1929, for both personal and educational reasons. Personally, Young had financial needs that a position at Lincoln could help alleviate. Since there was no retirement
system for the teachers of black public schools at this time and
since Young had lost money on certain investments in black business ventures, he needed a decent income to provide for his wife
and children, as well as for his mother and mother-in-law, who
were living with him in Jefferson City.[34] And, of course, there were
also educational reasons why Young returned to the helm of Lincoln in September 1929. Understandably, he took delight in the
challenge of establishing Lincoln as a standard four-year liberal arts
college, especially since he had received such great support from
the state's black community in his earlier struggles with the politicians over the future of Lincoln. Moreover, during his absence from
Lincoln, Young had made a statewide survey of the educational
needs of Missouri's blacks. As Negro inspector of schools he had
traveled throughout the state, observing the poor rural school conditions for black youth and lobbying for new legislation to meet

33. "Minutes of the Lincoln University Board of Curators," May 20, June
23, August 26, September, 19, 1929. Interviews with Professors L. S. Curtis
and James D. Parks, August 1981, and Mrs. Faye Carter, August 1982. They
all claim that Young was weaker and did not have the energy he had
shown in his first term.

34. N. B. Young to W. E. B. Du Bois, April 13, 1927, W. E. B. Du Bois to
N. B. Young, April 20, 1927, N. B. Young to W. E. B. Du Bois, April 27, 1927,
W. E. B. Du Bois Papers, Lincoln University. Interview with Mrs. Faye
Carter, August 1982, and Judge Nathan B. Young, Jr., August 1981.

their needs. Now he had new ideas on how Lincoln University could serve the rural black community, and in 1929 he lobbied successfully for the legislature to provide scholarships to Lincoln's high school for students in districts that did not provide education beyond the eighth grade for blacks. Young also convinced the board to offer scholarships to all black honor graduates of Missouri's high schools. In addition, he helped created a position for an educational extension teacher to go to southeast Missouri and aid black teachers there, many of whom had only a third-grade education.[35]

Young also brought a number of other important changes and programs to Lincoln during his second administration. Following the recommendation of the faculty and its executive council, he approved the establishment of fraternities and sororities. He closed the elementary school again and used Jefferson City's black elementary school as a teacher training facility. He resumed the practice of bringing in outstanding black intellectuals such as W. E. B. Du Bois and Alain Locke to speak. Young also worked with the board in providing travel expenses for faculty members to attend professional meetings, and he helped obtain $50,000 from the General Education Board of New York for a home economics building and $7,500 from the Rosenwald Fund for the school's library.[36]

Despite Young's efforts during his second administration, the conflicts that were so prevalent earlier resurfaced. He still had many enemies both on and off campus, and he did very little to appease them. Rather, he was uncompromising and even defiant at times. As a result, there was a year and a half of conflict, and Young's enemies gained increasing power and were able to continually frustrate him.[37]

There were still members of the faculty and staff who were no

35. N. B. Young, "Report of the Inspector of Negro Schools, 1928–29," *80th Report of the Public School State of Missouri* (Jefferson City: State of Missouri, 1930), 146–47. Mitchell, *Embattled Democracy*, 127; Savage, *History of Lincoln*, 202, 216–18, 223; "Minutes of the Lincoln University Board of Curators," October 29, 1929.

36. Savage, *History of Lincoln*, 218–20. When the issue of fraternities and sororities came up in Young's first administration, he was against them as being antidemocratic. He did not belong to such a social organization, but Young was an original member of the professional black fraternity, the Boulé. This time the faculty endorsed the organizations and Young bowed to their will. "Minutes of the Lincoln University Board of Curators," May 13, 1930. Savage, *History of Lincoln*, 220–21, 223.

37. Curtis, "Nathan B. Young," 110.

more satisfied with Young's leadership and direction in 1929 than they had been during his first administration, and these individuals renewed their efforts against him. Damel continued his opposition to Young's emphasis on liberal arts over agriculture and the mechanical arts, and Collins was still ambitious to have the presidency for himself. The role of former President Jason is not totally clear; while Jason wanted to remain as president and Young saw him as having joined forces with those against him, there is little direct evidence linking him to Young's active opponents. What is known is that certain members of the board of curators who were opposed to Young established a spy system on campus and used the information that was gathered to turn Governor Caulfield against Young and the pro-Young curators.[38]

The chief figure in turning Caulfield against Young was curator J. D. Elliff, who, when Nagel resigned from the board because of other commitments, became Caulfield's chief adviser on Lincoln. Elliff, of course, had been associated with Lincoln for many years and had been the person who had worked with Young on getting North Central accreditation for both Lincoln's high school and its teacher-training program. Thus, he was a natural choice for such an advisory role.[39]

Elliff, however, had a rather limited vision in regard to education for blacks. While working hard to see that Lincoln received fair appropriations from the legislature and higher salaries for its faculty, he felt that the school should emphasize agricultural and mechanical arts. As a curator he pushed the board to accept the Dalton Vocational School, of which he was a trustee, as the state agricultural experiment station for blacks. At his insistence, eventually the legislature handed the Dalton School, which had been under the University of Missouri for a few years, over to Lincoln in 1929. Young,

38. Wolters, *The New Negro on Campus,* 222. Interviews with Professors L. S. Curtis, James D. Parks, and Judge Nathan B. Young, Jr., August 1981; "Statement of N. B. Young," *St. Louis American,* April 11, 1931; "Lincoln (Mo.) University in Turmoil," (Baltimore) *Afro-American,* July 18, 1931, clippings filed in Lincoln University Archives.

39. Brigham, "Negro Education in Missouri," 214–18; George Melcher to J. D. Elliff, June 2, 1919, George Melcher to S. A. Baker, June 3, 1919, George Melcher to Frederick D. Gardner, June 2, 1919, Elliff Papers. Elliff was a longtime associate of former Governor Sam A. Baker. They had worked with each other as far back as 1919.

however, angered Elliff and black curator J. B. Coleman by refusing to divert Lincoln's appropriations to support the Dalton School.[40]

Unhappy with Young's uncompromising attitude, Elliff began working against him. As head of the Teachers' Committee, he blocked a number of Young's attempts to improve the college. For example, he put off the acceptance of a plan for a year's leave of absence at half pay for department heads seeking the Ph.D., even though this was one of the recommendations of the North Central and would move Lincoln closer to accreditation. Elliff also put off the consideration of a tenure system and uniform standards for promotions and salary increases. Though it cannot be proved, it is probable that Elliff, a longtime representative of the North Central, used his influence to block that organization's recognition of Lincoln in 1930. In addition to blocking Young's various efforts for improving Lincoln, Elliff also convinced Caulfield not to reappoint Young's friend Mrs. Curtis to the board when her term expired, so that finally, in April 1931, a newly organized board headed by Elliff met in secret and fired Young without a hearing. There was, to be sure, an outcry in the black press, both inside and outside of Missouri, but it soon blew over.[41]

Now nearly seventy years of age and in poor health, Young did not long survive this last blow from the politicians. Because of economic necessity and pride, he undertook lecture tours for the National Association of Teachers in Colored Schools and for the Association for the Study of Negro Life and History, but his health remained poor, and he died of a heart attack at the home of his daughter in Tampa, Florida, on July 10, 1933.[42]

40. J. D. Elliff, "A Concise Statement of the Needs of Lincoln University," Elliff Papers; "Minutes of the Lincoln University Board of Curators," May 30, June 13, September 14, October 22, December 20, 1929, April 10, 1930. Elliff was also against desegregation, whereas Young never fully accepted the system of racial separation and openly said so. In the 1930s Elliff told Dr. Lorenzo J. Greene that "cows would be grazing on the moon before a Negro was admitted to the University of Missouri." Interview with Dr. Lorenzo J. Greene, August 1981, Jefferson City.

41. "Minutes of the Lincoln University Board of Curators," April 29, May 5, 13, 22, June 18, September 20, 1930, April 6, 1931; Wolters, *The New Negro on Campus,* 227.

42. Curtis, "Nathan B. Young," 110–11. Funeral services were held at Florida A&M. The *Tuskegee Messenger*'s death notice called Young a "Militant Educator." Clippings from a 1933 issue of *Tuskegee Messenger,* Tuskegee Institute Archives.

After Young's tenure, political maneuvering continued at Lincoln for a decade, but in 1934, through the renewed effort of Elliff and President Charles Florence, the institution was fully accredited as a four-year liberal arts college, a posthumous tribute to all of the work that Young had contributed to the school. When he came to Lincoln in 1923, the institution was, at best, a secondary industrial school. When he was finally forced to leave, it was a college, with a nationally ranked faculty and a curriculum that merited accreditations.

Seven years after his firing, in June 1938 Young finally received full recognition for the service he had rendered at Lincoln. Upon the recommendation of Acting President Jason, a new board, headed by the first black president, Joseph L. McLemore of St. Louis, ordered that the widow or heirs of Young receive the one thousand dollars in back salary owed him since 1931. The board also changed the name of College Hall, built under Young's administration, to Young Hall. The citation in the board minutes stated that this was to be done "in honor of the late President Nathan B. Young, a scholarly exponent of higher education his entire life."[43]

43. "Minutes of the Lincoln University Board of Curators," June 4, 1938. There is also a men's dormitory at Florida A&M named after Young. He received two honorary degrees: a Litt. D. from Talladega College in 1915, and an LL.D. from Selma University in 1923.

CHAPTER 7

Summation of a Life

Any summation and assessment of Nathan B. Young's life and career must recognize that he had a well-developed philosophy of life and a strong value system. Young greatly valued family and held deep religious beliefs. Nathan Young also very much believed in equality of educational opportunity, race pride, public service, and the economic development of the black community.

Young believed that the first thing the schools should do for the race was to help its members become economically independent. Blacks had to be taught to work together, Young thought, because slavery had not been a good school for teaching either collective action or economic wisdom. Blacks had come out of slavery with nothing, and their poverty was compounded by their ignorance of reading, writing, and counting. These historical facts and Young's association with Booker T. Washington and R. R. Wright encouraged him to promote the ideals of economic self-sufficiency, race pride, and public service as major aspects of his life.

After the Civil War, most blacks went into the same lines of work that they had performed in slavery. The vast majority had worked the land, so they now had to make a living as sharecroppers and renters. Of these agricultural workers, only a fortunate few managed to own their own farms. Other black workers who had been the house servants and former slave artisans followed their earlier trades and became carpenters, blacksmiths, brick masons, and wheel-wrights. Others went to the urban centers, where the women washed, cooked, and served in household employment and the men, facing the competition of white workmen, often had to settle for common laborer work such as porters, janitors, waiters, longshoremen, rail-road workers, and semi-skilled industrial employees.[1]

By the 1880s and 1890s the race question was being raised, much as it had been used in the 1870s to overthrow the Reconstruction governments in the South. Partly because of the Populist move-ment, the race question was being exploited by the conservative Democrats to maintain their power. Racial tensions were greatly in-creased, and blacks were made the scapegoats. The movement to es-tablish white supremacy and to keep the blacks in their place was in full swing. There was increased violence against blacks and the rise of Jim Crow restrictions of all kinds.[2]

As part of the rising Jim Crow restrictions, black workers, small-business owners, and professionals met increasing competition and hostility from the white community. The hard economic times caused whites to seek a livelihood in jobs that had previously been reserved for blacks. The barber trade is a good example. The trade was dominated by blacks before and right after the Civil War. Then, as economic conditions changed, the black barber's white patrons abandoned him for a white barber. The same thing could be said for owners of restaurants, hotels, and a variety of other businesses.

Black business and professional classes had to increasingly de-pend on the patronage of the black community. The leaders of the black race, from conservatives such as Booker T. Washington to radicals such as W. E. B. DuBois, called upon their people to sup-port black businesses. In part, these efforts were in response to the rise of white racism, with its discrimination and segregation. The concepts of self-help, race pride, and economic self-sufficiency had always been an important part of black life since the end of the Civil War. In fact, these ideals could be traced back to Africa and the colonial period. Now, however, they took on even greater im-portance after 1880.

1. John Dittmer, *Black Georgia in the Progressive Era, 1900–1920*, 23–29, 30–33.
2. C. Vann Woodward, *Origins of the New South*, 257, 259. Woodward, *The Strange Career of Jim Crow*, 61–63, 84–87, 96–99.

The period of 1880 to 1930 was marked by the growth of black business enterprises. The Fourth Annual Atlanta Conference on Negro Life in 1898 was centered around the theme of blacks in business. Blacks were urged to support black businesses and professionals.[3]

In 1900, Booker T. Washington founded in Boston the National Negro Business League. This league encouraged the development and advancement of black business through a network of local chapters throughout the country. The league's annual meetings became clearinghouses from which black business persons could learn from one another and develop a sense of race pride. The league was built upon the ideals of self-help and economic self-sufficiency, as well as race pride. Soon local chapters of the league began organizing in a number of Southern cities.[4]

Despite the spirit that had called forth the league, most black businesses were small and financially weak. Most blacks lacked capital, training, and experience. Because of the hostility of the white community, moreover, black business owners had to band together to get the needed capital for their businesses. In response to the need of black business for capital and general self-sufficiency, a number of savings banks began to be established.[5]

A pioneering black business that Young was involved with was the Alabama Penny Saving and Loan Company of Birmingham. This was one of the most successful banking firms established by blacks, as it eventually established three separate branches and stayed in operation for twenty-five years.[6]

The Alabama Penny Savings and Loan Company was organized in 1890. Although it was the fourth black-owned and operated bank to be organized in the United States, by 1907 it was the second largest in terms of both capital and deposits. Much of this success was due to the fact that the bank encouraged savings and capital accumulation among blacks as a sign of race pride and advancement.

---

3. W. E. B. DuBois, ed., *The Negro in Business,* 50. See Juliet E. K. Walker, *The History of Black Business in America,* especially chap. 7, "The Golden Age of Black Business, 1900–1930," 182–224.

4. August Meier, *Negro Thought in America,* 124–26.

5. Ibid., 143.

6. Young, "A Fifty Year Jaunt," 4–5.

The bank was founded and presided over by the Reverend W. R. Pettiford. He had been born a free Negro in North Carolina before the Civil War and was educated in Alabama at the State Normal School at Marion. A former schoolteacher and an active Baptist minister, Pettiford was also a close associate of Booker T. Washington and was active in the field of real estate. All of this eventually culminated in his founding of Alabama Penny and later in his presidency of the Negro Bankers Association. The key to the bank's and Pettiford's success lay in the fact that he tied the development of the black bank business with the advancement of the race and campaigned to educate the black masses to support black-owned businesses.[7]

For his part, Young viewed his support of the bank as a means by which he could help the race gain economic independence, and he thus took an active interest in the bank's activities. Besides investing in the bank, Young became a member of the board of directors in 1907 because he hoped the bank would become one of the great financial institutions in the South.[8]

On January 1, 1913, the Alabama Penny Saving Bank and Trust Company moved into a newly furnished building. The bank had operated successfully for twenty-two years, a span of time considerably longer than average at that time. This, of course, was seen as a great achievement for race pride and the ideals of black economic self-help.

Accordingly, Young and many other longtime patrons of the bank were invited to help celebrate the opening of the new building. At the same time, they were also asked to make as big a deposit as they could, even if it were only for a short time. In this way the bank hoped to make a show of its money deposits on the opening of the new building in an attempt to inspire the race to even greater accomplishments.[9]

During the same period, Pettiford wrote to Young and the other

7. Meier, *Negro Thought in America,* 143.
8. James Blow, "Those Who Trespass Against Us: Based on the Life and Letters of Nathan Benjamin Young." This work is in the form of a historical novel, and largely deals with Young's career at Florida A&M. Concerning Young at Florida A&M, the work is fairly accurate, but when dealing with Young's career elsewhere there are mistaken dates.
9. Ibid., 199.

stockholders, urging that they increase their shares and deposits. He also asked them to get their friends and family to invest in the bank as well. The bank had passed the half-million-dollar mark in volume of business, Pettiford noted, and had a capital stock of one hundred thousand dollars. This clearly proved, he suggested, that blacks could run a bank and earn a profit for stockholders.[10]

Not too long after, however, the bank overextended itself in real estate and other ventures. Such speculations were common during this period, but the result in this case was the bank's failure in 1915.[11]

Although he lost money in the venture, Young was proud of his role in the development of this institution. The bank had encouraged and fostered many other black businesses throughout Alabama in its long period of service. Young's racial pride was maintained even in the bank's failure because, as he noted, it had "voluntarily liquidated due to frozen assets—not to dishonesty—frozen morals."[12]

Another pioneering black enterprise that Young helped to establish was the Standard Life Insurance Company of Atlanta. The establishment of black insurance companies was an example of the self-help, economic self-sufficiency, and race pride concept that was being emphasized at the start of the twentieth century. Black insurance companies provided services not available from white companies. They also provided capital to start and expand other black businesses.[13]

The development of black insurance companies filled an important need. Before these companies, blacks had to pay excessive rates or insure themselves through lodges and fraternal societies. In fact, one of the most important functions of fraternal orders for blacks was to provide death benefits for its members. The lodges and fraternities were very active in this area because blacks generally could not get insurance from the white mainline companies. Some white-

10. Ibid., 200. This shows a remarkable support of black savings banks. In 1899 only four out of 450 college-educated blacks surveyed said they supported such banks and only 48 had invested in any black business. Du Bois, ed., *The College-Bred Negro*, 94.
11. Meier, *Negro Thought in America*, 143.
12. Young, "A Fifty Year Jaunt," 5.
13. Ibid.

owned insurance companies, moreover, were formed overnight simply to exploit the black community.

If the black community was not a victim of prejudice in this area, it often lost because of poor business practices. Incompetency in business was the main problem of the lodge insurance programs. The people who became the treasurers of these lodges were not always the most competent, nor were they always honest. Yet they received millions of dollars from the black community for insurance. In Georgia alone, between 1870 and 1920 blacks paid about $16.5 million to lodges for insurance.[14]

In response to this need for competent and honest insurance companies for blacks, Standard Life Insurance Company of Atlanta was founded in 1912. It was a progressive experiment in racial cooperation; in less than ten years of its founding, Standard Life became the largest black company in the industry. Later it became one of the first legal reserve black companies, and, as we look back on it now, we note its significance as the final step in the development of the black insurance industry: an insurance company that achieved the same level of stability and profit as the most established white insurance companies of its time.[15]

The man most responsible for making Standard Life the leading black insurance company in the United States was Herman Perry, its founder and president. Under Georgia laws, a standard legal reserve insurance company had to have $100,000 in capital within two years to receive a state charter. When Perry began organizing the company, he had raised only $30,000, all of which he returned to his investors along with 4 percent interest. The next time he raised the full $100,000. Within a short time thereafter, Standard Life had two hundred agents operating in nine Southern states.[16]

Young was one of the original members of the company's board of directors. As such, he enjoyed the association that the company gave him with many intelligent, progressive young black men who were attracted to the company. In fact, his most pleasant memories of visits to Georgia were centered around the board table of

14. Dittmer, *Black Georgia in the Progressive Era,* 44–46.
15. Meier, *Negro Thought in America,* 142–43.
16. Dittmer, *Black Georgia in the Progressive Era,* 44–46.

Standard Life. Here he found confirmation of his life's work of educating the youth of his race. These young men, he knew, would be the future economic leaders of Georgia's black community in the next decade.[17]

In Florida, Young was one of Standard Life's best promoters, as he tried to get many of his friends in on the venture. In January 1913, for example, he wrote to his friend Sparton Jenkins of Apalachicola, urging him to invest in the company. Young spoke of the soundness of the company and listed its various assets. He noted that he personally was "putting every cent" he had and could borrow into the company in order to be in on the ground floor, and he said that, although all open stocks had been sold, he was sure that Mr. Perry, the president, had shares that he was willing to sell.[18]

Young, appealing to race pride, pointed out that a white company was being organized in Birmingham to sell insurance to blacks. He noted this company was putting up black men as fronts and had recently even tried to take over a black bank in Birmingham. Young wanted Standard Life to beat this other company out, and he solicited new inventors—some as important as Emmett Scott, the personal secretary of Booker T. Washington—with this in mind.[19]

Shortly after World War I, however, Standard Life began to run into financial trouble. While Herman Perry was honest, he was also a dreamer. He expanded into several other businesses during the war, and he continued to extend himself when the war was over. The young and talented black managers and accountants whom he had hired advised him against this overexpansion, but Perry was a self-educated and self-made man, and he would not take the advice of his younger associates. He therefore continued to purchase grocery stores, drug firms, laundries, farms, and print shops, and frequently used funds from Standard Life to back up these speculations.

Eventually, several of these speculations failed, and in 1924 Perry

17. Young, "A Fifty Year Jaunt," 4. Meier, *Negro Thought in America,* 153–54.
18. Blow, "Those Who Trepass Against Us," 202–4.
19. Ibid., 204–5. Emmett J. Scott to N. B. Young, letter dated February 3, 1915, Booker T. Washington Papers. In the letter Scott refers to materials sent to him by Young. There is a reference to the selection of directors of the company. Scott says that he will talk to Young at length later about the Standard Life proposition. He ends by saying he is very interested, like Young, "that this company should altogether succeed."

lost control of the insurance company. Within three years Standard Life had been handed over to a white-owned insurance company, and it soon after fell to another black insurance company. When the Great Depression came, Standard Life ceased to function altogether. It was another Young investment that became both a major achievement and an eventual failure in the attempt to create and sustain significant black economic independence.[20]

In 1906 the Florida chapter of the Negro Business League was chartered, holding its first meeting in Jacksonville. At the second annual meeting of the league, in Tallahassee in 1907, the League's president, *Florida Sentinel* editor M. M. Lewey, asked Young to be the speaker before the convention. In accepting, Young showed so much interest in the league's activities that Lewey asked him to attend the national convention scheduled for Topeka, Kansas, later that year.[21]

In a succeeding letter to Young, Lewey explained the program of the Florida Negro Business League: a statement of purpose that was as much Young's as it was the league's. The league knew, Lewey noted, that the majority of the race was still too poor to provide any large measure of support, so it was mostly aimed at developing a sense of racial pride. The league did not "expect any great rush of activity among our people, or enthusiasm in support of our business enterprises at the stage of our material growth." Nevertheless, the Florida League hoped "to awaken as best we can among the masses a sense of duty they owe to business enterprises owned and managed by colored men."[22]

After he became president of Florida A&M in 1901, Young traveled throughout Florida promoting the doctrine of economic independence and black enterprise. Thus he toured the state encouraging potential black businessmen to get the necessary training. They had to become competent in modern business techniques, he noted, if they hoped to be successful. Those interested in going into an economic venture had to search out all the facts surrounding that business; for that reason, there was a great need for extensive business education among the race. More emphasis on efficiency was needed, and a competent businessman had to keep up with the

20. Dittmer, *Black Georgia in the Progressive Era*, 47–48.
21. Blow, "Those Who Trespass Against Us," 195–96.
22. Quoted in ibid., 197.

latest scientific inventions and techniques, which were having a profound effect on business practices and society. In short, Young suggested that businessmen should get together and exchange ideas and experiences.[23]

Young's interest in promoting black businesses was known throughout the state. In fact, he used part of his meager salary to encourage such projects. One Florida-based company that Young supported was the Capital Trust and Investment Company of Jacksonville. This company was organized in 1906 by an energetic and ambitious black businessman, S. H. Hart, and Young became an investor in the company during its first year of operation.[24]

Once Young's interest in black business development was known through his public speaking and his actual investments, he soon began to attract correspondence from individuals who sought his advice and frequently his capital. Thus black businessmen who had investments in various enterprises soon called upon Young for his advice and counsel. Some bankers even asked him to use his influence with state officials in Tallahassee in getting state deposits into their banking concerns.[25]

Before World War I there was an investment fever running through the country. In February 1914, for example, G. H. Bowen, a Savannah, Georgia, real estate dealer, tried to interest Young in putting money into a land development proposition. Similarly, Frank D. Bank, president of the Bay Shore Summer Resort in Virginia, wanted Young to buy shares in the resort at ten dollars a share. In Bank's selling materials he pointed out that the "best people" of Hampton Institute were stockholders, including Major R. R. Moton.[26]

23. Ibid., 192–95.
24. Ibid. Young's efforts to promote black business enterprises and the support of these ventures by the black masses was also winning support for Florida A&M and its programs.
25. Ibid.
26. Ibid., 210–12. R. R. Moton of Hampton was a good friend of Young and was able to be friendly with Booker T. Washington and a number of radicals such as John Hope of Atlanta Baptist College (later Morehouse). Moton would follow Washington as president of Tuskegee. Before Washington's death, Morton tried unsuccessfully to reach an understanding between Washington and the NAACP radicals. He did get Washington to approve ten thousand dollars for Morehouse from the Carnegie Fund. Meier, *Negro Thought in America,* 114, 183–84, 209, 240.

There was also a lot of speculation going on in the state of Florida, and Young received a couple of interesting investment offers from within that state. In June 1914, for example, Nathan W. Collins, principal of the Florida Baptist College in Jacksonville, tried to interest Young in investing in the new Exchange Bank. Young was interested in the bank, but his small salary prevented him from investing in it. Two years later Young received another investment offer from a group of Jacksonville businessmen who had formed the West Indies Trading and Transportation Company. This was an organization of black business investors headed by George E. Taylor, a well-known black political figure, and the company also had a wealthy white Jacksonville lumber dealer backing the venture. Young was asked to become a director or vice president in the company, but he declined, probably because he did not have the money to invest and because he wanted to be careful about lending his good name to attract potential investors to a company that he did not know much about.[27]

While Young could not always invest money in black businesses, the idea of racial economic independence almost became an obsession with him. During the last decade of his life he even wrote a proposal for incorporating into the black secondary and collegiate institutions a teaching project with this aim. Young started by saying that the most serious handicap the black race faced was its economic poverty. He criticized both the secondary schools and the colleges for emphasizing the literary and professional to the exclusion of commerce and business. These schools should seek to interest more students in business careers. To schools that emphasized industrial and vocational training, he said such training should go "beyond the mere use of tools" and finding employment at the "lower levels of industrial life." Real economic independence came in the areas of trade and commerce, Young noted, even as he then observed that the race, as a group, presently lacked the spirit of enterprise. Although there were historical reasons for this lack of business initiative among blacks, Young felt that the proper educational program would correct the situation. If blacks successfully entered business, they would get their political and civil freedoms. Political power was tied to economic power. "To rule is to own," he noted.

27. Blow, "Those Who Trepass Against Us," 210–12.

The schools must instill in black students ideas that make them *"business-minded, race appreciative,* and *public spirited."*[28]

In encouraging black youths to engage in business careers, Young made references to the skilled trades as being a "blind alley" because of race prejudice, an obvious reference to the segregation of trade unions. Business careers would show the youth "that their own group offers potential business opportunities, that would go far toward gaining for the group economic independence." Successful black businessmen should be brought into the classroom to serve as an example and inspiration.

The "big job" of the schools, continued Young, was to teach black youths "to have an abiding faith in themselves, in their ability to have and to hold, and to become worth while in all life's activities, and to get from under the shadow of 'inferiority-complex.'" Young went on, giving more his philosophy of race than an endorsement of a business career:

> In a word, the Negro youth must be taught to think black, to feel that whatever is common to all forward looking people may not be alien to the Negro, to think of themselves as highly as they think of others. *That is thinking black.* They must be taught that their race group has not always played an inferior role on the stage of history, that after all, theirs has been no mean contribution to civilization.[29]

Young ended by emphasizing that black youths had to learn how to live collectively. Like all progressive people, they had to learn that no individual or group could live in isolation. He criticized the many black institutions of learning that encouraged their students "to cultivate an attitude of self-effacement" in politics and civil rights. These institutions had to stop "this kind of pussyfooting." Like all other youths, blacks had to learn "business adventure, race

28. N. B. Young, "A Teaching Project toward Economic Independence— A Challenge to Institutions of Learning for Negroes," Young Papers. In an interview Nathan Sweets, emeritus publisher of the *St. Louis American* newspaper said that Nathan B. Young, Sr., suggested he join in this business venture started by Young's son, Nathan B. Young, Jr. Interview in St. Louis, August 1981. The underlining is Young's.

29. Ibid. This statement represents Young's views of life for most of his career. He certainly had assumed this attitude by 1900. He also shows an awareness of the black history movement under Carter G. Woodson.

pride, and active interest in the general welfare." Above all else, they had to develop a sense of direction to help remove the heritage of slavery and move the race to "efficiency and full citizenship." Young especially wanted his own children to follow his lead in the promotion of black economic independence.[30]

Besides economic independence, Young urged an "active interest in the general welfare" of his race and showed his promotion of the general well-being of the black race in many ways. One of the great problems of the black community was health care. In 1914 Booker T. Washington established a National Negro Health Week movement that lasted long after his death. Emphasizing racial pride, Washington hoped to encourage blacks to better safeguard their health. Many black colleges established hospitals and nurse training programs, including Florida A&M. Meharry Medical School, in fact, was born out of the need for black physicians.

After 1900 an anti-tuberculosis movement spread throughout the country. The black population, still largely located in the South, became a part of this movement. Educated leaders such as Young often had to take the lead in such movements because of the lack of black doctors. In early August 1909 Young wrote to Dr. C. P. Wertenbaker of Norfolk, Virginia, and noted that he was planning to organize an Anti-Tuberculosis League for the black citizens of Florida.[31] Wertenbaker had written to Young and asked him to accept the responsibility for the establishment of such an organization. So despite Young's busy schedule as a teaching president of Florida A&M and his business activities, he found the energy to organize such a league. In less than four weeks, therefore, Young had established a provisional committee in and around Jacksonville. By late August he was able to make a progress report on his efforts.

To inaugurate the movement, Young persuaded almost a dozen religious leaders and other professionals to volunteer their services. Even though the religious leaders represented different denomina-

30. Ibid. Young, "A Fifty Year Jaunt," 4–5. Young left among his papers the stock certificates of the Alabama Penny Savings Bank and Trust Company and the Standard Life Insurance Company to encourage his children to follow his example in support of black business.

31. N. B. Young to Dr. C. P. Wertenbaker, August 5, 1909, Wertenbaker Papers, Manuscript Department, University of Virginia Library, Box 2. Wertenbaker was trying to promote and keep up on progress of Anti-Tuberculosis Leagues throughout the South involving the black population.

tions, Young, an active Black Congregationalist, always worked effectively with the leaders of other denominations because he was a believer in race unity in matters of education and general race advancement. Soon, therefore, this newly created Ministers' Union appointed a committee to push the movement throughout that section of Florida.[32]

Young then made the same efforts in different parts of the state. He presented the matter to the last meeting of the Florida Negro Business League in Tampa, and he also spoke before the Florida Teacher's Association (for Negroes) at its annual meeting at De Land. He then continued to further this important organization for the general health and welfare of the black people of Florida in every way that he could.[33]

Young found ways of combining his strong sense of public service with his deep sense of Christian piety. While in Florida, he organized and was pastor of a Black Congregational church in Tallahassee.[34]

He was also very active in the National Convention of Congregational Workers among Colored People. This organization held its first biennial convention in 1906, and its national convention provided a full forum on the activities of Black Congregationalist churches in spreading Christian education and social services. Among his activities with the national convention, then, Young was first vice-president and chairman of the Pilgrim Memorial Fund and president of the convention's ninth biennial session, which met in Chicago in 1922. He then remained active in the National Convention's work for many years thereafter.[35]

Another organizational movement in which Young was involved

32. N. B. Young to Dr. C. P. Wertenbaker, August 26, 1909, Wertenbaker Papers, Box 2.

33. N. B. Young to Dr. C. P. Wertenbaker, January 6, 1910, Wertenbaker Papers, Box 2.

34. Interview with Judge Nathan B. Young, Jr., August 1981, St. Louis.

35. "Official Program of the Eighth Biennial Session of the National Convention of Congregational Workers among Colored People," Atlanta, September 22–26, 1920, 1–7, American Missionary Association Papers, Amistad Research Center, Dillard University. N. B. Young to H. H. Proctor, June 5, 1922, H. H. Proctor to N. B. Young, June 14, 1922, N. B. Young to H. H. Proctor, July 5, 1922, H. H. Proctor to N. B. Young, July 21, 1922, H. H. Proctor to N. B. Young, August 4, 1930, N. B. Young to H. H. Proctor, June 30, 1924, H. H. Proctor to N. B. Young, July 31, 1930, N. B. Young to H. H. Proctor, August 4, 1930, Ibid.

was that of educational associations that had formed throughout the South in the 1890s. Young was president in 1897 of the Alabama State Teachers Association. While he was in Georgia between 1897 and 1901, he was also active with the Georgia State Teacher's Association. Soon after, when Young went to Florida A&M in 1901, he became active in the Florida State Teacher's Association, serving as its third president from 1907 to 1910. Finally, when Young went to Missouri in 1923, he once more became active with the state teachers association and was elected president in 1925.[36]

In general, these state teachers associations aimed at upgrading the training and qualifications of public school teachers, even as they also tried to raise teaching salaries and improve the materials, texts, equipment, and physical structures in the states' schools. For all these reasons, Young was very active in these groups throughout his life.[37]

Besides these various state teachers associations, there were national associations in which Young was also active. The most important was the National Association of Teachers in Colored Schools, which was organized in 1904. Among the founders and early leaders here were Richard R. Wright, J. R. E. Lee, and Young. In its Declaration of Principles, the Association emphasized race pride and self-help, and it also held annual meetings aimed at developing higher educational ideals, better techniques and methods, and more effective professional cooperation.[38]

The twelfth annual session of the association was held in Cincinnati from July 29 to August 1, 1915, and Young, as president of the

36. Wright, *A Brief Historical Sketch*, 46–47. Blow, "Those Who Trepass Against Us," 212.

37. Gilbert L. Porter and Leedell W. Neyland, *The History of the Florida State Teacher's Association*, 32–33, 171. In 1900, of 731 black teachers in the Florida public schools, only 30 were normal school graduates or had some normal school training. In 1907–1908, the average monthly salary of white male teachers was $67.90 and white females $27.22. White male teachers got from a high of $225 to a low of $25 per month, and white females from a high of $118 to a low of $10 a month. Black male teachers salaries ranged from a high of $90 to a low of $15 per month; while black females got from a high of $65 a month to $10. Black school terms were one to two months shorter on average than school terms for whites; per capita expenditures for public schools were $16.07 for whites and $4.63 for blacks.

38. Jones, *Negro Education*, 1, 21, 170–71. Meier, *Negro Thought in America*, 208–9. The 1916 meeting of the association in Nashville was held in connection with the meeting of the annual conference of the presidents of land-grant colleges; another organization that also met with the National

organization at that time, gave the major address. In his speech, entitled "An Upward Departure in Negro Education," he dwelt on the need for a graduate school for blacks in the central South, a radical idea for 1915. To support his concept, Young noted that there were actually no real normal schools or colleges for blacks in the South, because most existing institutions were primarily elementary or secondary schools that were colleges in name only. At best, Young thought, a few of these schools were junior colleges or near colleges.

A standard college and graduate school, Young stated, was needed to meet the educational demands of black students in education, science, and the arts. The Eastern and Western schools were too far from the center of the black population, and they admitted too few blacks in the first place to meet the present need. Furthermore, the South's system of segregated education was against broad training for blacks. Therefore, blacks had to supply their own teachers and their own professionals in the social, commercial, and industrial worlds. Because of the Southern states' very narrow view of the educational needs of blacks, it would be a long time before a public graduate institute would come into being; nor were the black churches and other organizations wealthy enough to adequately support such a group.

Therefore, Young called upon personal or corporate philanthropy to meet this need, either by upgrading some existing black institutions or creating a totally new institution. Once this happened, he said, the undemocratic caste system of Southern segregation would no longer make it impossible "for every man to be educated according to his several abilities, and not according to his race." For "whatever training is common to the entire system of our schools should not be wanting to the schools that are devoted specially to the education of Negroes."[39]

Association was the Council of College Presidents. This group discussed such problems as mission, responsibilities, teacher preparation, and other common problems. A similar organization formed in 1913 was the Association of Colleges for Negro Youths, which dealt with college entrance and graduation.

39. Nathan B. Young, "An Upward Departure in Negro Education," 4–15. Young would write his friend John Hope in 1929 when Atlanta University was formed into a center of black graduate study under Hope to remind him that such a university had been proposed by Young fifteen years earlier.

Throughout his life, Young of course was a professional educator, but he did not confine his "teaching" to the classroom walls. The purpose of education, he felt, was to develop better people in a better society; and thus "education," of necessity, needed to deal with all the needs—economic, physical, and spiritual—of all its "students," especially those who needed it most. Likewise, significant "educators" needed to deal with all these needs as well, and Young, of course, was one of those significant "educators."[40]

Young was awarded honorary degrees: a Doctorate of Letters in 1915 from Talladega College, and from Selma University a Doctorate of Law in 1923, in recognition of his contribution to education.

Nathan B. Young, Sr., was very much a family man. He was the father of seven children, five of whom survived to adulthood. With his first wife, Emma Mae Garrette, of Selma, whom he married December 30, 1891, he had Nathan B., Jr., and Emma. Young's first wife died of fever in 1904. He remarried on November 15, 1905, wedding Margaret A. "Maggie" Bulkley, of Charleston, South Carolina. Frank DeForest, William Henry, and Julia were born during this second marriage. Young was a devoted father who always encouraged the best from his children. Despite his demanding professional activities, he always had time to write encouraging letters to his children. Nathan B. Young, Jr., "Ben," kept all of his father's letters that he began receiving as he pursued and completed studies in law at Yale University. Young continued advising his son as Ben tried to establish a law practice in Birmingham. Establishing a business in the South was especially difficult for a black man, and Young's letters to Ben were filled with encouragement, advice, and support.[41]

When Ben doubted his ability to make it as a lawyer in Birmingham, Young wrote back with what might be called an attitude of

40. Young was a member of W. E. B. DuBois's "Talented Tenth." See Eugene F. Provenzo, Jr., ed., *Dubois on Education,* chap. 5.

41. N. B. Young to Nathan B. Young, Jr., January 23, February 25, 1919, Nathan B. Young Jr. Collection, St. Louis University Archives, Pope Pius XII Memorial Library. Hereafter cited as Nathan B. Young Jr. Collection. The full names and birth dates of Young's children are Nathan B. Young, Jr., November 27, 1894; Emma Garrette, July 1, 1900; Julia Bulkley, February 28, 1908; Frank DeForest, December 7, 1909; and William Henry, November 30, 1912.

tough love. "I am sure," he wrote, "you are not going to be a quitter." You are "going to stay in Birmingham till you succeed, and that to as a lawyer. It can be done and you are going to do it." These letters were often followed by ones with more tender tones such as, "I am with you as long as you are with yourself. If you get against yourself, nobody can help you."[42]

Young's advice to Ben replicated his personal philosophy. In 1921, when he began having trouble at Florida A&M, Young wrote to Ben to inform him that he intended to fight it out "to the last ditch." Young was not a quitter, despite the fact that he could have simply left Florida for a presidency he was offered in Dover, Delaware.[43]

Young continued to correspond with his son about his and other family members' travels, the situation at Florida A&M, and to offer him encouragement in his law practice and his recently established newspaper. Young wrote that he hoped that the "paper may stay on top." Regarding Ben's law practice, Young wrote, "Your exhibit is not a bad one in view of all the circumstances in your case. My only suggestion is that you keep progressive and aggressive in a legal way. Keep on your professional ball . . ."[44]

Young's daughter, Emma, called Gareth, kept in close contact as well. In 1921 she surprised the family with a visit during a Florida A&M–Talladega College football weekend. She had recently recovered from an illness. He told his son in a letter of a forthcoming trip to attend a YMCA conference. He also asked him to check on his grandma's property. Young's mother was living with Young in Florida and was well.[45]

When the Florida politicians finally removed Young from the presidency of Florida A&M, he notified Ben that he would visit him soon and look for a place to buy a home. Instead, Young accepted the presidency at Lincoln University. From Jefferson City he continued to

42. N. B. Young to Nathan B. Young, Jr., August 23, October 15, 1919, June 16, 24, 1920, July 18, 1921, Nathan B. Young Jr. Collection.

43. N. B. Young to Nathan B. Young, Jr., June 29, July 7, 16, 1921, Nathan B. Young Jr. Collection.

44. N. B. Young to Nathan B. Young, Jr., September 13, November 22, 1921, Nathan B. Young Jr. Collection.

45. N. B. Young to Nathan B. Young, Jr., November 21, 1921, Nathan B. Young Jr. Collection.

encourage and give career advice to his son. In coming to Missouri, Young laid the ground for Ben's relocation to the state as well. Since Ben had been involved with a newspaper in Birmingham, Young suggested that he get in touch with J. E. Mitchell, the owner of the *St. Louis Argus*. Mitchell, Young told Ben, was "developing a first-class plant . . . in which it might be possible for you to enter, some-day, somehow."[46]

In 1925, when Young began having his first serious trouble with Missouri politicians, he wrote a letter to all his children explaining the situation. Young was not all that hopeful that he would suc-ceed. In fact, he planned to go to St. Louis to look for a possible business venture. In 1926 Young traveled to Tampa. After visiting with a successful lawyer, he suggested Tampa as a possible location for Ben's practice. He advised Ben, however, that he could "get busi-ness in St. Louis" if he "went after it." Young was as much a gadfly for his oldest son as his mother had been for him.[47]

Of course, after Young's removal from the presidency of Lincoln University in 1927, he spent more than a year as Inspector of Negro Schools and returned to Lincoln University in September 1929 until 1931. While in Jefferson City, Young's household included both his mother and mother-in-law. His children visited often and worried when he was fired that his health would be affected. When Young was fired for the last time from Lincoln University in 1931, his daughter Emma, in Pensacola, Florida, wrote to her brother Ben of her concern for their father. Referring to his previous trouble at Lincoln University, she wrote, "What's wrong with Papa and Lin-coln now? He wrote and said he had been fired. I hope he won't worry this time as he did before. I don't believe he could stand it."[48]

Perhaps the greatest tragedy of Young's being fired in 1931 was the fact that he and his loving wife, Maggie, were left impover-ished. The firing came during one of the most severe years of the Great Depression. Young had invested in several businesses that had

46. N. B. Young to Nathan B. Young, Jr., June 15, 26, December 12, 1923, Nathan B. Young Jr. Collection.
47. N. B. Young to "Dear Children," May 5, 1925, N. B. Young to Nathan B. Young, Jr., January 9, 1926, Nathan B. Young Jr. Collection.
48. Emma Young to N. B. Young, February 6, April 14, 1929, Emma Young to Nathan B. Young Jr., April 12, 1931, Nathan B. Young Jr. Collec-tion.

failed. Although he owned real estate in Alabama, Florida, Georgia, and Missouri, he could not sell the land for cash nor could he, without a reliable income, keep up with the properties. Because Young believed that a man should never quit no matter the odds, he left Missouri in search of work.

Maggie Young remained in St. Louis with her son Frank. She vented her frustrations with the situation they were in during their advanced years. Claiming that she would have been a better steward of their money had it been placed in her hands, Maggie complained that she never thought the day would come "that I had no money of my own" even to buy clothes. Despite her complaints, Maggie very much wanted to be together with her husband in their old age. She told Young, "I will be happy, if in a swamp if you find work . . .it won't take much for us to live on if a place to stay is finished we could make it nicely on $100 per month . . ."[49]

Nathan Young shared his professional struggles and battles with his wife. In March 1933, Maggie Young would write her husband that matters "seems to be in a stir at Lincoln University as you said Dr. [William] Thompkin is taking the rein in hand." Thompkin, the black, Democratic political boss of Kansas City, was putting pressure on Lincoln President Charles Florence, a Republican, from his position as head of Lincoln's board of curators. Mrs. Young wrote, "I heard last night that Florence is shaky." In a reference to the educator-politicians within Lincoln University who had worked with outside political forces to undermine her husband's administration, she wished them ill. Referring to Thompkin's activities, she said, "I trust they get Collins and Jason, but they are too slick I think."[50]

If there is a real tragedy to the life of Nathan B. Young, Sr., it is that at the very end he was forced to be apart from his loving wife because of financial struggles. Otherwise, his family life was close, loving, and supportive. In fact, Young only shared details of professional ups and downs with his wife and his oldest son, Ben.

If Young had lived as long as his mother, he and Maggie well might have enjoyed their last years together with financial security. Young's mother lived until 1930 and died in Jefferson City at the

49. Mrs. Maggie Young to N. B. Young [no date], 1933, Nathan B. Young Jr. Collection.

50. Mrs. Maggie Young to N. B. Young, March 5, 1933, Nathan B. Young Jr. Collection.

age of eighty-seven. She died with property in Alabama and enough resources to pay for her own burial. Young died in July 1933 just two years before the coming of Social Security. At least Maggie lived long enough to benefit from this New Deal reform. Young's children ended up well. His oldest son, Ben, purchased, with Nathaniel Sweets, the *St. Louis American.* Besides becoming an influential newspaper publisher, Ben was an important voice in the St. Louis legal community. In addition to establishing an active law practice, Ben went on to serve for seven years as prosecutor in the St. Louis City Courts. Later he was the first black appointed a judge of the Municipal Courts of St. Louis. He also in the 1920s wrote short stories and a novella. In 1937 Ben published *Your St. Louis and Mine,* a history of the local black community. He was an authority on the black history of the area. Ben was also a self-instructed artist who painted many pictures from local and national black history. He was in 1976 named "citizen of the year in St. Louis."

Young's other children were equally successful in their own ways. Frank De Forest Young started in teaching in St. Louis, but ended up in business. He established the highly successful De Forest Wood Products, Inc. William started as a teacher in the St. Louis area as well, but went on to a career in the insurance business. He moved to Kansas City, where he cofounded the Crusade Life Insurance Company. William became a highly respected member of the black community in Kansas City. In 1950 he and his brother Ben published *Your Kansas City and Mine,* an anthology of black Kansas City's achievements.

Both of Young's daughters went into teaching. Emma was an activist in the Florida public schools. Julia taught in North Carolina, St. Louis, and Chicago. Nathan B. Young, Sr., would have been proud of the accomplishments of his children.[51]

An assessment of Young's professional life finds that it was extraordinary. His achievements are especially noteworthy given his very humble beginnings and the many obstacles he faced on his life journey. Nathan was born in slavery during the Civil War. In his early years he only had his mother for support, since he did not

51. Nathan B. Young, Jr., to N. B. Young, March 1, 15, 1929, Nathan B. Young Collection. Josephine Lockhart, "The Young Family, Kansas City; St. Louis, *Proud,* vol. 7, no. 3, 1976/1977, 20–22.

know the identity of his father. Amidst the chaos at the end of the war, his mother made good her escape from slavery with three-year-old Nathan. Susan Smith made her way to near Tuscaloosa, Alabama. Here she established her own home. She met and married Frank Young, who provided for his new family. Young was reared in rural Alabama during the Reconstruction period, and he witnessed some of the most violent activities of the Ku Klux Klan in Alabama. Because of this situation, Young's mother wanted him to receive an education and enrolled him in a small ungraded school. He also spent a short time at what would later be called Stillman Institute. Young's real formal education was at Talladega College, where he received a classical education in the normal school branch. During the summers Young would teach in ungraded rural schools in Alabama and Mississippi. These not always positive experiences would give Young the ambition and drive to be in a more formal educational situation. Upon receiving a diploma from Talladega College, Young took charge of a secondary school in Jackson, Mississippi. Although school officials wanted Young to stay as head of the secondary school, he realized from this experience that he needed more schooling. Having decided to make teaching his career, Young sought better preparation at Oberlin College in Ohio. He received a liberal arts training here, earning a bachelor's degree. Young became the head of a black elementary school in Birmingham, Alabama, while he earned his master's degree in history.

Earlier while Young was at Talladega, an American Missionary Association college, he was much influenced by its president, Henry S. DeForest. Like the leaders of the American Missionary Association, DeForest believed that the primary mission of the college was to educate the leaders of the black population. What was most important was to provide the best education to the "talented tenth." Henry DeForest obviously recognized Nathan B. Young as belonging to the "talented tenth" intellectually, and encouraged his development. In fact, Henry DeForest wanted Young to go to Yale for his further education. Young chose Oberlin mainly because his mother did not want him to go so far from the South, and Oberlin was more affordable than Yale. Of course, the liberal education of Talladega was more than reinforced at Oberlin. Young and DeForest had talked of working together on a campaign to carry common school education throughout the rural South. Unfortunately, Henry

DeForest died in 1896 before he and Young could move forward on this project. It is with this background that Young arrived at Tuskegee Institute.[52]

In 1892 Booker T. Washington employed Nathan B. Young to teach at Tuskegee. Young stayed at Tuskegee for five years and mostly served as the head of the Academic Department. Young admired Washington as an educational leader and administrator. In fact, Young looked upon Washington as a mentor in educational administration. He saw Washington as a great educational leader of blacks. Of course, when Young started at Tuskegee it was before Booker T. Washington became a national figure. After Washington's famous 1895 Atlanta Address, conflict developed between the two. Washington felt the need to impress the white Northern industrialists and Southern white leaders that industrial education was present in every aspect of Tuskegee Institute. The industrialists were pouring significant funding into Tuskegee. Then, too, Booker T. Washington was almost overnight considered the leader of Black America by the most influential white Americans. If all blacks did not consider Washington their leader, they certainly had to recognize that he was the most influential black American. In this context Washington began demanding that all aspects of the curriculum at Tuskegee be vocationalized. In academic courses such as English and mathematics, Washington demanded what he called dovetailing. In English class, students would write essays on the making of bricks. In math class, students used the farm or tin shop as examples in working their problems. Young's liberal arts background made him resist Washington's effort at dovetailing. Washington and Young had been very friendly early on in their relations. In fact, they lived next door to each other at Tuskegee. There was a relationship not only between Washington and Young but also between Mrs. Washington and Mrs. Young. Washington, however, was the principal, and his directions had to be followed. If Young could not follow them, then Washington suggested that Young leave Tuskegee. Young did leave Tuskegee Institute in 1897. Nathan Young left still feeling that he had earned his postgraduate educational administration with Booker T. Washington. Young and Washington maintained a friendly relationship. When Young's first wife died of a

52. Anderson, *The Education of Blacks in the South,* 69.

fever in 1904, Washington wrote him a gracious letter of condolence. After 1901, when Washington was in Florida, Young often served as his host or introduced him to audiences.

In 1897, Young accepted the position of professor of English and history and director of teacher training at Georgia State Industrial College (Savannah State University today). Here he worked cooperatively under Richard R. Wright, Sr. At Georgia State Industrial College, Wright, a graduate of the first class of Atlanta College, was a supporter of a liberal education. In order to make his presidency more acceptable to the college's all-white board of commissioners, Wright carefully tried to balance liberal arts with the industrial/agricultural curriculum. With Wright's keeping Latin and Greek in the curriculum and the general weakness of the industrial education program, the Northern industrialists and their sometime organ, the General Education Board, would not put funding into Georgia State Industrial College. Soon the board of commissioners began putting increased pressure on Wright to emphasize the vocational/industrial over the liberal/literary curriculum. By the time Young left Georgia State Industrial College, he had become disillusioned by the efforts of the white Southerners on the board of commissioners to proscribe black education to agriculture and the trades.[53]

In 1901, Young was called to serve as the second president of Florida Agricultural and Mechanical College. The person most responsible for hiring Young was the long-serving superintendent of public schools, William N. Sheats. Sheats was a strong advocate of Booker T. Washington. At Florida A&M, Young tried to balance the agricultural and vocational education program with a liberal arts program. What Young really wanted to do was develop Florida A&M into a standard four-year liberal arts college with a normal school program and an agricultural and industrial program. Even though in his twenty-two years at the head of Florida A&M Young continuously moved in this direction, he never obtained his goal. He was largely frustrated because most of the funding coming into the school was for the expansion of the agricultural and industrial program, not the liberal arts program. One of the main regular sources of outside funding was the federal government under the Morrill Act of 1890. All of this funding was for the development of

53. Ibid., 122–23.

the agricultural and industrial programs. The other main source of revenue was the state of Florida. Here, again, most of the funding for Florida A&M was directed at the development of his agricultural and industrial programs. Despite the lack of funding, Young moved forward with his liberal arts model. He was always careful to keep the development of the school programs strictly within the letter of the law. Cleverly, he would often advance his liberal arts model under the mantel of the normal school mission of Florida A&M. Young was fortunate that for most of his twenty-two years as president of Florida A&M, William N. Sheats was superintendent of Florida's public schools. Sheats had many of the prejudices and bias about blacks of the average white-educated Southerner, but he believed in quality of education and instruction above all else. Therefore, he believed that black teachers should adhere to the same standards as white teachers. Sheats advocated quality instruction in all of Florida's public schools. Young pushed his liberal arts program in the name of providing qualified black instructors for the black public schools of Florida.

Yet Young had to always struggle against a hostile racial climate in Florida. His son Ben recalled seeing, as a student at Florida A&M, black chain gangs working outside the gates of the school. After World War I, the racial and political climate became even more intolerant. With poor economic conditions, especially in rural areas, and increased racial violence, blacks were migrating to the cities and out of state. Given this situation, Florida's political establishment was more determined that blacks only receive agricultural and vocational education. When federal vocational authorities informed state officials, especially the recently elected governor, that Florida A&M was promoting a liberal arts curriculum, they moved to stop it. Young, too, had to go. Later Young wondered if he might have been able to stay at Florida A&M had he been more diplomatic. It is unlikely, though, that there was any compromise which could have changed the outcome. The governor, federal vocational agents, and Young's internal opposition wanted to turn Florida A&M back from any aspirations of college-level work to an agricultural and industrial vocational school not much above the high school level. After Young's dismissal, Florida A&M went through a long rough patch. Fortunately, Young had always kept the school's development within the law. Then, too, Young had developed support for the school's existing program among the college's alumni and Florida's black community. The alumni and friends of Florida A&M, recognizing the value of Young and his program, saw to it that no lasting harm was done to Florida A&M and its programs.[54]

When Nathan B. Young accepted the presidency of Lincoln University in 1923, he hoped to create the first-class black institution of higher education that he had called for in his 1915 presidential address to the National Association of Teachers in Colored Schools, "An Upward Departure in Negro Education." In Missouri Young found a reform governor, Arthur Hyde, who was in tune with the aspiration of the black community to convert Lincoln University into a standard, accredited institution of higher learning. With a majority of the board of curators in accord with these aspirations, Young was able to quickly start moving the school in that direction. With Young's twenty-two years of experience at Florida A&M, he knew what needed to be done. He improved the faculty, reorganized the school, and upgraded its curriculum. Learning from his Florida experience, he moved to get Missouri's black community behind his program for Lincoln University.[55]

In Missouri, Young also sought out the support of the liberal white community. He was able to gain this support by explaining the shortcomings in state support for black education at the college, secondary, and elementary level. Particularly distressing was the fact that Missouri had a law that a school district did not have to establish a school for blacks unless there were fifteen school-age children in the district. As a consequence, three thousand black school-age children in the state had no schools. There were high schools only in larger towns and cities. Most of these were inadequate. In most Missouri communities, blacks were not provided educational opportunities beyond the eighth grade. Lincoln University,

54. Mr. and Mrs. Brogg to Alumni Assoc. FAMC, June 25, 1923, Althea and Kathleen Johnson to E. B. Jones, June 30, 1923, W. A. Rochelle to E. B. Jones, June 29, 1923, Lucille V. Martin, Class '18 to E. B. Jones, June 29, 1923, Dr. W. S. Stevens to E. B. Jones, June 27, 1923, Carrie K. DeVaughan to E. B. Jones, June 26, 1923, W. H. L. Howard and E. Nelson Welsey to Fellow Alumni Fla. A&M, June 29, 1923, Mrs. Eunice S. Brown Tharp to E. B. Jones, June 27, 1923, Alpha O. Campbell to N. B. Young, April 17, 1929, Nathan B. Young Jr. Collection.

55. N. B. Young to Nathan B. Young, Jr., December 12, 1923, Nathan B. Young Jr. Collection.

of course, should receive the five hundred thousand dollars promised but not made available when its name was changed in 1921.[56]

In some ways, Nathan B. Young was ahead of his time. He believed that the dual system for blacks and whites was expensive, discriminatory, and undemocratic. He also favored the broad liberal arts over agricultural and industrial education for blacks. In Missouri, however, politics was as much of a roadblock for Young and his vision as it had been in Florida.

Because a governor could only serve one four-year term, by 1925 the reform-minded Hyde was replaced by Sam Baker. In Baker's view, Lincoln University was not to aspire to a first-class institution of higher learning, and Nathan B. Young had to be dismissed. With the help of black educator-politicians on campus and off, Baker finally got his way in 1927. As in Florida, Young had put up a fight because he had the general support of the black community. He even turned down job offers elsewhere to stay and fight it out, but it was hopeless. The political deck was stacked against him.[57]

Young was forced by financial necessity to go outside of Missouri and take a position at Knox Institute and Industrial School in Georgia. He also engaged in a speaking tour in Florida over the winter holiday period to improve his financial standing. Fortunately, Young was offered the position of Missouri's state inspector of Negro schools by Charles Lee, the Democratic superintendent of public schools. Young was a lifelong Republican, as most blacks were at this time. In fact, Young's friend, publisher J. E. Mitchell, advised him against taking the position. Mostly likely Mitchell was concerned about Lee's political ambition for governor. Lee promised Young that his position would be nonpartisan.

It is likely that Lee did have some political considerations in offering the inspector position to Young. Lee knew that the black leadership in St. Louis and Kansas City was very upset with the Republican Baker administration. He was also aware that the Democratic machine bosses in St. Louis and Kansas City were attracting

56. N. B. Young, "Remarks before Missouri Conference for Social Welfare, October 13, 1924," *Bulletin Lincoln University*, June 1925.

57. J. E. Mitchell to N. B. Young, May 27, 1927, N. B. Young to Nathan B. Young, Jr., May 28, 1927, Nathan B. Young, Jr., to N. B. Young, May 28, 1927, Marie C. Gillard to J. E. Mitchell, May 1927, Nathan B. Young Jr. Collection.

an ever-increasing number of black voters to the Democratic Party's ranks. Young had good reasons for taking the position. It offered a salary of twenty-four hundred dollars a year, and it reunited him with his family in Missouri. It also allowed Young to make a true survey of black educational opportunities and shortcomings throughout the state. He would not have to depend on official reports put together by someone else. Young would also travel to meet the black educational and community leaders in every corner of the state. Last, Young still hoped to return to Lincoln and complete his dream of establishing a first-class institution of higher education. From his family associates and friends, he knew that Lincoln was a mess under the new regime. He could only hope that in 1928 Missouri would elect a governor who respected the wishes of the black community regarding Lincoln University. So in January 1928 Young began his duties as the state inspector of Negro schools with a view toward getting a fuller picture of black education in the state and of how Lincoln University could improve that situation. The realities of black education in Missouri were grim. Racial discrimination within the state was most pervasive in education. Black teachers were generally paid 25 percent less than their white counterparts. Inadequate facilities were the norm in black schools. In some black schools wooden walls had to be painted black for blackboards. Most schools were overcrowded, and in some cases three students would share one desk. In other schools there were no desks and students sat at wooden benches. And by 1928 there were four thousand black school-age children that had no school available to them.[58]

The 1928 gubernatorial race was won by Henry Caulfield. Caulfield expressed a positive interest in black education, starting with his inaugural address in January 1929. Young was hopeful that Caulfield would do right by black Missourians' educational aspirations. Where Lincoln University was concerned, that would mean a return to the progressive program that he had earlier tried to carry out. Obviously, Young himself was the best person to put over such a program. While hopeful, Young's previous experiences made him aware that the political tide could go against him. To keep his options open at the national level, he communicated with impor-

58. Charles A. Lee to N. B. Young, November 15, 19, 26, 1927, N. B. Young to J. E. Mitchell, November 21, 1927, Nathan B. Young Jr. Collection.

tant black educational leaders. Many of these leaders, such as Robert R. Moton, president of Tuskegee Institute, J. S. Clark, president of Southern University, and John Hope, president of Morehouse College, were also Young's friends. Young even advised Clark that he had developed a series of lectures on educational, economic, and racial uplift which he intended to give at various black colleges throughout the South. Of course, Young knew such a venture would tax his health. Besides, what Young truly hoped to do was return to the presidency at Lincoln. As early as January 1929, Young had suggested to his old friend John Hope that things were breaking his way. Hope thought of Young as an unusual person to be willing, after twenty-two years at Florida A&M, to go into a new situation in another part of the country "and fight it out as you have done." The humorous Hope warned Young against making the mistake "of thinking that it is your brains that are accomplishing the great things that you are doing. Don't kid yourself about your brains. You have some, but not enough to brag about. The thing that you are making it with is this: honesty and a good warm, unselfish heart. Keep to those and you will continue to make it." Suggesting that Young should come to Atlanta for a visit, Hope said, "I have a bed that will hold you in spite of your pounds . . . a room . . . to yourself, so that you and the two Hopes may all three snore to their hearts content without disturbing anyone else."[59]

Nathan B. Young had enough political experience to know that he had to campaign to get the presidency at Lincoln. In 1928, Young had encouraged his son Ben and former Lincoln University graduate Nathaniel Sweets to buy the then year-old *St. Louis American.* Although Joseph E. Mitchell, publisher of the competing *St. Louis Argus,* was a friend and supporter, Young thought St. Louis could use another black newspaper. Besides running the newspaper, Ben began promoting his father among black political leaders in St. Louis. Young also communicated directly with black leaders who were thought favorably disposed toward him and the program he had tried to put in place at Lincoln. Nathan Young also put forth a plan to Representative Walthall Moore to remove Lincoln University from politics by having its board of curators reorganized on the

59. Robert R. Morton to N. B. Young, January 31, 1929, N. B. Young to J. S. Clark, February 1, 1929, J. S. Clark to N. B. Young, January 24, February 5, 1929, John Hope to N. B. Young, January 20, 1929, Nathan B. Young Jr. Collection.

same basis as that of the University of Missouri and the other state colleges. He also enlisted the support of the Lincoln University St. Louis alumni in this effort. Young, however, knew that Governor Caulfield's appointments to Lincoln's board of curators would have the greatest say in his being returned to the presidency.[60]

He recommended to Governor Caulfield a program to raise the quality of Lincoln University and that the good Hyde appointees who had supported his progressive program be reappointed. Young kept his good friend, former Lincoln University business manager Irving C. Tull, informed of all that happened at Lincoln through letters and newspaper clippings. As Governor Caulfield began making new appointments to Lincoln University's board, Young made contact with both potential and actual appointees. He was careful not to openly seek the presidency while W. B. Jason and current Lincoln business manager Duke Diggs tried to hold on to their positions. Young also made it clear that he understood the problems facing the university and that he had a program to solve those difficulties. He also pointed out that his nearly two years as inspector of Negro schools gave him an outstanding perspective on the general status of black education at all levels throughout the state. Young also made clear to curator Dr. J. Edward Perry of Kansas City that he had the physical strength to carry out his program.[61]

Young, of course, was reappointed as president of Lincoln in September 1929. He immediately began trying to obtain full accreditation of Lincoln University by having the liberal arts program recognized by the North Central Association. The university's physical facilities, however, were still inadequate. This was especially true in the sciences. The college also still needed more faculty with graduate degrees. Young also renewed his efforts to remove the school from politics by having the board of curators reorganized on the same basis as the University of Missouri. Wathall Moore was able to get a bill through the Missouri House of Representatives to

60. Nathan B. Young, Jr., to N. B. Young, no date [1929] and March 18, 1929, George B. Vashon to N. B. Young, January 10, 1929, N. B. Young to O. O. Nance, February 1, 1929, Nathan B. Young Jr. Collection.

61. N. B. Young to I. C. Tull, February 1, 1929, I. C. Tull to N. B. Young, January 12, 24, February 20, March 11, 20, April 9, 15, May 10, 30, 1929, Mrs. A. J. Tull to N. B. Young, no date [1929] and April 1929, William H. Holloway to N. B. Young, April 8, 1929, C. H. Kirshner to N. B. Young, March 2, 1929, J. B. Coleman to N. B. Young, April 13, 1929, N. B. Young to Dr. J. Edward Perry, May 2, 1929, Nathan B. Young Jr.Collection.

that effect. In the Missouri Senate, for some reason Young enlisted the support of Jefferson City Democrat Phil Donnelly. As later activities would show, Senator Donnelly was not interested in removing Lincoln University from political interference. In December 1933 Donnelly would write to Governor Park claiming that he was often called upon in reference to the "difficulties at Lincoln University." With his letter he enclosed a list of "Persons Employed at Lincoln University, other than the Faculty." This list of employees gave their position, former residence, and political affiliation. There were twenty-one people listed, from the president and business manager down to the janitors. The senator noted "that they are practically all Republicans. It seems to me that there is ample justification for more Negro Democrats to be employed in this institution." He claimed that conditions were not very good at Lincoln. There had recently been a strike by the students, and there was "dissention" between the students and President Charles Florence. There was trouble between the faculty and the president. He ended his letter by expressing hope that "something satisfactorily" could be worked out for "these people and the best interest of Lincoln University." Five days later, Charles A. Lee, superintendent of public schools, wrote a letter marked "Personal" to Governor Park. He stated there was a strong effort by some to inject politics into the administration of Lincoln. While a believer in party government, Lee felt that in regard to state educational institutions, "Party politics should be kept out of the picture." He felt that "Lincoln University should be conducted on the same high plane as our state university." Apparently, Governor Park agreed with Lee, since no changes in the Lincoln University administration occurred for another five years."[62]

Nathan Young was successful enough that on June 14, 1930, Mrs. Julia G. Curtis, secretary to Lincoln's board of curators, informed Young that at its last meeting the board had decided to retain him as president "for the scholastic year 1930–1931 at a salary of $4,000 for 12 months." But even before January 1931 there were forces at work to push Young out of the presidency for a second and final time. There were still members of the faculty and staff promoting their own self-interest and ambitions who wanted Young out. While

62. Phil M. Donnelly to Guy B. Park, December 14, 1933, Charles A. Lee to Guy B. Park, December 19, 1933, Park Papers.

Young identified Jason and Collins, there were others as well. C. G. Williams of the Baker era was replaced by J. B. Coleman of Columbia, Missouri. Young recognized that Coleman had henchmen and henchwomen inside Lincoln working against him. In January 1931 Ben Young wrote his father that he had learned from confidential sources that Coleman was about to be indicted for overissue of stocks. Ben thought he should be the one to resign. The influential St. Louis lawyer Homer G. Phillips agreed with Ben's position, and was to look into the matter. Sweets had called Lee to warn him about Coleman. Lee told Sweets of the different charges that Coleman was pressing against Young—"teacher's failure, too many committees, etc." Lee wanted Young to get rid of "disloyal teachers." Young did not do so. Coleman's grand jury indictment did not happen. Also, Dr. J. D. Elliff of Columbia wanted Young to pour Lincoln University resources into Dalton Vocation School. Coleman also supported the Dalton School. Once more, Young had to fight off the attack of the combination of black and white educators and politicians who wanted a lesser Lincoln University devoted primarily to the agricultural, industrial, and normal school model. Ben was now the one encouraging his father not to be a quitter. Ben would tell his father, "I trust you are holding firm. Don't talk of giving up. . . . I think some of your getting tired talk has made them bolder . . . You are going to stay with them and with a punch!"

Young pushed uncompromisingly toward his dream of establishing an accredited bachelor of liberal arts degree at Lincoln University, and he was dismissed without a hearing. The educational aspirations of the black community were ignored. In fact, Young was shortchanged a thousand dollars, since the board ended his service to Lincoln University with the June 1 commencement. He was denied the salary from June 1 to September 1, 1931, called for in his contract. Young now had to focus on getting the thousand dollars owed him. He tried with the aid of his son Ben to use both political influence and the threat of legal action to get his money.[63]

While Young hated to see Lincoln dragged down by politics, he had devoted his energy to finding useful employment. He apparently did not have any idea at first of the difficulty of that task. In

63. J. G. Curtis to N. B. Young, June 4, 1930, Nathan B. Young, Jr., to N. B. Young, January 12, 1931, N. B. Young to Nathan B. Young, Jr., May 4, 18, June 1931, J. B. Coleman to N. B. Young, June 1931, Nathan B. Young Jr. Collection.

mid-May 1931 he told Ben that he was offered a place at Western University in Kansas City, but he wanted to wait and see what turned up. Western was a small religious school that probably could not have offered Young much of a salary. Young's son Frank was unemployed and his youngest, William, was still in school at Lincoln. As time passed, Young's financial situation worsened and his employment possibilities were no better. He sent out inquiries to his friends throughout the country. He looked into the teacher placement business with Southern Colored Teacher's Agency without success. He took a train to Kansas City to look into a position with the Urban League. He even asked some of his friends in Kansas City to look into job possibilities for him. Young wired John R. E. Lee, president of Florida A&M, and a couple of influential educational leaders to put in a word for him with the head of the National Urban League, Eugene K. Jones in New York City. This was all to no avail. Young was very discouraged. He wrote to Ben, "It begins to look as if I am down and out . . . Looks very much like I am in educational discard—sunk." He mailed out "S.O.S." to several black colleges proposing a series of lectures on teaching. He knew this would mean a lot of travel for very little money. It was a race "for mere existence for me from now on a hectic end to a long service." Young, however, still had his pride and dignity, saying "it's all in a days work, I did my best to render a good days work." Young was still in good physical health if mentally and spiritually down.[64]

He was forced to travel and lecture for the National Association of Teachers in Colored Schools, followed by traveling and selling for Carter G. Woodson's Association for Study of Negro Life and History. In late December 1932 Young would write Ben that he had decided he could not "carry on the Woodson proposition, and I am winding up the North Carolina campaign. The traveling is too great and financial collecting end is more than I can meet." He was thinking of getting into "something else before my health is seriously impaired." Earlier in Raleigh, North Carolina, Young had experienced a "sick spell," and he knew that he needed to slow down. He was still hoping to get the thousand dollars owed him by Lincoln. His daughter in Tampa asked him to spend the holidays with her. By June 1933, Young was confined to a bed. The doctor in

64. W. B. Baker to N. B. Young, September 30, 1931, N. B. Young to N. B. Young, Jr., May 16, September 30, October 3, 1931.

Tampa was dehydrating him. Young told Ben that he was doing fine. His illness was a case of "overwork and overworrying—especially over worrying." The highly religious Young felt he had been blessed with a strong constitution or his health would have broken much earlier. Young wrote that "The Lord has been good to me. He brought me deliverance out of all of my troubles somehow." Young would die a month later.[65]

In conclusion, Nathan B. Young's educational adventures provide an opportunity to see the important forces that both shaped and undermined the development of black higher education during the late nineteenth and early twentieth century. An advocate of liberal arts education for blacks, Young had to fight powerful forces that saw elementary agricultural and industrial education as best for Black America. While Young's foes frustrated his educational ideas for black Americans in the short run, in the end his vision prevailed. Despite the best efforts of Young, the actions of racist white state officials, trustees of black colleges, and black educator-politicians in Alabama, Georgia, Florida, and Missouri were successful for a time in limiting the curricula of publicly supported black educational institutions in the South and Midwest to basic training in agriculture, industry, and teaching. While at times unsuccessful, Young's efforts were not futile. He kept the vision of first-class standard institutions of higher learning alive among like-minded faculty, students, and supporters in the black community. Nathan B. Young was a brave, farsighted black educator who laid the groundwork for the emergence of genuine collegiate institutions after 1930. Young's efforts were supported by increasingly assertive black communities that demanded quality education for its youth. By the 1920s blacks were determined that they should determine for themselves the nature and curricula of their institutions of higher learning. The battles that Nathan B. Young fought at Florida A&M and Lincoln University were to provide black youth with the same educational opportunities as white youth. Young had the support of enlightened white educators, and especially in Missouri of a few enlightened white politicians. Finally, the leaders of the white community would be convinced that the education of black youth could not be held to a narrow model of agricultural, vocational,

65. N. B. Young to Nathan B. Young, Jr., April 24, June 9, 1933.

and normal school education. Florida A&M and Lincoln University were allowed to develop as first-class standard institutions of higher learning. In both Florida A&M and Lincoln University, there was such uproar about Young's removals that highly educated replacements had to be put in his place. At Florida A&M, John R. E. Lee served from 1924 to 1944 and fulfilled Young's blueprint and dream of a four-year accredited liberal arts program. At Lincoln University, Charles W. Florence, who was working on his Ph.D. at Harvard University, was appointed president. In 1934, Lincoln University received full accreditation from the North Central Association for its bachelor of liberal arts program. Florence would remain president from 1931 to 1937. He was replaced by Sherman D. Scruggs, who remained president from 1938 until 1956 and the coming of integration. During the late 1930s and 1940s, Lincoln University was known as the Black Harvard of the Midwest. Nathan B. Young might have died poor in terms of worldly possessions, but he was rich in terms of accomplishments. His vision prevailed.

Primary Sources

UNPUBLISHED COLLECTIONS AND MANUSCRIPTS

Amistad Research Center, Dillard University, New Orleans:
  American Missionary Association Papers.
  Henry Hugh Proctor Papers.
Atlanta University, Atlanta. John Hope Papers.
Florida A&M University, Tallahassee. Nathan B. Young Collection.
Joint Collection–University of Missouri, Western Historical
    Manuscript Collection and State Historical Society of
    Missouri Manuscripts:
      Thomas Frazier Baker Papers.
      Charles Jasper Bell Papers.
      Marion T. Bennett Papers.
      James T. Blair Papers.
      Doris Crump Bradshaw Papers.
      William Clark Breckenridge Papers.
      A. S. J. Carnahan Papers.
      Roy Emerson Curtis Papers.
      John M. Dalton Papers.
      Phil M. Donnelly Papers.
      Joseph D. Elliff Papers.
      Sarah Guitar Papers.
      Herbert S. Hadley Papers.
      Charles M. Hay Papers.
      Arthur M. Hyde Papers.
      Frank M. Karsten Papers.

James Perston Kem Papers.
Ralph F. Lozier Papers.
Missouri Association for Social Welfare Papers.
Earl F. Nelson Papers.
Guy B. Parks Papers.
Vivian E. Phillips Papers.
H. E. Slusher Papers.
Forrest Smith Papers.
George A. Spencer Papers.
Lloyd C. Stark Papers.
University of Missouri Papers: Committee on Accredited
Schools and Colleges; Graduate School; President's
Office.
Nathan B. Young Papers.
Library of Congress, Washington, D.C.:
Jebez L. M. Curry Papers.
National Association for the Advancement of Colored
People Papers.
Robert Ogden Papers.
George Foster Peabody Papers.
Mary Church Terrell Papers.
Robert H. Terrell Papers.
Booker T. Washington Papers.
Carter G. Woodson Papers.
Lincoln University, Jefferson City, Mo.:
W. E. B. Du Bois Papers, Schomburg Collection
(microfilm).
Scrapbooks.
Missouri Historical Society, St. Louis:
Edward F. Goetra Papers.
Governors of Missouri Papers.
National Archives, Washington, D.C. U.S. Department of
Agriculture Collection. Office of the Secretary
Correspondence File, 1906–1929.
Oberlin College Archives, Oberlin, Ohio:
Henry C. King Papers.
James Monroe Papers.
Saint Louis University Archives, St. Louis. Nathan B. Young, Jr.
Collection

Southern Historical Collection, Chapel Hill, N.C. William Sheats
    Papers (microfilm).
Talladega College Archives, Talladega, Ala. Negro Education
    Papers.
Tuskegee Institute, Tuskegee, Ala. Tuskegee Institute Collection.
University of Virginia, Charlottesville. Dr. C. P. Wertenbaker
    Papers.
Washington University, St. Louis. Urban League of St. Louis
    Papers, John Thomas Clark File, 1926–1949.
Young, Nathan B., Jr. "My Eight Great Grands Ago."

UNPUBLISHED OFFICIAL MINUTES, REPORTS, AND RECORDS

Greene, Lorenzo J. "Needs of Negroes of Missouri in Respect to
    Education." Report, 1936 (mimeograph). Lincoln University
    Archives.
"Minutes of the Board of Control of the State Institutions of
    Higher Learning," 1905–1925. State Archives, Florida.
"Minutes of the Board of Curators of Lincoln University,"
    1921–1940. Lincoln University Archives.
"Minutes of the Board of Regents of Lincoln Institute,"
    1879–1921. Lincoln University Archives.
"Minutes of the Executive Committee of the Board of Curators of
    Lincoln University," 1921–1940. Lincoln University Archives.
"Minutes of the Weekly General Faculty Meeting and Prudential
    Committee," 1906–1911. Florida A&M University Black
    Archives.
"North Central Association of Colleges and Secondary Schools,
    Missouri Reports," Joint Collection–University of Missouri,
    Western Historical Manuscript Collection and State Historical
    Society of Missouri.
Oberlin College. Official Papers and Records. Oberlin College
    Archives.
———. "Records of Phi Delta Literary Society." Oberlin College
    Archives.
Savage, Sherman W. "The Workers of Lincoln University," Pts. 1
    and 2. Lincoln: University of Missouri, 1951 (mimeograph).
    Lincoln University Archives.

PUBLISHED OFFICIAL REPORTS, PUBLICATIONS

Baldwin, Roger N. *Report of the Committee on the Problems of Negroes of the Missouri Conference for Social Welfare.* Springfield, n.p., 1914.

Florida A&M University. *College Arms.* Monthly publication. Tallahassee. 1905–1920.

————. *General Catalogue for Florida State Normal and Industrial College 1900–01.* Tallahassee: Florida State Normal and Industrial College, 1900.

Foster, Richard B. *Historical Sketch of Lincoln Institute.* Jefferson City, Mo.: Lincoln Institute, 1871.

Lincoln University. *Catalogues.* Various issues, 1879–1938.

Lincoln University Quarterly. Various issues, 1918–1928.

Lincoln University. *University Record,* New Series, 1923–1925.

Oberlin College. *Oberlin Triennial and Quinquennial 1889, 1900–1905.* Oberlin College Archives, Catalogues.

Official Program of the Eighth Biennial Session of the National Convention of Congregational Workers among Colored People. Atlanta, September 22, 26, 1920, 1–7. American Missionary Association Papers. Amistad Research Center, Dillard University, New Orleans.

Talladega College Annual Catalog, 1882–83. Talladega College Archives.

Talladega College. *Catalogue of Talladega College, 1894–95.* Talladega College Archives.

PUBLIC DOCUMENTS

FEDERAL

U.S. Department of Commerce. Bureau of the Census. *Eleventh Census of the United States: 1890.* Washington, D.C.: Government Printing Office, 1896.

————. *Bulletin 129: Negroes in the United States.* Washington, D.C.: Government Printing Office, 1925.

————. *Negro Population: 1790–1915.* Washington, D.C.: Government Printing Office, 1935.

————. *Negroes in the United States: 1920–1932.* Washington, D.C.:
     Government Printing Office, 1935.
————. *Fifteenth Census of the United States: 1930. Population.* Vol. 3.
     Washington, D.C.: Government Printing Office, 1932.
————. *Sixteenth Census of the United States: 1940. Population.* Vol.
     2. Washington, D.C.: Government Printing Office, 1943.

FLORIDA

Board of Control of the State Institutions of Higher Learning Report,
     1905. Tallahassee: State of Florida, 1906.
Biennial Reports of the Board of Control of the State Institutions of
     Higher Learning. 1906–1908 through 1924–1926. Tallahassee:
     State of Florida.
Biennial Reports of the State Superintendent of Public Instruction.
     1900–1902 through 1924–1926. Tallahassee: State of Florida.
Constitution of the State of Florida: Adopted by the Convention of
     1885. Tallahassee: State of Florida, 1937.

MISSOURI

Appendix to the House and Senate Journals. Fifty-first through Fifty-
     fourth General Assemblies.
Biennial Report of the Missouri Negro Industrial Commission:
     1923–1924. 1923–1924, 1925–1926. Jefferson City: Hugh
     Stephens Press, n.d.
Constitution of the State of Missouri as Revised, Amended, and Adopted
     in Convention Begun and Held at the City of St. Louis. 1865.
     Jefferson City: Emory S. Foster, 1865.
Journal of the House of Representatives. Forty-eighth through Sixtieth
     General Assemblies.
Journal of the Senate. Forty-eighth through Sixtieth General
     Assemblies.
Official Manual. 1919–1920 through 1940–1942.
Revised Statutes of the State of Missouri. 1919. 3 vols. Jefferson City:
     Hugh Stephens Press, n.d.

Semi-Annual Report of the Missouri Negro Industrial Commission. Jefferson City: Hugh Stephens Press, n.d.

78th Report of the Public Schools State of Missouri. Jefferson City: State of Missouri, 1928.

79th Report of the Public Schools State of Missouri. Jefferson City: State of Missouri, 1929.

80th Report of the Public Schools State of Missouri. Jefferson City: State of Missouri, 1930.

CONTEMPORARY PERIODICALS

Colored American Magazine. Vols. 1–17 (1900–1909). New York: Negro Universities Press.

Crisis: A Record of the Darker Race. Vols. 1–47 (1910–1940).

Higher Education among Negroes. Various issues. Johnson C. Smith University, North Carolina.

Journal of Negro Education. (1932–1940).

Journal of Negro History. (1916–1940).

Messenger. Various issues.

Opportunity: A Journal of Negro Life. Vols. 1–17 (1923–1939). New York: Negro Universities Press, 1969.

Quarterly Review of Higher Education Among Negroes. Vols. 1–28 (1933–1960). New York: Negro Universities Press, 1969.

Southern Workman. Various issues. Hampton, Va.: Hampton Institute Press.

Voice of the Negro. Vols. 1–4 (1904–1907). New York: Negro Universities Press, 1969.

NEWSPAPERS

Afro-American (Baltimore). 1931.

Call (Kansas City). 1922–1940.

Chicago Defender. 1931.

Democrat-Tribune (Jefferson City). 1910–1940.

Norfolk Journal and Guide (Virginia). 1923.

Pittsburgh Courier. 1931.

Savannah Tribune (Georgia). 1923.

St. Louis American. 1928–1940.

St. Louis Argus. 1920–1940.
St. Louis Globe-Democrat. 1920–1940.
St. Louis Post-Dispatch. 1920–1940.
Tallahassee Daily Democrat (Florida). 1920–1923.
Western Messenger (Jefferson City and St. Louis). 1914–1917.

Secondary Works

DISSERTATIONS AND THESES

Brigham, Robert I. "Education of the Negro in Missouri." Ph.D.
  diss., University of Missouri–Columbia, 1946.
Carter, Proctor N. "Lynch-Law and the Press of Missouri." Master's
  thesis, University of Missouri–Columbia, 1933.
Dorsett, Lyle W. "A History of the Pendergast Machine." Ph.D.
  diss., University of Missouri–Columbia, 1965.
Greene, Debra Foster. "Published in the Interest of Colored People:
  The *St. Louis Argus* Newspaper in the Twentieth Century."
  Ph.D. diss., University of Missouri–Columbia, 2005.
Grothaus, Larry H. "The Negro in Missouri Politics, 1890–1941."
  Ph.D. diss., University of Missouri–Columbia, 1970.
Kittel, Audrey N. "The Negro Community of Columbia, Missouri."
  Master's thesis, University of Missouri–Columbia, 1938.
Lowe, James L. "The Administration of Arthur M. Hyde, Governor
  of Missouri, 1921–1925." Master's thesis, University of
  Missouri–Columbia, 1949.
Large, John J., Jr. "The 'Invisible Empire' and Missouri Politics: The
  Influence of the Revived Ku Klux Klan in the Electoral
  Campaign of 1924 as Reported in Missouri Newspapers."
  Master's thesis, University of Missouri–Columbia, 1954.
Miller, Barney E. "Negro Education." Master's thesis, University of
  Missouri–Columbia, 1919.
Ogilvie, John Albert. "The Development of the Southeast Missouri
  Lowlands." Ph.D. diss., University of Missouri–Columbia,
  1966.
Mitchell, Frank D. "Embattled Democracy: Missouri Democratic
  Politics, 1918–1932." Ph.D. diss., University of
  Missouri–Columbia, 1964.
Sawyer, Robert M. "The Gaines Case: Its Background and Influence

on the University of Missouri and Lincoln University, 1936–1950." Ph.D. diss., University of Missouri–Columbia, 1966.

Schall, Jesse M. "The Negro in New Madrid County." Master's thesis, University of Missouri–Columbia, 1930.

Slavens, George E. "Lloyd C. Stark as a Political Reformer." Master's thesis, University of Missouri–Columbia, 1957.

———. "A History of the Missouri Negro Press." Ph.D. diss., University of Missouri–Columbia, 1969.

Stith, Priscilla A. "The Negro Migrant in St. Louis." Master's thesis, University of Missouri–Columbia, 1918.

Worner, Lloyd E., Jr. "The Public Career of Herbert Spencer Hadley." Ph.D. diss., University of Missouri–Columbia, 1946.

BOOKS

Anderson, Eric, and Alfred A. Moss. *The Facts of Reconstruction: Essays in Honor of John Hope Franklin.* Baton Rouge: Louisiana State University Press, 1991.

Anderson, James D. *The Education of Blacks in the South, 1860–1935.* Chapel Hill: University of North Carolina Press, 1988.

Bardolph, Richard. *The Negro Vanguard.* New York: Rinehart, 1959.

Barnard, John. *From Evangelicalism to Progressivism at Oberlin College, 1866–1917.* Columbus: Ohio State University Press, 1969.

Beard, Augustus Field. *A Crusade of Brotherhood: A History of the American Missionary Association.* Boston: Pilgrim Press, 1909.

Bond, Horace Mann. *Black American Scholars: A Study of Their Beginnings.* Detroit: Balamy Publishers, 1972.

———. *The Education of the Negro in the American Social Order.* New York: Prentice Hall, Inc., 1934.

———. *Negro Education in Alabama.* Washington, D.C.: Associated Publishers, 1939.

Brawley, Benjamin G. *Negro Builders and Heroes.* Chapel Hill: University of North Carolina Press, 1937.

Broderick, Francis L., and August Meier, eds. *Negro Protest Thought in the 20th Century.* Indianapolis: Bobbs-Merrill Company, 1966.

Bullock, Henry Allen. *A History of Negro Education in the South.* Cambridge, Mass.: Harvard University Press, 1967.

Butler, Addie Louise Joyner. *The Distinctive Black Colleges: Talladega, Tuskegee and Morehouse.* Metuchen, N.J.: Scarecrow Press, 1977.

Chambers, Frederick. *Black Higher Education in the United States.* Westport, Conn.: Greenwood Press, 1978.

Crossland, William A. *Industrial Conditions among Negroes in St. Louis.* St. Louis: Mendle Printing Company, 1914.

Chalmers, David M. *Hooded Americanism: The First Century of the Ku Klux Klan, 1865–1965.* New York: Doubleday and Company, 1965.

Culp, D. W., ed. *Twentieth Century Negro Literature.* Atlanta: J. L. Nichols and Company, 1902.

Curtis, L. S. *Some Facts on the Education of Negroes in Missouri: Reports of the Statistician, 1930–1939.* Missouri State Association of Negro Teachers, 1940.

Dabney, Charles William. *Universal Education in the South.* 2 vols. Chapel Hill: University of North Carolina Press, 1936.

Dittmer, John. *Black Georgia in the Progressive Era, 1900–1920.* Urbana: University of Illinois Press, 1977.

D'Orso, Michael. *Like Judgment Day.* New York: G. P. Putnam and Sons, 1996.

Du Bois, W. E. B. *Black Reconstruction in America.* Cleveland: Meridian Books, 1968.

———, ed. *The College-Bred Negro.* Atlanta: Atlanta University Press, 1900.

———, ed. *The Common School and the Negro American.* Atlanta: Atlanta University Press, 1911.

———. *Dusk to Dawn.* New York: Schocken Books, 1968.

———. *The Education of Black People.* Amherst: University of Massachusetts Press, 1973.

———, ed. *The Negro in Business.* Atlanta: Atlanta University Press, 1899.

———. *The Souls of Black Folk.* New York: Premier Americana Edition, 1961.

Fairchild, James H. *Oberlin: The Colony and the College, 1833–1883.* Oberlin, Ohio: E. J. Goodrich, 1883.

Fleming, Walter L. *Civil War and Reconstruction in Alabama.* New York: Columbia University Press, 1905.

Fletcher, Robert S. *A History of Oberlin College: From Its Foundation through the Civil War.* 2 vols. Oberlin, Ohio: Oberlin College, 1943.

Foner, Eric. *Reconstruction: American's Unfinished Revolution, 1863–1877.* New York: Harper and Row, 1988.

Franklin, John Hope. *From Slavery to Freedom.* New York: Alfred A. Knopf, 1965.

———. *Reconstruction.* Chicago: University of Chicago Press, 1961.

Franklin, Vincent P., and James D. Anderson, eds. *New Perspectives on Black Educational History.* Boston: G. K. Hall, 1978.

Fredrickson, George M. *The Black Image in the White Mind.* New York: Harper and Row, 1971.

Gallagher, Buell Gordon. *American Caste and the Negro College.* New York: University Press, 1938.

Goggin, Jacqueline. *Carter G. Woodson: A Life in Black History.* Baton Rouge: Louisiana State University Press, 1993.

Goodenow, Ronald K., and Arthur O. White, eds. *Education and the Rise of the New South.* Boston: G. K. Hall, 1981.

Green, Dan S., and Edwin D. Driver. *W. E. B. Du Bois on Sociology and the Black Community.* Chicago: University of Chicago Press, 1978.

Greene, Lorenzo J., Gary R. Kremer, and Antonio F. Holland. *Missouri's Black Heritage.* Columbia: University of Missouri Press, 1993.

Guitar, Sarah, and Floyd C. Shoemaker, compliers. *The Messages and Proclamations of the Governors of the State of Missouri.* Vols. 11, 12. Columbia: State Historical Society of Missouri, 1928, 1930.

Hahn, Steven. *A Nation under Our Feet.* Cambridge, Mass.: Belknap Press, 2003.

Harlan, Louis R. *Booker T. Washington.* New York: Oxford University Press, 1972.

———. *Booker T. Washington, The Wizard of Tuskegee, 1901–1915.* New York: Oxford University Press, 1983.

———. *Separate and Unequal.* Chapel Hill: University of North Carolina Press, 1958.

Haynes, Elizabeth Ross. *The Black Boy of Atlanta: Richard R. Wright.* Boston: House of Edinboro, 1952.

Heller, Otto, ed. *Charles Nagel, Speeches and Writings, 1900–1928.* New York: G. P. Putnam's Sons, 1931.

Hine, Darlene Clark. *Black Women in White*. Bloomington: Indiana University Press, 1989.

Historical Savannah Foundation, Inc. *Historic Savannah*. Savannah: Historical Savannah Foundation, Inc., 1968.

Holmes, Dwight Oliver Wendell. *The Evolution of the Negro College*. New York: Teachers' College, Columbia University Press, 1934.

Index to Periodicals, Articles by and about Blacks, 1973. Boston: G. K. Hall, 1973.

Johnson, Charles. *The Negro College Graduate*. Chapel Hill: University of North Carolina Press, 1938.

Johnson, James Weldon. *Along This Way*. New York: Viking Press, 1933.

Jones, Jacqueline. *Soldiers of Light and Love: Northern Teachers and Georgia Blacks, 1865–1873*. Chapel Hill: University of North Carolina Press, 1980.

Jones, Thomas Jesse. *Negro Education*. 1917. Rprt., New York: Arno Press, 1969.

Klein, Arthur J. *Survey of Negro Colleges and Universities*. U.S. Department of Interior, Bureau of Education Bulletin 7. Washington, D.C.: Government Printing Office, 1928.

Kolchin, Peter. *First Freedom*. Westport, Conn.: Greenwood Press, 1972.

Kousser, J. Morgan, and James M. McPherson. *Region, Race and Reconstruction: Essays in Honor of C. Vann Woodard*. New York: Oxford University Press, 1982.

Lee, Charles W. *Portraits and Biographical Sketches of Representative Negro Men and Women of Missouri and Kansas*. Kansas City: Berry Printing Company, 1895.

Levy, Eugene. *James Weldon Johnson*. Chicago: University of Chicago Press, 1973.

Lewis, David Lavering. *W. E. B. Du Bois: Biography of a Race, 1868–1919*. New York: Henry Holt, 1993.

Litwack, Leon F. *Been in the Storm So Long: The Aftermath of Slavery*. New York: Knopf, 1979.

———. *Trouble in Mind: Black Southerners in the Age of Jim Crow*. New York: Vintage Books, 1988.

Logan, Rayford W. *The Betrayal of the Negro*. New York: Collier Books, 1965.

———, and Michael R. Winston. *Dictionary of American Negro Biography*. New York: W. W. Norton and Company, 1982.

Love, Donald. *Henry Church King of Oberlin.* New Haven, Conn.:
    Yale University Press, 1956.
McPherson, James M. *The Abolitionist Legacy.* Princeton, N.J.:
    Princeton University Press, 1975.
————. *Blacks in America: Bibliographical Essay.* Garden City, N.Y.:
    Doubleday, 1971.
McReynolds, Edwin C. *Missouri: A History of the Crossroads State.*
    Norman: University of Oklahoma Press, 1962.
Malone, Dumas, and Allen Johnson, eds. *Dictionary of American
    Biography.* New York: Charles Scribner's Sons, 1930.
Margo, Robert. *Race and Schooling in the South, 1880–1950: An
    Economic History.* Chicago: University of Chicago Press, 1990.
Marshall, Albert P. *Soldier's Dream.* Jefferson City, Mo.: Lincoln
    University Press, 1966.
Martin, Asa E. *Our Negro Population.* Kansas City: Franklin Hudson
    Publishing Company, 1913.
Meyer, Duane G. *The Heritage of Missouri: A History.* St. Louis: The
    State Publishing Company, 1963.
Meier, August. *Negro Thought in America, 1880–1915.* Ann Arbor:
    University of Michigan Press, 1963.
————, and Elliott Rudwick. *From Plantation to Ghetto.* New York:
    Hill and Wang, 1966.
Mitchell, Franklin D. *Embattled Democracy: Missouri Democratic
    Politics, 1919–1932.* Columbia: University of Missouri Press,
    1968.
Moore, Albert B. *History of Alabama.* Tuscaloosa: University of
    Alabama Press, 1934.
Moton, Robert Russa. *Finding a Way Out: An Autobiography.* Garden
    City, N.Y.: Doubleday, 1921.
Myrdal, Gunnar. *An American Dilemma.* 2 vols. New York: Harper,
    1944.
Neyland, Leedell W. *The History of Florida Agricultural and
    Mechanical University.* Tallahassee: Florida A&M Foundation,
    1987.
————, and John W. Riley. *The History of Florida Agricultural and
    Mechanical University.* Gainesville: University of Florida Press,
    1963.
North Carolina Central University. *Newspapers and Periodicals by
    and about Black People.* Boston: G. K. Hall, 1978.

Oberlin College. *Alumni Catalogue, 1833–1936*. Oberlin, Ohio: Oberlin College, 1937.

———. *Alumni Register, 1960*. Oberlin, Ohio: Oberlin College, 1961.

———. *A History of Honor: What Oberlin Has Meant to American Life*. Oberlin, Ohio: Oberlin College, 1923.

———. *Inauguration of President Henry Churchill King of Oberlin College*. Oberlin, Ohio: Oberlin College, 1903.

———. *Oberlin General Catalogue, 1883–1908*. Oberlin, Ohio: Oberlin College, 1909.

Orr, Dorothy. *A History of Education in Georgia*. Chapel Hill: University of North Carolina Press, 1950.

Osofsky, Gilbert. *Harlem: The Making of a Ghetto*. New York: Harper and Row, 1966.

Perdue, Robert E. *The Negro in Savannah, 1865–1900*. New York: Exposition Press, 1973.

Perry, J. Edward. *Forty Cords of Wood*. Jefferson City, Mo.: Lincoln University Press, 1947.

Porter, Dorothy. *The Negro in United States: A Selected Bibliography*. Washington, D.C.: Government Printing Office, 1970.

Porter, Gilbert L., and Leedell W. Neyland. *The History of the Florida State Teacher's Association*. Washington, D.C.: National Education Association, 1977.

Powdermaker, Hortense. *After Freedom; A Cultural Study in the Deep South*. New York: Viking Press, 1939.

Provenzo, Eugene F., Jr., ed. *Du Bois on Education*. Walnut Creek, Calif.: Altamira Press, 2002.

Pyburn, Nita K. *The History of the Development of a Single System of Education in Florida, 1822–1903*. Tallahassee: Florida State University Press, 1954.

Rabinowitz, Howard. *Race Relations in the Urban South, 1865–1890*. New York: Oxford University Press, 1978.

Range, Willard. *The Rise and Progress of Negro Colleges in Georgia, 1865–1949*. Atlanta: University of Georgia Press, 1951.

Ransom, Roger, and Sutch Ransom. *One Kind of Freedom*. New York: Cambridge University Press, 2001.

Reid, Ira de A. *A Study of the Industrial Status of Negroes in St. Louis*. St. Louis: Welfare Plan Council of St. Louis and St. Louis County, 1934.

Richardson, Joe M. *The Negro in the Reconstruction of Florida, 1865–1877*. Tallahassee: Florida State University Press, 1965.

Savage, Sherman W. *A History of Lincoln University*. Jefferson City, Mo.: New Day Press, 1939.

Scott, Emmet J. *Negro Migration during the War*. New York: Oxford University Press, 1920.

Sellers, James Benson. *Slavery in Alabama*. Tuscaloosa: University of Alabama Press, 1950.

Sherer, Robert G. *Subordination or Liberation?* Tuscaloosa: University of Alabama Press, 1977.

Shoemaker, Floyd C. *History of Missouri and Missourians*. Columbia: Walter Ridgeway Publishing Company, 1922.

Simmons, William. *Men of Mark: Eminent, Progressive and Rising*. 1887. Rprt., New York: Arno Press, 1968.

Spear, Allan H. *Black Chicago: The Making of a Negro Ghetto, 1890–1920*. Chicago: University of Chicago Press, 1967.

Spencer, Samuel R., Jr. *Booker T. Washington and the Negro's Place in American Life*. Boston: Little, Brown and Company, 1955.

Spivey, Donald. *Schooling for the New Slavery: Black Industrial Education, 1868–1915*. Westport, Conn.: Greenwood Press, 1978.

Stearn, Charles. *The Blacks of the South, and the Rebels*. Boston: N. E. News Company, 1872.

Sterne, Emma Gelders. *Mary McLeod Bethune*. New York: Alfred A. Knopf, 1959.

Swint, Henry Lee. *The Northern Teacher in the South, 1862–1870*. New York: Octagon Books, 1967.

Strickland, Arvarh E., and Robert E. Weems, Jr. *The African American Experience*. Westport, Conn.: Greenwood Press, 2001.

Taylor, Alutheus Ambush. *The Negro in the Reconstruction of Virginia*. 1926. Rprt., New York: Russell and Russell, 1969.

Terrell, Mary Church. *A Colored Woman in a White World*. 1940. Rprt., Washington, D.C.: National Association of Colored Women, 1968.

Thornbrough, Emma L., ed. *Booker T. Washington*. Englewood Cliffs, N.J.: Prentice-Hall, 1969.

Tindall, George B. *The Emergence of the New South, 1913–1945*. Baton Rouge: Louisiana State University Press, 1967.

Trelease, Allen W. *White Terror: The KKK Conspiracy and Southern Reconstruction.* New York: Harper and Row, 1971.

Vaughn, William Preston. *Schools for All: The Blacks and Public Education in the South, 1865–1877.* Lexington: University of Kentucky Press, 1976.

Walker, Juliet E. K. *The History of Black Business in America.* New York: Twayne Publishers, 1998.

Wall, Joseph F. *Andrew Carnegie.* New York: Oxford University Press, 1970.

Washington, Booker T. *Character Building.* New York: Doubleday, Page and Company, 1902.

———. *Education of the Negro.* Albany: J. B. Lyon Co., 1904.

———. *Up from Slavery.* 1901. Rprt., New York: Bantam Pathfinders Edition, 1963.

Waskow, Arthur J. *From Race Riot to Sit-In, 1919 and the 1960's.* Garden City, N.Y.: Doubleday, 1966.

Webster, Stater W. *The Education of Black Americans.* New York: J. Day, 1974.

Weiner, Jonathan M. *Social Origins of the New South: Alabama, 1860–1880.* Baton Rouge: Louisiana State University Press, 1978.

Wharton, Vernon Lane. *The Negro in Mississippi, 1865–1900.* Chapel Hill: University of North Carolina, 1947.

Who's Who in Colored America. New York: Who's Who in Colored America Company, 1927.

Wilkerson, Doxey Alphonso. *Special Problems of Negro Education.* Washington, D.C.: Government Printing Office, 1939.

Williams, William T. B. *Duplication of Schools for Negro Youth.* Lynchburg, Virginia: J. P. Bell Co., 1914.

Williamson, Joel. *A Rage for Order.* New York: Oxford University Press, 1986.

Wolters, Raymond. *The New Negro on Campus.* Princeton, N.J.: Princeton University Press, 1975.

Woodson, Carter G. *A Century of Negro Migration.* Washington, D.C.: Association for the Study of Negro Life and History, 1918.

———. *The Education of the Negro Prior to 1861.* New York: Arno Press, 1968.

———. *The Miseducation of the Negro.* Washington, D.C.: Associated Publishers, 1933,

———, ed. *Negro Orators and Their Orations.* Washington, D.C.: Associated Publishers, 1925.

Woodward, Comer Vann. *Origins of the New South, 1877–1913.* Baton Rouge: Louisiana State University Press, 1951.

———. *The Strange Career of Jim Crow.* New York: Oxford University Press, 1966.

Wright, Richard R. *A Brief Historical Sketch of Negro Education in Georgia.* Savannah: Robinson Printing House, 1894.

Young, Nathan B., Jr. *Your St. Louis and Mine.* St. Louis: n.p., n.d.

ARTICLES

Aptheker, Herbert. "The Negro College Student in the 1920's— Years of Preparation and Protest: An Introduction." *Science and Society* 33 (Spring 1969): 150–67.

Bacote, Clarence A. "The Negro in Atlanta Politics." *Phylon* 16, no. 4 (1955): 33–50.

Bigglestone, W. E. "Irrespective of Color." *Oberlin Alumni Magazine* 77 (Spring 1981): 35–36.

———. "Oberlin College and the Negro Student, 1865–1940." *Journal of Negro History* 56 (July 1971): 198–219.

Blassingame, John. "Before the Ghetto: The Making of the Black Community in Savannah, Georgia, 1865–1880." *Journal of Social History* 6 (Summer 1973): 463–86.

Bond, Horace Mann. "Negro Education: A Debate in the Alabama Constitutional Convention of 1901." *Journal of Negro Education* 1 (1932): 49–59.

Bottoms, L. W. "The Policies and Rationale Underlying the Support of Negro Colleges and Schools Maintained by the Presbyterian Church in the United States." *Journal of Negro Education* 29 (Summer 1960): 264–73.

Curtis, L. S. "Nathan B. Young: A Sketch." *Journal of Negro History* 19 (January 1934): 107–10.

Daniel, Walter C. "W. E. B. Du Bois at Lincoln University: Founders' Day Address, 1941." *Missouri Historical Review* 74 (April 1980): 343.

Du Bois, W. E. B. "Education and Work." *Journal of Negro Education* 1 (1932): 60–74.

———. "Enrollment in Negro Universities and Colleges." *School and Society* 28 (September, 1928): 401–2.

———. "Gifts and Education." *Crisis* 29 (February 1925): 151–52.

———. "Higher Education." *Crisis* 34 (September 1927): 239.

———. "The Negro College." *Crisis* 40 (August 1933): 175–77.

———. "Negro Education." *Crisis* 15 (February 1918): 173–78.

———. "Returning Soldiers." *Crisis* 18 (May 1919): 14.

Lamon, Lester C. "The Black Community in Nashville and the Fisk University Student Strike of 1924–1925." *Journal of Southern History* 11 (May 1974): 225–44.

McPherson, James M. "The Liberal and Black Power in Negro Education, 1865–1915." *American Historical Review* 75 (June 1970): 1357–79.

"Missouri's First Negro Representative." *Missouri Historical Review* 44 (April 1950): 340.

Patton, June O. "'And the Truth Shall Make You Free': Richard Robert Wright Sr., Black Intellectual and Iconoclast, 1877–1897." *Journal of Negro History* 81 (Spring 1996).

Rabinowitz, Howard N. "From Reconstruction to Redemption in the Urban South." *Journal of Urban History* 2 (1976): 169–94.

———. "Half a Loaf: The Shift from White to Black Teachers in the Negro Schools of the Urban South, 1865–1890." *Journal of Southern History* 40 (1974): 565–94.

Small, Sarah E. "The Yankee Schoolmarm in Freedmen's Schools: An Analysis of Attitudes." *Journal of Southern History* 45 (1979): 381–402.

"Slave to Banker." *Ebony* 1 (November 1945): 43–47.

"Survey of Negro Higher Education." *Journal of Negro Education* 2 (July 1933). Special issue.

Writings of Young

UNPUBLISHED

Blow, James Harold, ed. "Those Who Trespass Against Us: Based on the Life and Letters of Nathan Benjamin Young." Introduction by Dr. Leedell W. Neyland, Tallahassee, Fla.: Florida A&M University, College of Humanities and Social

Science, 1976. Unpublished manuscript. Florida A&M Black Archives, Tallahassee.

Young, Nathan B. "Booker T. Washington." Typed manuscript. Joint Collection–University of Missouri, Western Historical Manuscript Collection and State Historical Society of Missouri.

———. "The Plight of Public Education for Negroes in Missouri." Joint Collection–University of Missouri, Western Historical Manuscript Collection and State Historical Society of Missouri.

———. "The Quest and Use of an Education." Joint Collection–University of Missouri, Western Historical Manuscript Collection and State Historical Society of Missouri.

———. "A Teaching Project toward Economic Independence—A Challenge to Institutions of Learning for Negroes." Joint Collection–University of Missouri, Western Historical Manuscript Collection and State Historical Society of Missouri.

PUBLISHED

Young, Nathan B. "The Birmingham Public Schools—Colored Department." *Our Work* 6 (October 1892). Talladega College Archives.

———. *Common School Extension.* Tuskegee: Normal School Steam Press, 1897.

———. "A Dream Fulfilled." *Southern Workman* (January 1916): 53–54.

———. "An Upward Departure in Negro Education." Annual Address, National Association of Teachers in Colored Schools, Cincinnati, July 15, 1915. Unpublished transcript. Talladega College Archives, Savery Library. Copy of speech also available at Moorland-Spingarn Research Center, Howard University, Washington, D.C.

Interviews

Allen, Ruth. Jefferson City, Mo., August 1981.

Blue, Cecil. Jefferson City, Mo., August 1981.

Brown, Sterling. Jefferson City, Mo., July 1981.

Carter, Faye Tull. Jefferson City, Mo., August 1982.

Curtis, L. S. St. Louis, August 1981.

Damel, Carroll. Jefferson City, Mo., August 1981.

Dowdy, W. W. Jefferson City, Mo., August 1981.

Eaton, James N. Tallahassee, Fla., May 1982.

Greene, Lorenzo J. Jefferson City, Mo., August 1981.

Greene, Thomasina Talley. Jefferson City, Mo., August 1982.

Hardiman, Milton. Jefferson City, Mo., August 1981.

Matheus, John. Tallahassee, Fla., May 1982.

Neyland, Leedell W. Tallahassee, Fla., May 1982.

Parks, James D. Jefferson City, Mo., August 1981.

Perry, B. L., Jr. Tallahassee, Fla., May 1982.

Reedy, Sidney J. Jefferson City, Mo., August 1981.

Riley, John. Tallahassee, Fla., May 1982.

Robinson, Harriet. Jefferson City, Mo., August 1981.

Sweets, Nathaniel. St. Louis, August 1981.

Williams, Julia Young. Letter to author dated December 2, 1981.

Young, Nathan B., Jr. St. Louis, July and August 1981.